Globalization and Feminist Activism

GLOBALIZATION

Series Editors
Manfred B. Steger
*Illinois State University, University of Hawai'i—Manoa,
and Royal Melbourne Institute of Technology*
and
Terrell Carver
University of Bristol

"Globalization" has become *the* buzzword of our time. But what does it mean? Rather than forcing a complicated social phenomenon into a single analytical framework, this series seeks to present globalization as a multidimensional process constituted by complex, often contradictory interactions of global, regional, and local aspects of social life. Since conventional disciplinary borders and lines of demarcation are losing their old rationales in a globalizing world, authors in this series apply an interdisciplinary framework to the study of globalization. In short, the main purpose and objective of this series is to support subject-specific inquiries into the dynamics and effects of contemporary globalization and its varying impacts across, between, and within societies.

Globalization and Culture
Jan Nederveen Pieterse

Rethinking Globalism
Edited by
Manfred B. Steger

Globalization and Terrorism
Jamal R. Nassar

Globalism, Second Edition
Manfred B. Steger

Globaloney
Michael Veseth

Globalization and Law
Adam Gearey

Globalization and War
Tarak Barkawi

Globalization and International Political Economy
Mark Rupert and M. Scott Solomon

Globalization and Feminist Activism
Mary Hawkesworth

Forthcoming in the Series
Globalization and American Popular Culture
Lane Crothers

Globalization and Militarization
Cynthia Enloe

Globalization and American Empire
Kiichi Fujiwara

Globalization and Labor
Dimitris Stevis and Terry Boswell

 Supported by the Globalization Research Center at the University of Hawai'i, Manoa

GLOBALIZATION AND FEMINIST ACTIVISM

MARY E. HAWKESWORTH

ROWMAN & LITTLEFIELD PUBLISHERS, INC.
Lanham • Boulder • New York • Toronto • Oxford

ROWMAN & LITTLEFIELD PUBLISHERS, INC.

Published in the United States of America
by Rowman & Littlefield Publishers, Inc.
A wholly owned subsidiary of
The Rowman & Littlefield Publishing Group, Inc.
4501 Forbes Boulevard, Suite 200, Lanham, Maryland 20706
www.rowmanlittlefield.com

P.O. Box 317, Oxford OX2 9RU, UK

British Library Cataloguing in Publication Information Available

Library of Congress Cataloging-in-Publication Data

Hawkesworth, M. E., 1952–
    Globalization and feminist activism / Mary E. Hawkesworth.
      p. cm.— (Globalization)
    Includes bibliographical references and index.
    ISBN-13: 978-0-7425-3782-8 (cloth : alk. paper)
    ISBN-10: 0-7425-3782-X (cloth : alk. paper)
    ISBN-13: 978-0-7425-3783-5 (pbk. : alk. paper)
    ISBN-10: 0-7425-3783-8 (pbk. : alk. paper)
    1. Feminism.   2. Globalization.   I. Title.   II. Globalization
(Lanham, Md.)
HQ1155.H39   2006
303.48'2082—dc22

                                                          2005034333

Printed in the United States of America

∞ ™ The paper used in this publication meets the minimum requirements of
American National Standard for Information Sciences—Permanence of Paper
for Printed Library Materials, ANSI/NISO Z39.48-1992.

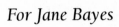

For Jane Bayes

CONTENTS

ACKNOWLEDGMENTS

Things are seldom what they seem. A maxim, first noted by the Pre-Socratics, resonates powerfully among feminist scholars. In the early 1990s, as mainstream political scientists began hailing the virtues of a new age of globalization and democratization, feminist scholars tracked worsening conditions for women around the globe. The palpable discrepancies between generic claims about economic and political life and women's growing marginalization and impoverishment inspired feminist scholars to investigate the gendered dimensions of globalization and democratization and to reconceptualize these processes on the basis of evidence inclusive of women's and men's lives. This book is part of that continuing project.

My research in this area was fueled and enriched by probing questions raised by two feminist colleagues and friends in the Women's Caucus for Political Science, Jane Bayes and Rita Mae Kelly, who invited me to participate in a transnational research project on gender, globalization, and democratization. Involving feminist social scientists from all regions of the world, this project has become one of three continuing research programs of the International Social Science Council (ISSC). Over the past ten years, I have benefited greatly from working with and learning from my ISSC colleagues, including Achola Pala Okeyo, Yassine Fall, Laura Gonzalez, Gunnel Gustafsson, Seiko Hanochi, Monique Leijenaar, Kihnide Mushakoji, Marian Simms, and Birgitte Young.

My intellectual horizons have also been profoundly influenced by the path-breaking work of feminist scholars in the fields of international political economy, international relations, and development studies, including Isabel Bakker, Janine Brody, Cynthia Enloe, Jane Jaquette, Kathy Jones, Helen Kinsella, Deb Liebowitz, Spike Peterson, Jane Parpart, Jindy Pettman, Shirin Rai, Gillian Youngs, and Marysia Zalewski, many of whom I have had the good fortune to work with on the editorial board of the *International Feminist Journal of Politics*. Patricia Begné, Lois Harder, Laura Mac-Donald, and Breny Mendoza have given me great insights into the complex interactions between globalization and democratization in North America, Central America, and Latin America.

I am particularly grateful to Manfred Steger for his continuing efforts to include feminist perspectives on globalization in invitational conferences and in panel sessions at the American Political Science Association and the International Studies Association. I would also like to thank Manfred Steger, Terrill Carver, and Jennifer Knerr for helpful comments on the manuscript.

The Women's and Gender Studies Department at Rutgers University is a particularly congenial place for pursuing the study of gender and globalization. I am indebted to Barbara Balliet, Ethel Brooks, Charlotte Bunch, Cheryl Clarke, Ed Cohen, Judy Gerson, Mary Gossy, Mary Hartman, Angelique Haugerud, Leela Fernandes, Jennifer Morgan, Elmira Nazombe, Jasbir Puar, Joanna Regulska, Philip Rothwell, Louisa Schein, Sarolta Takacs, and Barry Qualls for the intellectual stimulation and the feminist solidarity they so warmly provide. To Joanna Regulska, Barry Qualls, and Holly Smith, I owe a special debt of thanks for approving a research leave to enable me to write this book.

Some of the material included in chapter 5 was drawn from two previously published articles, "The Semiotics of Premature Burial: Feminism in a Postfeminist Age," *Signs* 29(4): 961–986 (2004); and "Theorizing Globalization in a Time of War," *Studies in Political Economy* 75 (Spring): 127–138 (2004).

My debts to Philip Alperson can neither be enumerated nor repaid, but his heroic efforts to retrieve years of intellectual work nearly lost when my hard drive crashed in February, his willingness to assume far more shifts in the kitchen than justice warrants, and his unfailing good humor are richly deserving of mention. Absent his ministrations, this book would have been many more years in the making.

ENGENDERING GLOBALIZATION

As a woman I have no country. As a woman I want no country.
As a woman, my country is the whole world.

—Virginia Woolf (1938, 109)

But women do not say "We," except at some congress of feminists or some similar formal demonstration; men say "women,"
and women use the same word in referring to themselves. . . .
The proletarians have accomplished a revolution in Russia . . .
but, the women's effort has never been anything more than a
symbolic agitation. They have gained only what men have been
willing to grant; they have taken nothing, they have only
received. . . . The reason for this is that women lack concrete
means for organizing themselves into a unit which can stand
face to face with a correlative unit. They have no past, no history, no religion of their own; and they have no solidarity of
work and interest. . . . They live dispersed among the males,
attached through residence, housework, economic condition,
and social standing to certain men—husbands and fathers—
more firmly than they are to other women.

—Simone de Beauvoir (1949, xxv)

Feminism in one country is not sustainable—we need feminism
on a global scale.

—Women in Development Europe (WIDE) (1995, 3)

One question often asked in Bihar [India] (mostly by men) is:
"Are you feminists?" by which they mean man haters. But we
proudly say: "Yes we are—feminists are those who can analyze

1

society and see that it discriminates against women and girl children; and then, most importantly, feminists are doing something
to change this ambiance."

—Viji Srinivasan (2001, 86)

Globalization is a gendered phenomenon. It positions and affects men and
women differently, and it produces new modes of gender power and disadvantage. For the past four decades, feminist activists and feminist scholars
have struggled to make the gendered dynamics of globalization visible. Yet
their work seldom captures public attention. Consider, for example, the
transnational commodification of care, a prime manifestation of the complex gendered dynamics of contemporary globalization. Relations of concern, affection, companionship, intimacy, sexuality, and reproduction,
once highly localized and shielded from the intrusions of the market, have
become objects of global exchange. The outsourcing of reproductive labor
sends affluent Westerners to China, Latin America, Romania, and Russia
in search of adoptable infants and recruits millions of women from Indonesia, the Philippines, Sri Lanka, Mexico, and Central America to work in the
households of affluent women as nannies and maids. With the assistance
of the Internet, lonely men cruise cyber-cafés in a quest for foreign brides
who conform to nostalgic fantasies of traditional, that is, submissive, wives.
For less marriage-minded men, sex tourism becomes the site of global adventure, as pimps and brothel owners in the guise of disinterested capitalist
business entrepreneurs procure sex workers to meet the ever increasing
global demand. For the ill and elderly, care of the body has created a global
market for nurses and health care paraprofessionals, recruited from Jamaica, Haiti, the West Indies, Puerto Rico, Mexico, Ghana, Nigeria, India,
South Korea, and China, in response to the growing demand for health
care services in wealthy nations. (Bales 2002; Brennan 2002; Diamond
1992; Ehrenreich and Hochschild 2002; Parennas 2001a).

Care work is now a highly lucrative transnational business, generating
multibillions of dollars annually. Recruiting some 60 million women from
poor nations to overseas contract work each year, care work has become
one of the largest sources of foreign currency for highly indebted poor
countries. In addition to helping to resolve unemployment crises in poor
nations, care work generates billions of dollars in remittances, which indebted nations are using to solve their debt crises, earmarking these funds
to pay annual interest on loans accumulated from the World Bank and the
International Monetary Fund (IMF). Despite its centrality to global flows
of capital and labor, the marketization of intimate exchange remains remarkably invisible. Like other gendered dimensions of globalization, it is
little noted and less discussed in mainstream accounts of globalization.

There are many narratives of globalization. In the midst of the intense social, economic, political, cultural, and technological fluidity characteristic of the contemporary world, each account of globalization tells a story of how things are and why things are as they are. Using particular focal points and framing assumptions, competing narratives of globalization privilege the internationalization of capital, economic restructuring or marketization, the emergence of nonstate actors as a transnational political force, centralization of power in the hands of international financial institutions such as the World Bank and the International Monetary Fund, the erosion of the sovereignty of nation-states, exponential increases in labor migration, the compression of time and space through the creation of computer-mediated interactions, or simultaneous pressures toward homogenization and differentiation of cultures. While these authoritative analyses of globalization disagree about many things, including the central features, fault lines, costs, and benefits of globalization, they converge on one point: the near total absence of any reference to women or to feminism.[1]

The absence of women and feminism from mainstream accounts of globalization contributes to a variety of misconceptions, suggesting that (1) globalization is a neutral phenomenon that affects the lives of men and women similarly; (2) gendered power relations are not at play in the complex processes of globalization; and (3) globalization is not and has never been a women's issue. Misconceptions of this sort mask critical dimensions of contemporary globalization; distort the historical record concerning feminist activism in earlier eras of globalization; and contribute to a form of social amnesia that erases from the public record structures of raced and gendered power, along with women's sustained struggles to contest that power. In an effort to counteract forces that enable such sanctioned forgetting, this book seeks to "engender" globalization debates. Toward that end, it makes visible the gendered dimensions of globalization—the ways that globalization affects the lives of women within particular races, classes, ethnicities, and nationalities. It explores the power dynamics of gendering processes, such as feminization, which operate at great remove from the bodies of individual women and men to restructure social, economic, and political relations. It also traces transnational feminist mobilizations over two centuries, which have sought to contest economic and political developments that exclude, marginalize, subordinate, and oppress women.

Globalization

The nature, causes, and consequences of globalization are subjects of intensive and continuing debate among scholars. Perhaps the broadest definition construes globalization as "the spatial extension of social relations across the globe" (James 2004, 29). Understood in this way, globalization has strong affinities with millennia of imperial adventures. The ancient Roman Empire, spanning 800 years, fifteenth- and sixteenth-century European colonialism, and nineteenth- and twentieth-century capitalist imperialism are various manifestations of globalization because in each instance a particular social, economic, and political order tried to control the known world and reshape it in its own image.

Other scholars suggest that globalization is linked to the emergence of an understanding of the world as a sphere or globe, and the age of discovery in which European explorers set out to map and to claim territories on the far side of the world (Robertson 1992). Within this frame, globalization is typically traced to the fifteenth century and the efforts of the Spanish, French, British, Portuguese, Dutch, Swedish, and Germans to conquer and colonize North, Central, and South America, Africa, and the Middle East, as well as South and East Asia. This Eurocentric view, linking globalization to initiatives of European states to spread their people, ideas, religion, cultures, and goods, as well as economic and political systems, around the world, is often cast as a beneficial process through which the West helped to develop or modernize underdeveloped regions. Such a benign depiction, however, masks oppressive features of colonial and imperial globalizing processes, such as the violent acquisition of territory, extraction of natural resources, and exploitation and extermination of indigenous peoples by European powers, which were essential to the accumulation of vast wealth that set the stage for the emergence of capitalism, a mode of economic production and exchange that privileges profit making as its primary objective (Shohat and Stam 1994).

Focusing on ideological dimensions, other scholars have linked globalization to modernity, to Enlightenment beliefs about the relationship between reason and progress, and to the emergence of new forms of individualism and arguments for self-governance associated with the American and French revolutions in the late eighteenth century. Breaking with feudal religious, economic, and political traditions that reinforced naturalized hierarchies, proponents of globalization as a process of modernization emphasize the possibilities for progress when human reason is used to resolve human problems and science is wed to a notion of human mastery of the material world. Associated with the development of experimental science and technological innovation, with industrialization and the development of global trade networks, and with the celebration of the "civilizing effects" of democratization, modernization theorists also tend to characterize the consequences of globalization as uniformly positive. They neglect the foundational ethnocentrism of modernity's assimilationist agenda, its intricate ties to the slave trade, colonial exploitation, and the invention and instrumental deployment of racism to legitimate new modes of inequality (Gilroy 1993; D. Goldberg 1993). The focus on "European culture emanating out to the colonial periphery from a self-generating center" also obscures "the constant movement of people and ideas in the other direction" (Pratt 1992, 91, 138).

Yet other scholars advance a conception of globalization tied to much more recent history, restricting its application to developments that are traced to the last three decades of the twentieth century. In this view, globalization refers to ongoing and often interrelated economic, political, cultural, and technological transformations that are reshaping the contemporary world. Chief among these is the "death of distance" occasioned by technological developments in communications—telephone, television, Internet—and transportation (Cairncross 1997). In the economic sphere, some suggest that this phase of globalization began with the demise of the Bretton Woods Agreement in 1971 and the creation of a new global financial architecture. Others suggest that the collapse of the Soviet Union and the end of the Cold War (1989–1991) facilitated the expansion of capitalist economic systems around the world, an expansion that has produced growing inequality within and between nations. In the political domain, globalization is manifested in the spread of competitive elections and democratization, decentralization of power within nation-states, neoliberal policies of privatization and deregulation, the growing power of transnational actors, often in conjunction with U.S. hegemony, and the emergence of global civil society. Fast-breaking developments in the spheres of information technology and communication technology provide the infrastructure essential to these economic and political transformations and create opportunities for new modes of production, finance, transnational mobilization, and cultural transformation.

To foreground continuities and differences in globalizing processes in ways that illuminate their impacts on women's lives and their relation to feminist activism, this book focuses on changing dynamics of globalization since the early nineteenth century. The complex and contradictory economic, political, and ideological transformations wrought by capitalism play a central role in this narrative, providing a framework in which women in various regions of the world struggle to sustain themselves, their families, and communities while forging new alliances to eliminate multiple forms of injustice.

In 1848, Karl Marx and Friedrich Engels identified several salient features of globalization related to capital's impulse to "create a world in its

5

own image." Deploying a rhetoric of individual freedoms, Marx and Engels suggested that capitalism ultimately pursues a "single, unconscionable freedom, free trade," as the bourgeoisie fan out "across the surface of the globe in search for constantly expanding markets for its products." Long-established factories within industrial nations are destroyed, as transnational industries flood markets with products made in countries whose workers are paid far lower wages. Exposure to global products heightens dissatisfaction with local brands, as "new wants requiring products of distant lands and climes" proliferate. "Old local and national seclusion and self-sufficiency" are supplanted by global exchange giving rise to "universal interdependence of nations." Technological innovation generates new means of communication "drawing all nations into bourgeois civilization, compelling all nations, under pain of extinction, to adopt bourgeois modes of production" (Marx and Engels 1955, 12–14).

Although Marx and Engels were describing features of capitalism just beginning to emerge in the mid-nineteenth century, these global processes have expanded and intensified over the past 157 years. National economies have grown increasingly interconnected through trade, financial flows, foreign direct investment by transnational corporations, and structural adjustment loans provided by the International Monetary Fund (IMF) and the World Bank. International mechanisms to promote and regulate multilateral trade agreements, such as the General Agreement on Tariffs and Trade (GATT) and the World Trade Organization (WTO), have challenged the power of national governments to control conditions of labor, production, and exchange within their borders. Computerized data processing and information technology have exponentially increased global financial transactions, transforming the nature of trade and exchange. Nineteenth-century industrial capital, which generated profit from trade in raw materials, means of production (tools and technology), and human labor power, has given way to postindustrial forms of capitalism, in which profits are accumulated in the sphere of circulation involving currency and securities markets, as well as trade in futures (i.e., forecasts of future profits from future production and stock prices).

Corporate loyalties to particular nation-states have been superseded by global strategies developed by transnational corporations to increase profits. Long-term investment in industrial plants in particular locations has been supplanted by the hypermobility of capital as transnational corporations rapidly move production sites across the globe in search of cheaper labor forces. With the assistance of governments desperate to secure employment and investment opportunities within their borders, transnational corporations locate in export processing zones or free trade zones exempt from national wage, labor, and environmental regulations. Rather than negotiating long-term employment contracts that afford workers job security, decent wages, health-care and pension benefits, transnational corporations rely upon a flexible labor force, offering only temporary or part-time employment, low wages, and no benefits. In their efforts to increase profits, some corporations have informalized their labor forces, outsourcing or subcontracting out work to small producers operating in the informal sector. Once characterized as the underground economy because it operated outside formal state regulations governing taxation, wages, and working conditions, the informal sector is now the site of employment for the majority of workers worldwide. In the late twentieth century, industry was redomesticated as production left factories and returned to home-based workshops, where small numbers of employees (ten to twenty) work for subcontractors manifesting little concern for healthy working conditions or living-wage levels. Controlling 70 percent of world trade, transnational corporations have increased profits by outsourcing production and creating global commodity chains, linking multiple, fragmented production sites around the globe, while keeping products and laborers in constant motion.

Although outsourced industrial production remains an important source of profit globally, the nature of work in postindustrial capitalism has been shifting from industrial production to the service sector. In the contemporary United States, for example, 72 percent of the labor force is employed in the service sector. In the twenty-first century, 46 percent of the economically active workers worldwide are engaged in service work (Wichterich 2000). The service sector encompasses a wide range of activities from financial markets, information technology, data processing, law, and insurance, to health care, child care, education, entertainment, catering, retail sales, commercial cleaning, tourism, and sex work. In 2000, the value of trade in cross-border services equaled the value of traded goods, but the service sector was growing at a much faster rate. The increasing importance of the service sector in the global economy has led some analysts to discuss globalization in terms of the "immaterial" or "virtual" economy, although this formulation privileges the highly paid, male-dominated services such as information technology and the financial sector over the thoroughly embodied services of health-care provision, child care, or sex work, domains dominated by women.

In addition to changes in global financial flows, sites and forms of production, and emergence of the service sector as an economic force, recent globalization has been characterized by a particular ideological formation, neoliberalism. Harking back to the classical economic theories of the eighteenth century, neoliberalism privileges the market as the key to economic growth and social well-being for all people. Borrowing certain arguments from Adam Smith's *The Wealth of Nations*,[2] neoliberals suggest that the market transforms individual pursuit of private interest into social benefits. Assuming that individuals are primarily self-interested "maximizers" who seek to increase their own wealth, neoliberals insist that each individual should be given complete freedom to pursue selfish objectives. The beauty of the competitive market, in this view, is precisely that it transforms the pursuit of private vice into public benefits. The market is a stern taskmaster, requiring producers to use their ingenuity to find cheaper ways to produce goods, to sell them for less than other producers. Consumers benefit from cheaper goods and reward the producer of the cheapest goods with their business, thereby helping that producer to amass wealth. Costly and inefficient producers are gradually driven out of business, as the market's "invisible hand" organizes the competition that generates new technology to produce cheaper and cheaper products.

Proponents of neoliberalism suggest that the primary task of the state is to support the unrestricted operations of the market, providing a legal framework that protects private property, enforces contracts, promotes law and order, and provides for a common defense. Arguing that market operations have been unnecessarily constrained by the policies of social welfare states, neoliberals endorse strategies to cut back the state, privatizing public enterprises, deregulating the market, freeing industry and trade from regulatory constraints, eliminating progressive taxation, reducing public expenditures for health, education, welfare, arts, and public broadcasting, as well as labor and environmental protection.

In a sense, the freedom afforded to transnational corporations in export processing zones constitutes the neoliberal ideal. Government is either absent or a handmaiden to private enterprise. Individual laborers freely contract to sell their labor to employers. Competition among workers for jobs keeps wages low, which helps producers to generate cheaper products to sell in the global market. International financial institutions, such as the IMF and the World Bank, develop policy papers on how best to transform worker consciousness to meet the demands of marketization and train field workers to cultivate "export mentality" and "market mentality" while whittling away "protest mentalities" among the poor (Bedford 2005).

Confident of the power of the unfettered global market to generate wealth, neoliberals, like their eighteenth-century forebears, emphasize that capitalism will generate jobs, raising the income of the poor over time. Giving priority to individual freedom to pursue selfish advantage, and trusting

8

to the market to produce the promised public benefits, neoliberals are not concerned about radical inequalities in the distribution of that wealth.

Critics of globalization are far less sanguine about the potential benefits that might accrue from growing inequalities within and across nations. During the last two decades of the twentieth century, a period of vast increases in the production of wealth, UNDP *Human Development Reports* (1999, 2002) note that the economies of the majority of the world's nations worsened. The economies of more than 100 nations were worse off in 2000 than they had been in 1980. The wealthiest 20 percent of the world population controls 86 percent of the world income, while the poorest 20 percent controls only 1.1 percent, and 85 percent of the world population controls only 14 percent of the world's income. Between 1970 and 1995, average per capita income in the poorest third of countries fell from 3.1 percent to 1.9 percent of the average per capita income of the richest third. Nor are inequalities restricted to income. As Valentine Moghadam (2005, 41) has pointed out, "In the 1990s one-fifth the world population, living in highest income countries, have 86% of the gross domestic product (GDP), 82% of the world export markets, 68% of foreign direct investment, and 74% of the telephone lines; the bottom fifth, living in the poorest countries, had about 1% of each category." Surveying the stark increases in inequality since 1980, Georgina Waylen has suggested that neoliberalism's promotion of free market and antistate policies have produced "development in reverse for much of the Third World" (Waylen 1996, 34).

Gendered Dimensions of Globalization

When mainstream approaches to globalization emphasize global finance, trade, economic restructuring, technological innovations, changing dynamics of national sovereignty, democratization, neoliberal policy consensus, and growing inequalities, it is easy to assume that gender has nothing to do with globalization. Typically understood as an aspect of individual identity or as a cultural construction of masculinity and femininity, gender may seem altogether irrelevant to these dramatic economic, political, and technological transformations.

Feminist scholars working in fields of political economy, international relations, development studies, philosophy, history, and women's studies have also been investigating the changing dynamics of globalization, however. They have developed new analytic tools to help illuminate how gender operates as a site of power within processes of globalization and to explicate the mechanisms within traditional scholarship that naturalize and normalize gender hierarchies, rendering raced and gendered power relations invisible. Drawing upon the conception of an analytic category developed by Imre Lakatos (1970), feminist scholars have deployed gender as an analytical tool. In contrast to popular understandings of gender as cultural constructions of masculinity and femininity, gender as an analytic category functions as a heuristic device that illuminates areas for inquiry, frames questions for investigation, identifies puzzles in need of exploration, and provides concepts, definitions, and hypotheses to guide research (Hawkesworth 1997).

In an important and influential essay, Joan Scott (1986, 1067) defined gender as a concept involving two interrelated but analytically distinct parts: "Gender is a constitutive element of social relationships based on perceived differences between the sexes, and gender is a primary way of signifying relationships of power." In explicating gender as a constitutive element of social relationships, Scott emphasized that gender operates in multiple fields, including culturally available symbols, normative concepts, social institutions and organizations, and subjective identities (1067–1068). Attuned to the structuring power of gender in these various domains, feminist scholars investigate in concrete circumstances how inequalities between men and women are produced, reproduced, contested, and transformed over time. According to Scott (1070), gender is a useful category of analysis precisely because it "provides a way to decode meaning," and to illuminate how gender hierarchies are created, preserved, and changed through the complex interaction of norms, symbols, interpersonal relations, social practices, and religious, economic, and political institutions.

Using gender as an analytic tool, feminist scholars have illuminated power relations between men and women, as well as mechanisms of advantage and disadvantage structured by race, ethnicity, nationality, and sexuality that create and sustain interpersonal and social hierarchies. Within a feminist analytic framework, gender power involves a set of asymmetrical relations permeating international regimes, state systems, financial and economic processes, development policies, institutional structures, symbol systems, and interpersonal relations (Duerst-Lahti and Kelly 1995; Kabeer 2003; Peterson 2003). Gender power is embedded in systems of value that privilege men by celebrating characteristics traditionally associated with maleness or masculinity, while devaluing women and characteristics associated with femininity. Culturally varying constructions of gender shape expectations about what is appropriate for men and women to do, structuring divisions of labor and social space, and constraining the opportunities, choices, and actions available to particular men and women. In this way, gender is integrally related to inequalities, which become embedded in institutions and structures that operate independently of individual volition and intention. Organizational and social roles, routines, and policies serve and promote men's interests and normalize male power, often rendering women's needs and interests invisible. Thus gender power operates through prohibitions, exclusions, denigrations, and devaluations that circumscribe women's lives.

Investigating its complex economic, political, technological, and ideological dynamics, feminist scholars construe globalization as a thoroughly gendered phenomenon. Seeking to trace the effects of globalization on gender, they have investigated the feminization of poverty, the feminization of the labor force, and the growing traffic in women. They have also sought to illuminate how gender structures globalization, examining changing sexual divisions of labor, male bias, masculinist priorities in economic policies, and gendered symbolic representations, such as "Davos Man" (Moghadam 2005, 18). In this way, feminist scholars have reframed issues and introduced new concepts to explicate facets of globalization omitted from mainstream accounts. By documenting the feminization of poverty and the care economy, and examining mobilizations concerning women's rights as human rights, strategies to engender development, and the need for gender justice, feminist scholars have demonstrated that globalization has varied effects, differentiated by gender, race, ethnicity, and nationality. A brief consideration of some of these findings helps explain how globalization is gendered.

The Feminization of the Labor Force

Over the past two decades, more and more women have been recruited to the formal and informal labor force, supplementing the work they do in the home and in the production of subsistence. Feminist scholars characterize this phenomenon as "the feminization of the labor force." In export processing zones across the global South, for example, women constitute 70 to 90 percent of the factory workers producing textiles, leather goods, toys, electronic goods, and pharmaceuticals (Wichterich 2000). Export processing zones approximate a new form of extraterritoriality, existing within the borders of particular states, but exempt from taxes, tariffs, national labor laws, and environmental regulations. With official and unofficial bans against labor unions, working hours are long, and working conditions are often hazardous. As transnational corporations have increasingly moved to outsourcing labor, 200 million women are employed by subcontractors. Working in textile and pharmaceutical production, small numbers of women employees work in their employers' homes, garages, or workshops for very low wages. To meet production deadlines, mandatory overtime without compensation is often required. The tolls of such working conditions are manifold. Long hours at work impose strains upon family life as women workers have little time to perform the domestic chores expected of them. Some families find it difficult to withstand such strains. In Salvador, for example, 80 percent of the married women in textile production are living without their husbands (Wichterich 2000; E. Brooks forthcoming). Thus feminist scholars have pointed out that globalization is changing family formations: 52 percent of poor households are now headed by women, compared to 20 percent in the 1990s, and 10 percent in the 1970s (Poster and Salime 2002, 211). The health effects of work in the export processing zones are also palpable. Women working in export processing zones have twice the normal rate of miscarriages and deliver twice as many underweight babies. Poor lighting, eye strain, and repetitive stress syndrome combine to impair the performance of women factory workers after a comparatively short period. The average work life for women factory workers in Thailand, for example, is five years. Job-induced problems with eye-hand coordination provide managers with a reason for firing workers. Nor is Thailand atypical. In Central America, a woman factory worker is let go after an average of seven years (Wichterich 2000).

The feminization of labor under globalization involves more than a shift to a majority female labor force. It also encompasses informal and flexible conditions of employment long associated with women workers, including part-time and temporary jobs, low wages, and no benefits. In 1975, 80 percent of economically active workers were eligible for unemployment compensation; in 1995 only 25 percent of economically active workers qualified for that benefit (Wichterich 2000). Both men and women workers have been subjected to "informalization" and "flexibilization" as the conditions of labor are feminized.

Saskia Sassen (2002) has pointed out that one manifestation of informalization is home-based work, which reintroduces the household as important economic space not only for outsourced workers in subcontracting facilities in export processing zones, but for telecommuting professional workers, and for growing numbers of domestic workers and self-employed. Similar to the effects of deregulation, home-based work increases flexibility while reducing costs of labor, as infrastructure expenses (physical space, utilities, equipment) are passed on to the workers themselves.

The feminization of the labor force and feminization of the conditions of labor are also related to the kinds of work characteristic of globalization, in particular to the shift to a service economy. Although male-dominated services in finance and information technology can be highly remunerated, women-dominated services such as childcare, paraprofessional health care, retail sales, or cleaning services tend to be paid very poorly. The vast majority of women service workers earn subsistence-level wages or less, which contributes to the feminization of poverty (Wichterich 2000). More than 70 percent of the poor globally are women.

The economic restructuring involved in transition to a market-based service economy has been particularly tough on women workers. In 1990, prior to the collapse of state socialism in Russia, women held 60 percent of the highly skilled positions in fields such as medicine and chemistry. In the transition to a market economy, 80 percent of women workers lost their jobs. After a decade of severe economic dislocation, the job opportunities available for many women were far less attractive than the positions they had lost. Taking positions as hairdressers, cosmeticians, secretaries, and sex workers, many Russian women experienced a significant decline in wages. Before 1990, Russian women earned 70 percent of the average male wage; in 2000, they earned 40 percent of the average male wage (Wichterich 2000). The intensification of sex segregation in the labor force under recent globalization has contributed to a growing wage gap between male and female workers. In Western nations women earn 10–25 percent less than average male earnings; in the global South, as in Russia and former Soviet states, women earn 30–60 percent less than the average male wage.

Another aspect of informalization associated with globalization is the rise of the female microentrepreneur. Adapted from a model of women's pooled savings[3] and incorporated into the business model of the Grameen Bank, microfinance has been hailed as a form of economic salvation, embraced with "evangelical zeal" by governments, donors, nongovernmental organizations (NGOs), and the World Bank (Tamale 2001, 75). Microcredit provides very small loans to individuals to enable them to launch profit-generating business ventures. Multiple studies have shown that women are far better than men at repaying their loans. With repayment rates near 90 percent, microcredit programs for women have been demonstrated to be sound capital investments. In advocating microcredit, proponents emphasize that it enables individual women to engage in market competition via microenterprise, promoting self-confidence and economic achievement, while fostering economic growth and promoting community development. Lending individual women investment capital, which they repay from their successful economic ventures, is a virtually cost-free means to economic development within a market framework. Yet microcredit advocates also insist that it is a strategy for empowering women.

In contrast to the glowing descriptions of microcredit schemes, feminists have called attention to the "onerous terms of these loans," which are seldom publicized. In Uganda, one of the twenty poorest nations in the world, for example, the 18 percent interest rate on microcredit loans is higher than prevailing commercial rates in the country. The interest is compounded monthly. The borrower is allowed no grace period on interest payments; indeed, the first payment is due within seven days. To mobilize peer pressure to encourage repayment, each loan must be cosigned by two to three individuals who are not relatives of the borrower and who face financial liability if the borrower defaults (Tamale 2001, 75–78). Microfinance rules specify that only one loan is allowed per family; and only one person within the family may borrow microcredit funds. Thus at the same time that microcredit fosters women's microenterprises, it also restructures family relations, precluding the equal financial involvement of men and women in family businesses. Under "constant pressure to repay their loans, women have no time for literacy, health, job training, or seminars on political rights" (Tamale 2001, 78). Development strategies grounded in women's microenterprise may help expand capitalist markets and foster economic growth, but they also heighten the economic responsibilities of individual women, magnifying their burden as providers for family subsistence. They increase the debt of poor women, imposing new levels of stress as well as responsibility. Thus gender disadvantage is intensified for women who already work longer hours than men, earn less, and are restricted to lower quality employment than men (Buvinic 1999, 570).

The Feminization of Migration

High levels of unemployment in their home nations and demand for workers in affluent nations have made the feminization of migration another feature of contemporary globalization. Some 60 million women, drawn predominantly from poor nations, constitute a mobile labor force criss-crossing the globe in search of livelihoods. Certain migratory circuits have been well mapped: South Asia to the Middle East, former Soviet states to Western Europe, Mexico and Central America to Canada and the United States, and Africa to Europe (Ehrenreich and Hochschild 2002). Migrating women are not an entirely new phenomenon. African women experienced forced migration through the slave trade from the sixteenth to the nineteenth centuries; and many European women migrated in search of better economic opportunities from the eighteenth to the twentieth centuries. In the current era of globalization, the sheer number of women migrants, the very long distances they travel, and their migration without family members are distinctive, however. Women migrant workers in the Middle East, for example, increased from 8,000 in 1979 to 100,000 in 1999 (Moghadam 2005, 71). Some 3.8 million Filipinas are currently working overseas as maids, nannies, nurses, and entertainers, composing more than 60 percent of the migrant labor force from their country. They are working in more than 130 nations, spanning Asia (especially Hong Kong and Singapore), the Middle East, North America, and Europe (Parrenas 2001a, 2001b). The remittances they send home are a mainstay of the Philippine economic system, providing the government with its largest source of foreign currency, totaling more than US$8 billion per year in 2000 (Magat 2001). Among other things, these remittances are used by the Philippine government to cover the $1.8 billion in annual interest on loans accumulated from the World Bank and the IMF (Rosca 1995). In addition to generating foreign currency, the migration of Filipinas helps solve the problem of unemployment in the Philippines. In the absence of migrant labor, unemployment in the Philippines would increase by 40 percent (Castles and Miller 1998).

Given the vital economic importance of the remittances provided by Filipina migrant workers, the Philippine government has been actively promoting the marketization of care work, taking the lead in negotiating labor contracts with the governments of receiving states in Asia, the Americas, Europe, and the Middle East. Among the provisions of these labor contracts are a number of significant violations of women's rights,[4] including extensive curtailment of reproductive freedom, the freedom to marry and engage in sexual relationships of one's own choosing, freedom of movement, and freedom of domicile. The contracts also violate a number of fair labor practices. Feminist scholars have pointed out that the terms of these overseas domestic employment contracts bear startling resemblance to the conditions of indentured servitude. Under the terms of these contracts, Filipina domestic workers become the dependents of their employers. The Singapore contract, for example, requires Filipinas to live in the household of their employers. They are not allowed to bring family members to their host nation. They are allowed one day off per month—after they have completed a three-month probationary period. They may not leave the country during the period of the contract (typically two years) without the written permission of their employers. They are forbidden to marry any citizen or permanent resident of Singapore. They must submit to pregnancy tests every six months. Moreover, the contract stipulates that they will be fired and deported should they become pregnant.

In stark contrast to neoliberal celebrations of individual freedom, one effect of globalization is a peculiarly gendered form of serfdom emerging at the heart of productive relations in the global service economy. Moreover, this prescribed mode of gender subordination is negotiated and enforced through the cooperative action of sending and receiving states. In contrast to the much vaunted individual freedom to contract their labor power, governments structure the foreign domestication of Filipinas, who leave their own children to care for the children of foreigners and who leave their husbands to assume domestic responsibilities in the households of foreign men.[5] The government-negotiated contracts transform Filipina overseas domestic workers from autonomous adults and citizens in the sending nation into dependents excluded from all rights of citizenship in the receiving nation, as they are denied control over the conditions of their lives and work, over decisions concerning love, marriage, reproduction, and physical mobility, and excluded from rights of political participation in both nations during the terms set by their contracts.

Filipinas are by no means the only women migrating to work in the global care economy. They are joined by millions of women throughout Africa, Asia, and Central and Latin America who are working in more affluent nations. "Pulled by the 'care deficit' in wealthier nations and pushed by poverty in their home states," women migrants involved in the global care economy contribute to a "global transfer of emotional resources" (Ehrenreich and Hoschschild 2002, 8). The transnational commodification of care thus appears to be a distinctive aspect of contemporary globalization. In the words of Barbara Ehrenreich and Arlie Hochschild (2002, 4):

> In an earlier phase of imperialism, northern countries extracted natural resources and agricultural products—rubber, metals, and sugar, for example—from lands they conquered and colonized. Today, while still relying on third world countries for agricultural and industrial labor, the wealthy countries also seek to extract something harder to measure and quantify, something that can look very much like love.

It would be a mistake, however, to romanticize the commodification of care. Overseas domestic workers often face abusive and exploitive working conditions. Indeed, a British study of 755 overseas domestic workers revealed that 88 percent had experienced psychological abuse by their employers; 38 percent had suffered physical abuse; 11 percent had been subjected to sexual assault; and most were underfed and overworked, required to work seventeen hours per day (G. Chang 2000, 138).

Sex work and sexual trafficking also help illuminate the gulf between the simulacrum of love and the real thing. High rates of poverty and unemployment have long served as triggers for increasing numbers involved in sex work. The exponential growth in transnational sexual trafficking in the last three decades of the twentieth century has more proximate causes, however. The Vietnam War generated a vibrant sex industry in Thailand and Japan, where American, Australian, and Korean soldiers were sent for rest and relaxation. When the supply of soldiers dwindled in the aftermath of war, sex tourism in Thailand was launched as a global business venture. The Thai government developed marketing schemes to make Thailand the preferred destination of sex tourists. Burgeoning tourism attracted 2 million tourists in 1981, 4 million in 1988, 7 million in 1996—two-thirds of whom were unaccompanied men. In the early twenty-first century, some 5 million men visit Thailand annually generating 656 billion baht (US$26.2 billion) in revenue. Sustaining this booming economy are young Thai women who service ten to eighteen clients per day to repay the cost of their "purchase" from their parents, plus the expense of their room and board (Bales 2002, 219–220).

The Thai model of sex tourism has been replicated by governments in the global South whose immiserated economies encourage them to promote commodification of women as sex workers as a strategy for survival (Sassen 2002, 273). Indeed, tourism is an economic solution to the troubles of poor countries, which has been highly recommended by the International Monetary Fund and the World Bank. Catering to the market demands of affluent tourists, sex tourism has been adopted as a development strategy by nations experiencing widespread poverty and unemployment (Sassen 2002, 269). It is certainly a lucrative strategy, generating remittances of $70 billion in 1998.

Sex tourism involves complicated public-private partnerships, however, because sex work remains illegal in most nations. Although government officials may be eager for the revenue generated by this illegal enterprise, their support for such ventures often takes the form of nonenforcement of existing criminal laws. The global traffic in women, then, turns on a suspect partnership involving government corruption and transnational criminal networks. Consider, for example, the significant increase in sexual trafficking of women from Armenia, Russia, Bulgaria, Croatia, and Ukraine to Europe during the last decade of the twentieth century. With women's unemployment in these states running 70–80 percent during the economic restructuring in the 1990s and without any safety net to rely on during the "shock transition," pressing financial need motivated some women to enter prostitution. Promising transportation, visas, local accommodation, and cell phones essential for meeting clients, and providing inaccurate information concerning the legality of sex work in most European nations, criminal networks secure the attention of prospective sex workers. The UN estimates that 4 million people trafficked in 1998 generated $7 billion for criminal networks. Traffickers in Ukrainian and Russian women, for example, earned $700–$1000 for every woman delivered to a European destination. Expected to service fifteen clients per day on average, sex workers in Europe generate $215,000 per month for the gangs that control trafficked women (Sassen 2002, 268). Once in the hands of criminal traffickers, sex workers' "freedom" to contract is severely compromised. Working illegally in their host nations, with their passports confiscated by sex traffickers, transnational sex workers become a transnational underclass cut off from civil protections and political life in both sending and receiving states (Barker 2003, 19). Although the terms of their employment may be onerous, they have lost the putative freedom of every worker—to quit.

Privatization

Privatization or the "shrinking of the state" is another aspect of the neoliberal agenda for globalization that has gendered effects. As noted above, neoliberal arguments for cutting back the state involve more than pragmatic concerns about budget cutting during periods of financial crisis. A defense of the "night watchman state" is integral to neoliberal ideological claims about the primacy of the market. In this view, the state has minimal legitimate functions such as providing for defense and public order, protecting private property, and the right to contract, but neoliberals insist that more expansive initiatives to meet human needs are best left to the market.

Over the past few decades, neoliberalism has profoundly altered perceptions of the kinds of contestations possible within the nation-state (Hoover and Plant 1989). Resurrecting the classical view that inequality among people is natural rather than politically constituted and maintained, neoliberals insist that state efforts to reduce inequality are futile and necessarily oppressive. Rather than indulge utopian fantasies, the role of the state, in this view, is to promote individual freedom, understood as the individual's pursuit of material self-interest. The state can best advance this end by facilitating economic development, which in turn will resolve social problems. State strategies to foster economic development include deregulation of the corporate sector, provision of special incentives for economic development in free enterprise zones, reductions of income, estate, and corporate taxes, and elimination of welfare dependency. Within the parameters set by neoliberalism, the political agenda should be winnowed down to the provision of essential business services and security (domestic and global). The hallmark agencies of the welfare state should be privatized.

In the past twenty-five years, privatization has occurred voluntarily in some circumstances, and it has been imposed as a condition of debt restructuring in others. Under the influence of neoliberal doctrines, the Thatcher administration in the United Kingdom (1979–1990), for example, began voluntarily divesting the government of various public assets, privatizing British Telecom, ports and airports, petroleum companies, railways, gas, gas stations, and hotels. Similarly, the Reagan administration in the United States (1980–1988) introduced policy changes to privatize education and welfare by contracting out public schools to be run by for-profit corporations such as Edison and outsourcing the administration of welfare services to corporations like Lockheed Martin, a major defense contractor. Under the influence of neoliberalism, even prisons in the United States have been privatized (Bayes 2004). In New Zealand, privatization has transformed the conditions of employment of the civil service. Top ministry officials are hired on five-year contracts, and consultants are contracted short-term to do the policy work once done by career civil servants.

For many nations in the global South, privatization has been required by the IMF and World Bank as a condition for debt restructuring, a privatization that transfers control of vital resources and services to transnational corporations. In Senegal, for example, privatization of state enterprises transferred phones and telecommunication services to France Telecom, public transportation to French RATP (transport authority), water to the French company SDE, and national energy policy to Quebec Hydraulique (Fall 2001). As Yassine Fall has documented, privatization has not produced the economic benefits promised, but it has generated new burdens for the poor.

> Prices of water, electricity, telephone, and transport have gone up, while service delivery is as distorted as before. . . . Public fountains made available by the government to the very poor in urban areas are no longer free. Having to buy water at the public fountain creates a new income deficit, aggravating poor women's living standard and obliging them to carry heavy buckets of water considerable distances after having bought it at highly prohibitive prices. (Fall 2001, 70)

In many nations, privatization is correlated with loss of employment for women. The expansion of the welfare state in the aftermath of World War II created new career opportunities for women professionals. In Egypt, for example, the state was the largest employer of women, providing positions for 43 percent of the economically active women (Wichterich 2000). In the United States,

> Great Society programs in the 1960s heightened the importance of social welfare employment for all groups, particularly women. Between 1960 and

19

1980, human services accounted for 41% of the job gains for women compared with 21% for men. Among women, there were significant differences in the importance of human services employment for whites and blacks. For white women, the social welfare economy accounted for 39% of the job gain between 1960 and 1980; for black women, an even more dramatic 58%. (Erie, Rein, and Wiget 1983, 103)

When state programs in human services are cut back, women employees are disproportionately affected. Thus neoliberal privatization contributes to a "regendering of the state," shoring up male-dominant institutions (finance, commerce, defense/military), while delegitimizing and diminishing the social welfare agencies in which women have gained ground.

Privatization also increases women's unwaged work. Feminist economists have long pointed out that a great deal of the work done by women is unwaged. Production of subsistence foods in small garden plots, food preparation, childcare and elder care, early childhood education, and nursing care for the ill and infirm, as well as household cleaning and maintenance, involve significant amounts of women's time and energy, yet they exist largely outside market exchange relations. The UN Development Program (UNDP) has calculated that 70 percent of the work performed by women globally is unwaged. The economic value of women's unwaged labor is $11 billion annually. Cuts in state provision of health care, education, and welfare shift responsibility for the private provision of these services largely onto women, thereby increasing women's unwaged work (Waring 1988; Bakker and Gill 2003).

Mainstream economists do not track costs of labor that occur outside the parameters of market exchange. Thus the added burdens imposed upon women by privatization remain invisible within dominant accounts of globalization. Feminist economist Ingrid Palmer (1992, 69) characterizes women's unwaged labor as a "reproductive tax," created as the market "externalizes the costs of reproduction and life sustenance and entrusts it to women." The reproductive tax imposes an exacting toll on poor women in the global South, who are already working a triple shift in subsistence, productive, and reproductive labor. One study in Mexico, for example, demonstrated that 90.5 percent of the economically active women were working a double shift in the formal sector compared with 62 percent of the men (Purewal 2001, 106). The demands of unwaged work in the home must be met over and above the hours devoted to waged labor in the market. The assumption that women's time is infinitely elastic and can expand indefinitely to absorb the responsibilities imposed by privatization is fast hitting up against the limits of human exhaustion (Elson 1995; Bedford 2005). Evidence of the harmful physical effects of overwork is mounting. Since structural adjustment policies were introduced in the early 1980s, infant and child mortality rates have increased, reproductive tract infections have increased, sterility has increased as women's health is taxed beyond endurance (Purewal 2001, 101). Moreover, across the global South women are turning to their daughters for assistance in unwaged work. Thus the numbers of girls in school have decreased and female illiteracy is rising as social provision is privatized.

Privatization also has discursive effects that subtly alter the possibilities for social justice and gender justice in the era of globalization. Efforts to create liberal democratic practices in the nineteenth century and social democracy in the aftermath of World War II targeted the state as the primary site of political contestation. Through political party platforms, as well as the politics of direct action, proponents of social justice engaged the nation-state to curb the enormous power of the capitalist market. Feminists, like other progressive activists, perceived the state as a unique vehicle in the struggle for social justice because the state had the capacity to bestow equal rights, to legislate policies to redress historic exclusions and inequities, to use its tax revenues toward redistributive ends, to provide all citizens with a decent quality of life, and to change exploitive conditions of labor. In devising multiple strategies to politicize women's issues, feminists intentionally sought to transform what had been construed as matters of private, intimate, or personal relations into objects of public concern. In forging their political agenda, feminists intentionally sought to redefine public issues. Thus they suggested that an issue is public "1) if it is treated as politically important; 2) if it is understood as causally related to societal structures in which all citizens are implicated; and 3) if its solution is viewed as requiring a collective effort to bring about reform" (K. Kelly 2003, 77).

In targeting the state, feminists sought to force the official institutions of government to treat women and women's concerns as matters of political importance. They sought to demonstrate how the law constructs and sustains public and private spheres and the relations of gender inequality that pervade them. By illuminating state complicity in the subordination of women, feminists tried to foster public awareness of the depths of collective responsibility for centuries of women's exclusion, marginalization, and exploitation in the hope that public knowledge of injustice would trigger collective action to change the laws, the social structures, and the personal relations shaped by them. In nations around the globe, feminists have devoted and continue to devote extensive efforts to the formation of a feminist public sphere or "counterpublic" as a crucial step in the politics of social change. It is a step that presupposes engagement with the state as a critical venue for democratic politics. The tenets of neoliberalism, however, transform the conditions under which feminist activists attempt to engage gender-based injustices.

Neoliberalism characterizes feminist political activism as private interest group activity. What social movement feminists understand as a political struggle for social justice, the rights of women citizens, or "women's rights as human rights," neoliberals construe as private mobilizations to gain public resources. For example, neoliberals frame feminist efforts to secure state funding for women's health, prenatal and infant care, early childhood education, rape prevention, and domestic violence prevention as special interest lobbying. In changing the framing assumptions from a discourse of social justice to a discourse of private pursuit of economic resources, feminist goals are depoliticized and resignified as private endeavors. By privatizing feminist appeals to the state for redress of grievances, neoliberals can depict feminist activists (as well as antiracism activists and gay and lesbian activists) as proponents of special interests, who unfairly demand special rights. As appeals to social justice are reduced to claims for special treatment within the neoliberal frame, they lose their justification and can be dismissed as violations of individual (i.e., white male) rights and universal norms. Caught within the privatization imperatives of neoliberalism, feminist claims for social justice are dismissed as special pleadings of private interest groups. Stripped by neoliberalism of a social justice context, feminist mobilizations have no greater claim on the public than the campaign of any interest group for private advantage. The moral suasion afforded by demands to remedy injustice is effectively neutralized as pluralist politics assumes the guise of providing an equal playing field for all private interests.

Feminization and Globalization

As the discussion of the feminization of labor and the feminization of migration suggests, there is more to feminization than a preponderance of women in any particular field. Feminization of labor involves increasing numbers of women in the labor force, as well as deterioration of working conditions (casualization, flexibilization, violation of international labor standards, declining wages, diminishing status) (Moghadam 2005, 7). Feminization of migration involves not only the transnational movement of millions of women, but their loss of physical security, political rights, and rights of bodily integrity. Indeed, some feminist scholars have suggested that overseas domestic workers are emblematic of the feminization of citizenship, the emergence of a mode of partial citizenship that requires payment of taxes, yet affords no voting rights and tolerates diminished liberties pertaining to movement, conditions of labor, marriage, and reproduction. (Parrenas 2001a, 2001b; R. Rodriguez 2002; Barker 2003). Since sending states lack power to protect their overseas nationals, feminized citizens face the abject vulnerability of the nationless, a status masked by the neoliberal rhetoric of self-reliance and cosmopolitan citizenship (Parrenas 2001a, 54–55).

The feminization of poverty refers to more than the fact that 70 percent of the poor globally are women; the poor are constituted as a feminized category, as dependent, subrational, and in need of direction (Kingfisher 2002). The transnational marketization of the care economy provides that direction through "the return of the serving classes" (Sassen 2002, 259). The increase in low-wage work globally constitutes a "feminization of job supply" (Sassen 2002, 259), as poorly paid workers are expected to adopt the self-sacrificing demeanor of the subaltern. Informalization and casualization constitute a "feminization of business opportunities" (Sassen 2002, 263), as microfinance subjects increasing numbers of women to the stern discipline of the market's invisible hand. The World Bank (2002) promotes the "feminization of survival" as the solution to the problem of global poverty, and households, communities, and governments become increasingly dependent on women for their survival as the structural forces of globalization make the possibilities of poverty alleviation increasingly remote.

The logic of feminization is complex and contradictory. Women are simultaneously hailed as resourceful providers, reliable microentrepreneurs, and cosmopolitan citizens and positioned as disposable domestics, the exploited global workforce, and as displaced, devalued, and disenfranchised diasporic citizens. In the early 1980s, Christine Delphy argued that what made "women's work" distinctive was not the particular tasks involved but the requirement that those tasks be done in a relation of subservience (Delphy 1984). Feminization replicates a mandate of subservience. Regardless of the tasks involved, feminization entails a logic of menialization, requiring that tasks be performed with a measure of servility. Where patriarchy required women's generic subservience to men, feminization renders the feminized (men and women) subservient to market imperatives, profit maximization, and commodification.

Tim Kaufman-Osborn (2005, 5) has suggested that feminization is a "strategy of power" involving "scripted practices of subordination designed to create helplessness and dependence," which work by cutting people off from the known and reassuring, casting them into the strange, and disorienting them to foster compliance. There is much about globalization that fits this description. Transnational migrants quite literally are cut off from all that is known and familiar, cast into strange homes in strange lands. Marketization in former socialist states superimposes the strange upon the remnants of a lost way of life. Deindustrialization and flexibilization of labor in emergent service economies disorient workers who can no longer rely on long-term employment at living wages. Structural adjustment policies cut people in the global South off from livelihoods built upon subsistence agriculture and subject them to the vicissitudes of export cropping, off-shore enterprises, urban and transnational migration, and radical restructuring of family and community life.

The dimensions of feminization contrast starkly with neoliberal claims concerning the beneficial effects of globalization. Rather than promoting freedom, equality, self-determination, maximization of self-interest, and individual flourishing, feminization produces marked inequalities, which workers rendered docile and subservient accept with resignation. Rather than conforming to the "developmental logic" of modernization discourses (Cruz-Malavé and Manalansan 2002), which suggests that the market obliterates traditional cultures and relations and establishes liberal individual freedoms in their place, feminization restores features of oppressive feudal relations, such as indentured servitude, servile relations, political disenfranchisement, and sexual slavery.

If feminization challenges the central logic and the purported benefits of globalization, then it is important to ask questions about the precise relationship between globalization and feminization—questions that cannot even be framed within the parameters set by mainstream accounts of globalization. Feminist scholarship suggests a number of possibilities for understanding the interrelated dynamics of feminization and globalization. As the material covered in this chapter demonstrates, the two processes are concomitant; they are occurring simultaneously. Noting that correlation, some feminist scholars describe feminization as a characteristic feature of globalization. Others make a stronger claim, suggesting that globalization causes feminization, either intentionally or unintentionally. Feminist scholars across a range of disciplines are currently investigating this issue. The stakes in this debate are high for they involve the long-term prospects of the majority of the world population, encompassing questions concerning the nature of women's waged and unwaged work, the conditions of labor within the global economy, the scope of democratic practices within neoliberalism, and gendered power relations within families, communities, nations, global institutions, and transnational arenas.

Feminisms

Feminism is a collective noun. At first glance, then, it appears that any reference to "feminisms" involves a grammatical mistake. But the concept of feminisms has a history and a politics directly tied to transnational feminist encounters. As Francesca Miller (1999, 225) has pointed out, the pluralization of feminism was introduced in the late 1980s to indicate that feminism was not the sole preserve of any one group and "to signify the multiplicity of ways in which those who share a feminist critique may come together to address issues." As a strategic term introduced by transnational feminist activists to help negotiate a complex array of ideological differences and differences in national and regional policy priorities, "feminisms" was intended to "create discursive space in a fraught arena" by "resisting homogenization, generalization, nostalgia" (Miller 1999, 225).

Foregrounding the plurality of feminisms is essential for any book seeking to trace global feminist activism. For feminism operates within and across a variety of intellectual, historical, political, geographic, and temporal frames. Culling the rich literature on feminism, it is possible to find authoritative accounts of feminism as an idea, a set of political convictions, a mode of identification with other women, a way of being a woman, a collective identity available to men and women, a form of political mobilization, a policy agenda, a legacy, a means of forging the "we" that Beauvoir thought women lacked, a strategy for forging alliances and building allegiance, a praxis, a vision of alternative possibilities, an imagined community, a process of creating something new, a tactic for transforming social relations, an inclusive, participatory politics, and an expansive conception of justice encompassing economic distribution, political rights and liberties, collective responsibility, and dispute resolution. The following chapters explicate these rich and various meanings of feminism in the context of two centuries of transnational feminist activism.

Focusing on the plurality of feminisms is also important because feminism is a contested term, even among women committed to improving the conditions of women's lives. While many transnational advocates for women claim the feminist label, many others reject it. Many who identify as feminist find strength and affirmation by claiming a vibrant tradition that has contributed to intellectual ferment and social transformation for five centuries. Many find a wealth of strategic insights by situating their work in the theories and practices of socialist feminists, liberal feminists, black feminists, social feminists, radical feminists, Marxist feminists, cultural feminists, ecofeminists, psychoanalytic feminists, postcolonial feminists, poststructuralist feminists, and postoccidental feminists. By claiming the long and rich legacy of feminism, many transnational activists are enabled to refuse the vicious caricature of feminism (man-hating, bra-burning, family-destroying) that circulates in the media and in the popular imagination in many parts of the world. Yet other proponents of women and women's rights have good reasons for rejecting the feminist label. Some object to a particular strain of imperial feminism that has been zealously promoted by white, liberal, Western, middle-class feminists since the 1870s, which has lent support to colonial and racist projects. Some seek to contest the class, racial, ethnic, and national biases of versions of bourgeois feminism that endorse capitalism as the precondition for women's emancipation. Some repudiate Judeo-Christian presuppositions of certain Western feminisms that caricature and underestimate the transformative potential of other religious and nonreligious traditions. Still other women's rights activists eschew the feminist label on pragmatic grounds to avoid having their political agendas derailed by charges of Western, imperialist bias advanced by traditionalists within their own nations.

Noting contestation over the term *feminism*, some scholars have sought to create an encompassing definition of feminism, which would enable them to classify as feminist all activities that conform to this definition, whether or not the women engaging in those activities identify as feminist. Surveying feminist engagements since the eighteenth century, for example, historian Karen Offen (2000) has suggested that feminism can be understood as a series of campaigns to eliminate women's economic, political, and social subordination—campaigns, one might say, that specifically target the menializing contours of feminization. "Feminist claims are primarily political, put forward in concrete settings" and posing specific political demands for change: calls to redress and reconfigure the sexual balance of power in virtually every area of human life (Offen 2000, xv). Other feminist scholars have constructed a category of de facto feminists that includes all activists who promote women's rights, explicitly challenge gender hierarchy, seek to change women's status, and promote women's empowerment, whether those activists claim or refuse the feminist label (Misciagno 1997; Moghadam 2005; Sperling, Ferree, and Risman 2001). Others have defined feminism as "women's self-organizing to further their own empowerment" (Weldon 2004), a definition that spans women's mobilizations to satisfy "practical gender interests" (i.e., action to address immediate needs) and "strategic gender interests" (i.e., action to eliminate gender-based subordination) (Molyneux 1985). Suggesting that the boundaries between practical and strategic gender interests tend to blur in women's activism, this definition emphasizes that activists themselves are transformed through action, which regardless of original intention may produce strategic outcomes and feminist consciousness.

Encompassing definitions of feminism have the advantage of inclusivity, demonstrating the expansiveness of feminist projects and mapping feminist presence in all nations and in all regions. They also illuminate common features of women's transformative practices, which may not be immediately apparent to activists themselves. Efforts to subsume diverse forms of women's activism under the feminist rubric have drawbacks, however, not least of which is the unseemly consequence of classifying as feminist women who actively refuse the label. Assimilating those who repudiate feminism into an encompassing definition of feminism replicates the problem of imperialism that troubles many critics of Western feminism in the first place. Moreover, it understates the significance of the differences that separate those who claim and those who refuse feminist identification. Thus it masks an important research question for those interested in transnational feminism. How are women who embrace feminism different from women who do not? Developing an answer to that question is part of the project of this book. In pursuing that project, my goal is to learn more about the defining characteristics of global feminism in the present and in the past, to explore the stakes in claiming feminism, and to examine what the claims of transnational feminists reveal about the nature and processes of globalization.

Toward that end, the book explores global feminist activism in multiple senses. It examines explicitly international feminist mobilizations involving women in more than one nation or more than one region who seek to forge a collective identity among women and to improve the condition of women. It also investigates feminist activism that targets problems at the global level, considering various transformative tactics that rely upon international organizations and transnational networks and the kinds of change they enable.

As noted earlier in this chapter, feminism is also an approach to scholarship, an approach that informs the structure and content of this book. Starting from the diversity of women's lives as a focal point of analysis and deploying gender as an analytical tool, the following chapters illuminate dimensions of globalization missed by other accounts. They investigate technological, cultural, political, and economic forces that enable transnational and global feminist engagements, analyzing the infrastructure of global feminism. They examine feminist politics that reach beyond the arena of the nation-state, mapping the scope and evaluating the impact of feminist efforts to use international institutions, international nongovernmental organizations (INGOs), and transnational feminist civil society to produce social change. In so doing, they excavate a far longer tradition of transnational feminist activism than is typically discussed and explore the world that feminists envision and enact through their global mobilizations.

The book also considers how feminist activism and feminist scholarship challenge fundamental assumptions concerning globalization. Illuminating gendered dimensions of social, economic, political, technological, and cultural transformations, it reveals a side of neoliberal capitalism at odds with the claims of its chief proponents. Taking issue with optimistic predictions concerning advances of freedom and democracy, the book traces how racialized and gender-based injustices are being created and legitimated in the present with profound consequences for the future. Through the analysis of historical and contemporary examples, *Globalization and Feminist Activism* provides new insights into the gendered nature of the global system and the gendered dynamics of international institutions and nation-states.

FEMINISTS GO GLOBAL:
RECLAIMING A HISTORY

> Our goal is association. Until now women have had no organization that allows them to give themselves to something great, they have only been able to concern themselves with petty individual matters that have left them in isolation. . . . We have faith that many women will rally to us, and that others will imitate us by forming their own groups. . . . Women alone will say what freedom they want.
>
> —*Tribune des femmes* (1832, 6–8)

> The reformation which we propose, in its utmost scope, is radical and universal. It is not the mere perfecting of a progress already in motion, a detail of some established plan, but it is an epochal movement—the emancipation of a class, the redemption of half the world, and a conforming reorganization of all social, political, and industrial interests and institutions.
>
> —Proceedings of the Woman's Rights Convention,
> Worcester, Massachusetts (1850)

> Amnesia, not lack of history, is feminism's worst enemy today.
>
> —Karen Offen (2000, 17)

Many of the key issues on the contemporary transnational feminist agenda are sketched in the discussion of the gendered dimensions of globalization in chapter 1: poverty, racism, neoliberalism, inequitable conditions of labor, women's triple shift, migration, women's full citizenship, prostitution and sexual trafficking, social justice, equal access to social goods, equal share of social benefits, Western imperialism, women's health and reproductive rights, equal access to education, occupational equity, equal representation in governance and in national and international decision making, violence against women, militarism, pacifism, and sustainable development. Feminist websites, feminist conferences held in conjunction with the World Social Forum, feminist activism to implement the Beijing Platform for Action, feminist work within the UNDP and UNIFEM, and feminist work in a host of transnational nongovernmental organizations (NGOs) foreground these issues, share information, and devise innovative strategies to address them. Many excellent books trace activism on these issues as evidence of the emergence of global feminism over the past thirty years and as evidence of the growing role of nonstate actors in the global arena (A. Fraser 1987; Antrobus 2004; Keck and Sikkink 1998; Moghadam 2005; Naples and Desai 2002; Rowbotham and Linkogle 2001; Wichterich 2000).

It is easy to assume, then, that transnational feminist activism and the identification of a global feminist agenda are fairly recent developments, emerging in the last decades of the twentieth century. Scholarship by feminist historians, however, suggests that transnational feminist activism has a much longer history (Anderson 2000; Buhle 1981; Bolt 2004; Jayawardena 1995; Newman 1999; Offen 2000; Rupp 1997). Examining that history reveals not only that most of the issues noted above were placed on the international feminist agenda during the nineteenth century, but also that some were articulated as far back as the fifteenth century. By tracing a longer trajectory of feminist activism, it is possible to learn more about changes in social, economic, and political life that have triggered feminist efforts to forge transnational alliances as a means to produce social change. Understanding the factors that have contributed to feminist mobilizing over the past two centuries can also provide insights into certain continuities and changes in economic, cultural, political, and ideological dimensions of globalization. Investigating longer historical trends can help identify obstacles to transnational feminist activism and factors that have undermined fragile gains achieved over decades of struggle. By troubling erroneous assumptions about the "newness" of transnational feminist activism and dispelling the modernist myth of irreversible progress in women's rights, a historical approach to global feminism generates useful lessons for contemporary transformative efforts.

The goal of this chapter is to demonstrate that the intricate global architecture of contemporary transnational feminism is the product of nearly two centuries of women's activism that has sought to cut across national and regional divisions and to build international networks and alliances to attain specific political objectives—often in the face of explicit opposition from their national governments and from international organizations. The transnational solidarities created and the victories achieved have been hard won and often fleeting. That some transnational feminist objectives have remained remarkably stable is as much an indicator of recurrent periods of backlash and policy reversals as it is of constancy of purpose.

Recent scholarship in women's history challenges entrenched views of the past, reshaping understandings of women's lives, feminism, internationalism, and backlash, as well as factors that contribute to progressive transnational mobilizations of women and to oppressive assimilationist and imperialist tendencies. Drawing on this transformative research, this chapter provides a brief sketch of one circuit of transnational feminist activism originating in Europe and the United States over the past two centuries to shed new light on contemporary debates about global feminism.

Reclaiming the History of Global Feminisms

Karen Offen (2000, 24) has suggested that it is a mistake to conflate feminism with women's social movements: "As a mode of critique and demand for remediation feminism precedes and succeeds mass mobilizations." While there is no question that the conceptualization of feminism as a social movement is particularly apt under certain conditions, excessive reliance on this analytical frame has a number of drawbacks (Hawkesworth 2004). Defining feminist activism in social movement terms makes it impossible to ask questions about how feminist ideas are conceptualized and put into circulation. Construing feminism exclusively in social movement terms plays to the media's fascination with spectacle, but it has the unsavory effect of making feminism disappear when women are no longer in the streets. Conflating feminism with forms of protest and mass demonstrations sustains a representation of feminism as perpetual outsider. Since such outsider status is fundamentally incompatible with working within the system, feminism is condemned to temporary and fleeting manifestations, for the institutionalization of feminist principles and mobilization within institutions appear to remain forever beyond reach. Social movement frames also tend to equate feminist success with a form of publicity that secures widespread recognition of a problem. But naming a problem and resolving or eliminating it are quite different things. Thus while the conceptualization of feminism as a social movement highlights one form of feminist activism in certain periods, it has the ironic effect of declaring feminism obsolete long before feminists have achieved the social transformations they envision. Feminist victories are declared while feminist activists continue the struggle to achieve their unrealized agenda.

To overcome the limitations associated with exclusive focus on social movement conceptions of feminism, a more capacious conceptualization is needed. An alternative is to understand feminism in relation to an emerging consciousness of injustices, grounded in raced and gendered hierarchies, which generates transformative efforts (Jayawardena 1995, 9). This conceptualization facilitates recognition of the many forms feminisms take. From anger against unwarranted constraints to preliminary efforts to articulate an account of harms done and wrongs to be rectified, from fledgling efforts to speak in public to sustained efforts to be recognized as political actors, from initial attempts to identify like-minded associates to the difficult work of forging consensus around a political agenda, from summoning the courage to imagine a different world to organizing resistance against structures of oppression, feminists have invented themselves as advocates of women's political freedom. In tracing the historical trajectory of that invention, it is important not to underestimate the enormous amount of work involved in envisioning a world governed by different principles, developing critiques of hierarchy, elitism, racism, class bias, sexism, and ethnocentrism, much less of putting these ideas into practice. The enormity of this effort is related to the multiple and complex dimensions of the world that feminists seek to change and to the specific historical circumstances in which they launch their transformative efforts. To reclaim the history of transnational feminist activism, then, it is critical to recognize that there have been and continue to be multiple starting points all over the globe, but prevailing geopolitical structures of power influence which feminist initiatives gain momentum.

Early Transatlantic Articulations of Feminism

Long before the word *feminism* was coined, much less accepted as a term of common parlance, treatises on the equal capacities of women and men and treatises concerning an equal entitlement to freedom were circulating beyond national borders.[1] These tracts can be read as a response to changing claims about women's "nature," their appropriate social roles, and the kind of work that women should be allowed to do. For much of human history, the social roles and opportunities available to women were structured by their membership in a particular caste, class, race, and family as much as by their gender. In societies governed by ascription, an individual's life prospects were fixed by birth. The family into which one was born determined the kind of education and work available. In subsistence and agricultural economies, the household was the primary work site. Women and men played parallel and overlapping roles in the production of food, fuel, clothing, shelter, and other necessities of life.

During the fourteenth century a debate erupted among the literati of Europe about the nature and capacities of women and their qualifications for a full range of occupational opportunities, including political rule, military duty, and the administration of justice. As early as 1405, Christine de Pizan, a native of Venice then living in France, wrote *The Book of the City of Ladies*, a systematic refutation of male "slanders against women," as a strategic intervention in this debate. In contrast to authors who claimed that women "are good and useful only for embracing men and carrying and feeding children," Christine drew upon evidence from myth, history, and contemporary experience to demonstrate that women had excelled in far more important roles. Cataloging tales of women of courage, integrity, authority, and power, Christine documented the feats of women who had ruled empires, led armies, conquered enemies, engaged in scientific inquiry, invented language, created poetry, and contributed to all dimensions of community life. Acknowledging that women played vital roles within the family, giving birth, raising children, and caring for aging parents, Christine insisted that performing these activities had not in the past and should not bar women from assuming other responsibilities.

Despite Christine's cogent arguments, which circulated widely in Europe, a growing number of male writers—philosophers, scientists, and theologians—in the early modern period began arguing that women's capacity to give birth literally incapacitated them, constricting their intellectual potential and making them unfit for demanding occupations, including political leadership (Hitchcock 1997; Laqueur 1990). These misogynous arguments evoked lucid responses. During the seventeenth century, Marie Le Jars de Gournay crafted another rejoinder, *De l'Égalité des hommes et des femmes* (*On the Equality of Men and Women* [1622]). Margaret Brent, a practicing attorney who had served as governor's counsel on several occasions, petitioned the governor of the colony of Maryland for a "voice and vote" in political life for propertied women on the same terms as were available to men.[2] François Poulain de la Barre advanced an argument for human equality on the basis of equal rationality, insisting that "the mind has no sex" (*De l'Égalité des deux sexes* [*On the Equality of the Two Sexes*] [1673]). And Mary Astell developed a case for women's universities and autonomous women's communities for women who did not wish to marry and devote their lives to family responsibilities (*Serious Proposal to the Ladies* [1694]). Circulating throughout Europe and on both sides of

33

the Atlantic, these texts emerged in response to explicit efforts to constrict the social, economic, and political opportunities available to women.

In contrast to popular notions that modernity rescued women from unrelenting male domination, in many cultures "traditional" gender relations were far more fluid than modernist assumptions suggest. Some of the fluidity in women's social, economic, and political roles began to dissipate with the arrival of modernity and the emergence of a rigid gender ideology in Europe and the Americas. From the early eighteenth century, the family economy began to change in Europe, as clothing and later food production moved out of the home and into the factory. Within these new industrial ventures, job segregation by gender and race was introduced. Women were excluded from certain assignments in textile, garment, and cigar manufacturing and concentrated in other areas of production within these units.

Political transformations in the second half of the eighteenth century were equally dramatic. Critiques of aristocratic excesses and monarchical abuses gave rise to demands for republican modes of governance that would allow some popular participation in decision making. Although men held the preponderance of power within feudal aristocracies, a peculiarly gendered discourse associating corruption with women's rule circulated widely among republican reformers on both sides of the Atlantic, providing a rationale for the exclusion of women from rights of citizenship (Anderson 2000; Offen 2000). Republican political theorists and practitioners actively sought to create an exclusively male political assembly, "free from women's corrupting influence." Rousseau developed the theoretical argument, which was enacted first by American revolutionaries and subsequently by French revolutionaries.

Despite his claim in *The Social Contract* (1762) that the only legitimate political system is one that promotes liberty and equality, Rousseau afforded women no place among the citizenry in his proposed democratic polity. Instead, he assigned women the role of producing and nurturing future citizens. Rather than fostering women's liberty, Rousseau invented the ideology of "republican motherhood,"[3] insisting that women's contribution to democratic politics lies in childbearing and childrearing. When designing their constitutions in the aftermath of the American Revolution, twelve of the original states forming the United States followed Rousseau in excluding women from the rights of citizenship,[4] setting a precedent in nation building that has been widely replicated around the globe. Despite women's critical contributions to the revolutionary struggle against Great Britain, at the moment of victory, women were excluded from participation in the design of political institutions and from equal participation within those institutions. The only reference to women in the *Federalist Papers*, the newspaper articles written to explain and justify the provisions of the U.S. Constitution, involves a discussion of the "dangers posed to the safety of the state by the intrigues of courtesans and mistresses" (Hamilton, Madison, and Jay 1961).

The cryptic reference to political dangers posed by women reflects the transnational circulation of misogynous discourses among "revolutionary" men who characterized themselves as proponents of human liberty. Coupling flagrant abuses during the reign of Russia's Catherine the Great (1762–1796) with depraved sexual mores associated with life at the French court, some male reformers on both sides of the Atlantic began castigating women for the evils of monarchical rule. In the context of the French Revolution, for example, the radical republican journalist Louis-Marie Prudhomme "invoked the bad effects of women's intrigues during the monarchies of Louis XV and Louis XVI as an argument against women's inclusion in the nation" (Offen 2000, 58). Alleging that "The reign of courtesans precipitated the nation's ruin; the empire of queens consummated it," Prudhomme (1791) argued against the extension of full rights of citizenship to women, a demand pressed forcefully by Olympe de Gouges and Condorcet. Following the tradition set by the American revolutionaries, the French National Assembly voted not only to exclude women from rights of citizenship, but in 1793 also voted to ban women's participation in political clubs as well as the existence of popular societies of women, effectively foreclosing all avenues of women's political participation (Offen 2000, 61–63).

The gender inequalities enshrined in the laws of new republics often exacerbated inequalities entrenched in custom and tradition (Smart 1992). Feudal and colonial hierarchies were grounded in class, family ties, nationality, gender, and race. Although the republican revolutionaries claimed to break with such feudal hierarchies, the constitutions created within the first liberal republics replicated and strengthened hierarchies tied to gender, race, and class by denying equal citizenship and rights of political participation to women, blacks, and those without property. Women who loudly protested the imposition of de jure gender inequality were dealt with harshly. Indeed, Olympe de Gouges, active participant in the French Revolution and author of *Déclaration des droits de la femme* (*Declaration of the Rights of Woman*, 1791), was sent to the guillotine by her fellow revolutionaries.[5] Even after the failure of the first French republic, exclusionary practices were carried forward. In 1804 the Code Napoleon, later imposed on much of Europe, classified women as incapacitated and excluded them, along with children, convicted criminals, and the insane, from political life.

By excluding women from full citizenship, male lawmakers used the law as a means not only to produce sex-segregated political spaces, but to reshape gender identities within the confines of emerging conceptions of separate spheres. Asserting that men and women have different natures, proponents of the emerging gender ideology insisted that men and women be assigned to sex-segregated social and economic roles for their own happiness, as well as for the good of society. Indeed, French aristocrat, revolutionary, and diplomat Talleyrand (1754–1838), who assisted in writing the *Declaration of the Rights of Man*, went on to persuade the French National Assembly that women's "share should be uniquely domestic happiness and the duties of the household." In his "Report on Public Instruction" (1791) presented to the Assembly on behalf of the Committee on the Constitution, Talleyrand argued that "in accordance with the will of nature," women should renounce political rights to ensure their happiness and their long-term protection (Offen 2000, 59).

Contrary to the popular notion that this gender ideology simply reflected tradition and customary practice, a new form of biological determinism, suggesting that sex has a profound influence upon the operations of the human mind, was espoused by philosophers, political revolutionaries, and men of science in the late eighteenth century (Laqueur 1990). The new domestic model of womanhood, which assigned women to the home, desexualized her, and reframed her political work as mothering, profoundly reshaped the terms of political discourse. Indeed the ideology of republican womanhood infiltrated even the arguments of proponents of women's rights. Mary Wollstonecraft, for example, begins her *Vindication of the Rights of Woman* (1792) railing against pernicious conceptions of femininity associated with the aristocracy, which reduced women to idleness, loose morals, vacant minds, and sexual intrigues. But in staking her ground against aristocratic norms and values, she accepted republican terms of discourse, arguing for women's access to education, the professions, and political rights so that they could be better mothers and more intelligent companions in marriage. Where Christine de Pizan had roundly rejected male efforts to define women in terms of their reproductive capacity, nearly four centuries later, Wollstonecraft incorporated the premises of republican motherhood within her argument for women's rights. Taking issue with systematic constraints upon women advocated by Rousseau and Talleyrand, Wollstonecraft demanded educational and political opportunities for women, but she did so within the parameters set by an emergent gender ideology that conceived women first and foremost as mothers. Keenly aware of the injustice of the prohibitions against women's political participation and of the damage done by denigrations of women's intellectual abilities, Wollstonecraft extended the republican arguments for liberty and equality to women, and she made a case for coeducation as essential to the promotion of gender equality, but she accepted republican claims that "the rearing of children, that is, the laying a foundation of sound health both of body and mind in the rising generation, has justly been insisted on as the peculiar destination of women" (1792 [1975], 189).

From Ideas to Action: Women's International Activism, 1830–1860

Internationalism involves "a commitment to reach out to colleagues from other nations, to attempt to forge understandings of differences and commonalities, to build consensus on projects and priorities, to work across national borders to attain goals," and often, to use international resources to bring pressure to bear on governments of individual nations (Rupp 1997, 107). Contrary to the common assumption that "internationalism is a twentieth century phenomenon facilitated by phone, fax, email and air travel," nineteenth-century women developed vibrant transnational networks dedicated to changing women's status in society (Anderson 2000, 1–2). Facilitated by the development of print culture, the rise of literacy, and the growth of a broad reading public (Offen 2000, xii), the earliest transnational feminist activism emerged in conjunction with utopian socialist experiments. Reading a common body of public writings, exchanging letters, and visiting each other, women in Europe and the Americas in the early nineteenth century cultivated a shared understanding of gender-based injustices, discussed tactics for social change, supported each other's work, and offered each other affirmation in victories and solace in defeats (Anderson 2000, 28–30). Exploring various mechanisms to transcend national and class differences in a period when those differences were being intensified and increased, a small number of women created coherent and convincing claims for women's rights and equality, advancing a major challenge to male dominance in Western culture (Anderson 2000).

In *Joyous Greetings: The First International Women's Movement, 1830–1860*, Bonnie Anderson traces the emergence of feminist activism to socialist and abolitionist circles in which women embraced a vision of social justice, calling for the massive transformation of social life. Developing their ideas in the context of radical social movements associated with Saint Simon, Fourier, and Robert Owen, these "New Women" decried the "barbarous injustice" that makes "one half the human race the servants of the other" (Anderson 2000, 67). Working within socialist networks stretching from Constantinople to Mississippi, the New Women embraced democracy, socialism, and feminism as one cause, derived from the fundamental principle of human equality (Anderson 2000, 75). Schooled in various egalitarian experiments associated with New England abolitionism, the free congregations of Germany, the missionary activism of Saint Simonians and the Fourierists, the early socialist women were inspired by visionary promises of equal treatment and dismayed when those promises were routinely breached. Blatant contradictions between principle and practice, such as professing equality but paying women only half the salary paid men for identical work or excluding women from full participation in decision making, fueled the first feminist transnational organizing.[6] Chafing against the persistence of male domination within their movements, socialist women developed critiques of oppressive practices and sought to form connections with other radical women like themselves (Anderson 2000, 82).

Reacting against an all-male retreat organized by Saint Simon's successor Prosper Enfantin, for example, Saint-Simonian women in Paris organized to "work for freedom and association of women" (Anderson 2000, 84). In 1832 they launched a newspaper, initially called *Free Woman* and later renamed *Women's Tribune*. Publishing thirty-two issues over the next two years that featured articles written exclusively by women, they appealed to women to "rally to them" or to "imitate them by forming their own groups" but to act to show that the "cause of women is universal" (Anderson 2000, 84–85). Indeed they suggested that organizing by women for women was itself an emancipatory act. "Men have advised, directed, and dominated us long enough. It is now up to us to work for our liberty by ourselves; it is up to us to work for it without the help of our masters" (Anderson 2000, 84).

Through such communications, circulating across national borders and linking radical women in Britain, France, Germany, and the United States, women activists crafted a vision of democratic socialism, forging a political agenda that included marriage reform, access to birth control, educational and employment opportunities, a new organization of housework, as well as economic and political transformation sufficient to eliminate poverty and enable the participation of all. Defying powerful norms that prohibited women from speaking in public and publishing in their own names, these women's rights activists gave public speeches and developed newspapers to circulate their ideas. Fighting for freedom of expression precisely because it was denied them, the advocates for women cultivated a vision of freedom that circulated widely on both sides of the Atlantic. In their correspondence and in their publications, they insisted that women must be free to choose how they want to live, to have access to education and professions, to have rights to voice their ideas, and rights to participate as equals in the political community.

Appealing to a transnational audience in the hope of hastening social transformation, these early activists urged women to form connections with like-minded women in other nations to press for recognition of women's humanity, equal rights, freedom, and emancipation. French socialist women were among the first to protest unjust marriage laws that made women the property of their husbands. Urging a union of women of all classes in a struggle for freedom, two French women issued a "call to women" in 1832, encouraging women not to marry unless their husbands agreed in principle to equality in marriage and demonstrated their willingness to work for equal marriage laws. Reprinted by radicals throughout Europe and in the United States, the call endorsed a cross-class alliance of "New Women," drawn from the people and from the privileged class to end "the property in women and the consequent tyranny it engenders. Let our common interest unite us to obtain this great end . . . liberty and equality and equal chance of developing all out faculties" (Anderson 2000, 67).

Acting against explicit and tacit prohibitions of women's political participation, the early proponents of women's rights devised creative initiatives to make the political system more democratic and accountable, sharing these strategies with women in other nations. In 1833, for example, British antislavery women invoked the medieval right to petition the Crown and gathered hundreds of thousands of signatures on petitions, which they delivered to Parliament, demanding that slavery in the West Indies be abolished. Inspired to replicate the practice, American women abolitionists delivered so many signed antislavery petitions to the U.S. Congress that the House of Representatives responded by passing a "Gag Act," which tabled all petitions—unread—from 1836 to 1844 (Anderson 2000, 116).

Attuned to economic injustices associated with emerging capitalism, socialist women drawn from the ranks of textile workers, seamstresses, milliners, nurses, and teachers also began to develop arguments about gender inequities in industrializing societies. Irish feminist Anna Wheeler suggested that capitalism was intensifying male domination, pointing out that bourgeois men were using "the domestic model of womanhood" to concentrate economic and political power in male hands (Anderson 2000, 86). French working-class women, such as Jeanne Deroin and Suzanne Voilquin, decried male workers' efforts to monopolize industrial jobs. Emphasizing that working-class women desperately needed jobs with decent wages, they pointed out the harms done when male workers advanced arguments for preferential treatment for male breadwinners.

From the early nineteenth century, working men also harnessed emerging notions of women's biological destiny to consolidate their economic advantage, insisting that paid employment outside the home be established on the basis of sex segregation (Bolt, 2004, 128). From the 1830s to the 1850s they advanced arguments about the propriety of the male breadwinner model in full awareness of the plight of working women, who outnumbered men in many textile mills. Indeed, Flora Tristan suggested that male workers pressed the case for a family wage in direct opposition to women workers' demands for equal pay and improved working conditions (Hawkes 1982; Tristan 1983). Conservative and radical forces coalesced around a gendered agenda—the privatization of women. Economists and male labor leaders pressed the case for a family wage precisely to displace women workers and return them to the home. Male workers, unions, and social democratic parties supported the family wage as means to prevent male wages from falling as a result of competition from women workers and to preserve male power in the home (Offen 2000, 235–236).

Flora Tristan, daughter of a Peruvian father and a French mother, traveled widely across France, Britain, and Peru, documenting the "mortifications" suffered by lone women travelers, women workers, and women prostitutes. *Promenades dans Londres* (*Walks in London*), her 1840 account of the abysmal working and living conditions of British factory workers, devoted two chapters to the unique miseries experienced by women workers (Hawkes 1982). Her final book, *Union Ouvrière* (*The Workers' Union*, [1843] 1983), provided a vision of socialist solutions to the immiserating conditions of industrial capitalism, including provision of low-cost, high-quality housing for workers, universal education, health care, and residential homes for the elderly, as well as transformation of the conditions of labor—all strategies conducive to the emancipation of women (Anderson 2000, 141–144). Active in radical religious circles and in socialist circles in Germany, Louise Otto published a series of articles calling for the elimination of poverty, slavery, war, and the oppression of women (Anderson 2000, 139). Arguing against a form of racist ethnocentrism surfacing in feminist and nonfeminist circles, she excoriated those who criticized the condition of women in other countries, such as India or China, while ignoring women's oppression in their own European nations. Rather than drawing attention to practices such as Chinese footbinding and Indian suttee to demonstrate the "superiority" of Western culture (a tactic that would later become a staple of a version of imperial feminism developed in the nineteenth century), Otto compared Chinese women's "crippled feet" with the "crippled character" of German women who "remain so undeveloped that they lost the free use of their mental abilities" (Anderson 2000, 140–141).

Founding feminist journals and newspapers as a means of national and transnational activism, socialist women in the 1830s and 1840s broke social taboos and risked censure and disapproval to circulate their analyses of the worsening conditions of women and workers (Anderson 2000, 101). By 1848 ten feminist journals and newspapers were circulating, including *La Voix des femmes* (*The Voice of Women*), which appeared six days each week in Paris; Louise Otto's German weekly, *Frauen-Zeitung* (*Women's Newspaper*); and *Lily*, the fifty-page monthly published in the United States. Combining reports of local issues with reviews of recent events from overseas sources, these publications facilitated the transnational flow of feminist analyses and critiques of contemporary affairs. *The Voice of Women* typically supplemented news of France with reports from Germany, Switzerland, Belgium, England, Ireland, Poland, Italy, and the United States. Less frequently, it included accounts of women in Africa, India, and China. Material initially published in one journal was routinely translated and reprinted in feminist journals across Europe and the United States (Anderson 2000, 158–159). Women's activism coalesced around these journals, as issues and strategies circulated via these transnational feminist networks.

The 1848 Seneca Falls Convention in the United States, which is often mistakenly identified as the origin of the feminist movement, was the culmination of more than twenty years of transnational feminist activism. The demands incorporated in the Seneca Falls Declaration, including property rights, voting rights, rights to divorce and to custody of one's children, equality in marriage, access to education and the professions, equal representation in political offices, equality in church offices, and an end to derogatory stereotypes of women, reflected an international women's agenda crafted through transnational correspondence and debate. Designed to replicate the language and style of the American Declaration of Independence, the Seneca Falls *Declaration of Sentiments* omitted some of the more radical demands advanced by European socialist women.

Participating in the revolutionary uprisings of 1848, European socialist women demanded to be equals in democratic and socialist reforms, pressing for "the complete, radical abolition of all the privileges of sex, of race, of birth, of rank, and of fortune" (Jeanne Deroin and Anne Knight cited in Anderson 2000, 156). Their activism continued through various feminist publications, which played a crucial role in mobilizing women during the heady days of revolution; but many women also took their activism to the streets, participating actively in the insurrections. In France, Pauline Roland tried to cast a ballot in municipal elections in Boussac in the spring of 1848. Jeanne Deroin, Jenny d'Héricourt, Désirée Gay, and Eugénie Niboyet helped found the Society for the Emancipation of Women, which launched a campaign to advance women's rights. Writing to editors of radical journals, they argued cogently that women deserve the same political liberties as men. Attending meetings of men's political clubs, they repeatedly tried to press the men to vote for a resolution supporting the equality of men and women. Forging an alliance with the Committee for the Rights of Women, the Society for the Emancipation of Women petitioned the government to implement gender equality in politics, social life, work, the family, and education (Anderson 2000, 157). And they warned that unless the revolutionary government extended full rights of citizenship to women, it would fail just as the 1789 revolution had failed. Indeed Deroin insisted that "only genuine female equality could prevent a resurgence of militarism, despotism, and restoration of monarchy that had followed the first French Revolution" (Anderson 2000, 160). Enacting her duty to participate as an equal citizen, Deroin ran for the National Assembly in April 1849, organizing her campaign around one bold claim: "A legislative assembly entirely composed of men is as incompetent to make laws for a society composed of men and women as an assembly entirely composed of the privileged would be to discuss the interests of workers, or an assembly of capitalists to uphold the honor of the nation" (Anderson 2000, 190).

In Germany, as in France, socialist women refused to accept their consignment to the domestic sphere. Louise Otto founded the *Frauen Zeitung*, served as its editor, and used the paper to raise awareness about gender-based and class-based injustices. Published weekly through 1852, the *Women's Newspaper* under Otto's direction was the longest surviving revolutionary paper launched in Germany in this era (Anderson 2000, 198). Incorporating material from all parts of the world, Otto challenged her readers to question "the spiritual and material chains that bind the entire female sex" and urged them to join "the great all-encompassing World-Movement which has suddenly shaken the artificially preserved ruins based on privilege to their foundations" (Anderson 2000, 159). Transgressing the strict prohibitions against women's political activism, Otto took the unprecedented step of trying to influence government policy, sending a public letter about the conditions of women factory workers to a governmental committee in the spring of 1848 (Anderson 2000, 160).

In a show of transnational solidarity that breached the gendered protocol of the nation-state, American educator Emma Willard also wrote an open letter directed to the government of France, urging it to enfranchise women in accordance with fundamental principles of justice (Anderson

2000, 161). The optimism concerning the possibilities for women's freedom and gender justice unleashed by the revolutions of 1848 were quickly
dashed as the revolutionary uprisings across Europe were harshly re-
pressed.

In France the first signs of reaction came in May 1848 from male revolutionaries who invaded women's political clubs and disrupted their meetings. The police then seized the pretext of public unrest to close all
women's clubs ostensibly to prevent disorder. In late June, the all-male Assembly, which had voted down proposed legislation to enfranchise women
by a resounding 899 to 1,[7] passed a law prohibiting women's membership
in political clubs. By enacting legislation requiring newspapers to post
bonds for the privilege of publishing news, the government of France also
succeeded in closing down the women's newspapers (*The Voice of Women*,
Women's Politics, and *Women's Opinion*), which like other radical papers
lacked the fiscal resources to cover the cost of the bonds. When Jeanne
Deroin and Pauline Roland defied the government ban on women's
involvement in political clubs by creating a federation of worker's cooperative associations, they were arrested, imprisoned, eventually tried, and sen-
tenced to an additional six months in Saint Lazare prison (Anderson 2000,
190–198).[8] Preserving their transnational networks from their jail cell, Deroin and Roland sent letters to women's rights activists in England and the
United States in 1850 affirming their commitment to "the right of Woman
to civil and political equality," and urging women's rights activists to forge
alliances with the working classes to carry on the struggle for justice (Anderson 2000, 9). The letters were published and circulated widely through
feminist networks in England, Germany, and the United States.

The Viennese Democratic Women's Association was shut down in
1848, when the Austrian army conquered the city and stifled all dissent
by arresting key activists, including women's rights activist Karoline Perin
(Anderson 2000, 178). The *Frauen Zeitung* was also shut down when the
state of Saxony passed a law prohibiting women from editing newspapers.
Targeting Louise Otto, the only woman newspaper editor in the country,
"Lex Otto" succeeded in stopping the circulation of feminist ideas. In 1850
Prussia followed France in passing a law banning women "from all meetings in which politics is discussed," a law which remained in effect until
1908 (Anderson 2000, 198). The Austrian empire passed a similar law. Police imprisoned or executed men and women whom they determined to be
"dangerous," effectively silencing feminist activism for a period. In 1851,
the Prussian government outlawed kindergartens, the educational innovation of German feminists, as centers of radical indoctrination (Anderson

2000, 24). Facing harsh repression, many radical women emigrated to Britain or the United States.

As forces of reaction trounced feminism in continental Europe, the sites of continuing transatlantic activism were concentrated in Britain and the United States. Reacting to political repression, some feminists shifted their efforts away from direct political involvement toward a struggle for women's education, launching Bedford College for Women in London in 1849 and the Philadelphia Female Medical College in 1850. With the exception of 1857, annual women's rights conventions continued to be held in the United States from 1850 through 1860. Bringing women's rights and antislavery advocates together, these conventions provided news of women's activism from other nations, tracing small victories as well as massive defeats, thereby cultivating a sense of participation in collective struggle. Bearing witness to the courage of imprisoned and exiled activists in other nations, participants renewed their commitment to the cause of women as a global struggle. In the words of Pauline Wright Davis (1853), "this great movement is intended to meet the wants not of America only, but of the whole world" (Anderson 2000, 182).

Wars brought a halt to the remaining transnational feminist activism. As Britain pursued the Crimean War (1854–1856) and the United States dissolved into civil war (1861–1865), feminist efforts to embrace a universal cause, appealing to all women within and across nations, gave way to nationalist preoccupations. Many women's rights activists shifted their energies to women's war work. According to Bonnie Anderson (2000, 203), the women's movements that managed to survive in Britain and the United States in the aftermath of war grew increasingly conservative and national in focus. The agenda narrowed on both sides of the Atlantic as property rights, custody, divorce, employment, and suffrage gained priority over socialist concerns. Racism not only fractured women's suffrage efforts in the United States, but dramatically reshaped the vision informing transnational feminist activism as it reemerged in the 1870s.

A Second Strand of International Women's Activism (1870–1940)

Despite critical setbacks caused by recurrent episodes of repression within particular nation-states and the disruptions caused by the conduct of wars, the communication of feminist ideas across national and linguistic boundaries and the internationalization of women's activism surfaced once again in the period from 1875 to 1890 (Offen 2000, 150). Emerging from "well-worn trans-Atlantic tracks" (Rupp 1997, 4), the second effort to cultivate transnational alliances among women had a decidedly different ideological cast than its socialist predecessor. As capitalism gained ascendancy, the radical vision of early nineteenth century activists gave way to "imperatives of 'free trade', imperialism, and the emerging science of race" (Sinha, Guy, and Woollacott 1999, 3). Discourses on evolution initially deployed to demonstrate the futility of feminist aspirations by "proving" that nature dictates women's reproductive and domestic role were absorbed into what might be called "missionary liberal feminism."

"Like socialists, communists, and affiliates of other 'internationals', liberal feminists took advantage of improved and cheaper communication and transportation technology to build a network of contacts across the globe and to forge an international liberal feminist network" (Ehrick 1999, 62). Oriented toward acquisition of equal political and civic rights within a capitalist and secular framework, liberal feminists launched various international organizations and sponsored regular international conferences during the second half of the nineteenth century. Swiss feminist Marie Goegg founded the Association International des Femmes (International Association of Women) in 1868 "to work for moral and intellectual advancement of women, and for the gradual amelioration of her position in society by calling for her human, civil, economic, social, and political rights" (Offen 2000, 150; Winslow 1995, 2). The first International Conference on Women's Rights was organized in Paris in conjunction with the World Exposition in 1878. With delegates from twelve nations participating, discussions of dimensions of women's inequality generated commitments to work for women on the international stage (Rupp 1997, 14). The commitment took the form of additional International Women's Congresses held in Chicago, London, Berlin, Brussels, and Rome over the next decade. The international conferences helped build dense networks of contacts between women of different nations and cultures, who sought solutions to significant issues that cut across national boundaries yet required national solutions. Targeting the nation-state as a critical arena of struggle, transnational liberal feminists urged women around the world to focus on suffrage as a means to accomplish various political objectives, suggesting that the vote would afford women a way to change society and to rectify women's civic and political subordination.

Ostensibly an "association of national associations," the International Council of Women (ICW) was launched in 1888 at a suffrage convention in Washington, DC. Reversing assumed relations between the local and the global, the International Council existed before the creation of any national councils. Indeed the creation of national councils of women became the primary objective of the ICW in its early years (Rupp 1997, 20). The model the ICW recommended for national women's councils shows just how different this second strand of transnational feminist activism was from its socialist predecessor. Appealing to the aristocratic structure of European, Latin American, and Commonwealth nations, the ICW recommended that elite women drawn from the ranks of the aristocracy serve as figureheads to lend respectability to the organization, educated middle-class women be mobilized as a "power center" to carry out the work of the national council, and selective representatives of working-class women be integrated to enable the organization to speak with one voice on behalf of all women in the nation (Ehrick 1999, 70). Thus the ICW advocated cross-class alliances, but for very different reasons and with very different effects from the cross-class alliances endorsed by socialist feminists in the 1830s. Assuming that they could speak for and set an agenda for all women, as long as they avoided certain controversial issues,[9] the ICW was emblematic of a kind of imperial feminism that took shape in the late nineteenth century.

Ideological Roots of Imperial Feminism

Claims concerning a "hierarchy of civilizations" circulated widely in the West during the nineteenth century. Tied to long-established agendas of Christian missionaries; fueled by Hegel's arguments (1807) that history is the progressive unfolding of reason and freedom, manifested in particular cultures at "world historical moments"; elaborated by European ethnologists and anthropologists; accorded a scientific base in Darwin's theory of evolution; incorporated via social Darwinism into imperial projects abroad and social policies domestically, the notion that some civilizations were more advanced than others became global currency as capitalism sought to modernize the world. Although any conception of hierarchy rooted in race and culture is fundamentally at odds with feminism's professed commitments to equality, claims concerning a "civilizing mission" shaped a good deal of this second strand of transnational feminist activism, marking it as an imperial project.

In the 1820s Fourier was the first to suggest that the condition of women is a "barometer of society," indicating the "level of advancement of a civilization." In the aftermath of Fourier's observation, efforts to measure the status of cultures by the "degradation of women" became standard tropes among those who constructed themselves as "more advanced" (Newman 1999, 163). Tied to discourses of Western superiority, such intercultural comparisons legitimated social reform efforts within nations and colonial projects transnationally as the "more civilized" sought to uplift those who lagged behind.

Over the course of the nineteenth century, the form of gender relations deemed to demonstrate "more advanced civilizations" shifted dramatically. Utopian socialists like Fourier and the early socialist feminists hailed equality between men and women as a sign of superior civilization. Indeed observations concerning sex equality in certain African and Native American cultures were deployed by feminists in Europe and the United States as proof of the defects of their own civilizations. As biological determinism gained credence, this egalitarian logic was inverted by liberal reformers who argued that *different* social roles for men and women, indeed, separate spheres, were the true mark of advanced civilization (Newman 1999). Nineteenth-century proponents of what Louise Newman (1999, 96) has called "patriarchal domesticity" argued that in an "advanced civilization," men assumed the dual roles of "financial provider and physical protector," while women's energies were expended in the home.

The shift from gender equality to gender separation as a sign of advanced civilization had profound consequences for women. Consider how this shift transformed debates about women factory workers. As noted above, critics of capitalism such as Flora Tristan (*The Workers Union*, 1843) and Friedrich Engels (*The Condition of the Working Class of England*, [1844] 1958) wrote about horrific working conditions, particularly those of women and children in textile factories, to raise public awareness of and to mobilize opposition against capitalist exploitation. They also offered socialist prescriptions, including elimination of oppressive working conditions for all workers as necessary to achieving a humane civilization. By contrast, social reformers inspired by the domestic model of womanhood took quite a different tack in crafting their prescriptions for social change. To rectify the brutal working conditions of "mill girls" in Massachusetts textile factories, which he meticulously documented in *Sex in Industry: A Plea for the Working Girl* (1875), for example, Azel Ames, a special commissioner of investigation for the State Bureau of Statistics of Labor, recommended that men be paid a family wage and women be removed from all factories in the long run and banned from dangerous jobs in the short run. Ames urged the state of Massachusetts to create incentives to induce women to stay at home rather than address dangerous working conditions. Making claims about the superiority of emerging middle-class standards of domesticity, he urged working-class women to conform to them (Newman 1999, 95–96).[10]

At a time when many states had extensive legislation in place to restrict women's labor, liberal reformers like Ames generated perniciously circular arguments suggesting that "since women could not support themselves or others, they could not be equal" to men (Newman 1999, 33). Diverting attention from obvious causes of women's inability to support themselves—wages well below subsistence levels—reformers advanced arguments about women's desires, interests, and needs. Insisting that women industrial workers were not working out of choice and that they would much prefer to remain at home, Ames urged employers to provide men a family wage that would enable women to leave paid employment (Newman 1999, 86–88). Drawing on the new "science" of sexual difference, medical doctors wrote treatises alleging that education and paid employment—even in the professions—were incompatible with women's delicate physiology. "Overworking women's brains," as well as their bodies, was deemed "to risk normal development of the reproductive system and endanger the future evolution of civilized society" (Newman 1999, 88–92). Social Darwinism provided a bridge between separate spheres as an indication of superior civilization and racist and elitist policy prescriptions to enforce policies to restrict women to the domestic sphere. If systemic differences between men and women are the mark of civilization, then erasing such differences contributes to the decline of civilization. In this view, equality, whether on the factory floor, in institutions of higher education, or in political life, is at odds with civilized existence, and as such, a policy problem in need of a solution.

Once bourgeois norms mandating separate spheres were taken as evidence of advanced civilization, any society that failed to emulate this gendered, classed, and raced division of labor was diagnosed by Western observers as less advanced. When mixed with elements of evolutionary theory and applied to other nations and cultures, the separate spheres model construed sexual equality as a sign of barbarism or savagery associated with a lower rung of the evolutionary ladder. For this reason, the Western, Christian civilizing mission required assimilation of peoples in less advanced civilizations to bourgeois norms. Modernization, then, involved elimination of egalitarian customary practices and the imposition of liberal reforms associated with capitalist market relations and republican politics. Feminist activism in the second half of the nineteenth century emerged in the context of this imperious ideology and was permeated by it. Conducted under the auspices of this Christian civilizing mission, feminist internationalism tended to shore up racist, imperialist projects (Newman 1999, 134).

Missionary Circuits

Leila Rupp (1997, 11) has suggested that the ideology of separate spheres operated not only to restrict the educational and employment opportunities available to women; it also had the unintended consequence of legitimizing new forms of women's organizing: "The notion of fundamental differences between men and women became the *raison d'être* for women's international organizing." The factors contributing to this second strand of transnational feminist activism were complex. In Europe and the United States, women found themselves in a contradictory position: War, militarism, direct state repression, and the ideology of separate spheres combined to thwart their activism in domestic politics. Those who dared defy prevailing norms were subjected to vitriolic criticism and ridicule. A "torrent of anti-feminist cartoons and writings" was produced throughout the second half of the nineteenth century (Anderson 2000, 205). The reinvigorated cult of patriarchal domesticity mandated marriage as the appropriate moral role and only rewarding career for women at a time when savage wars in Europe and the United States produced severe shortages of marriage partners. Under these conditions, some women were attracted to internationalism as an area in which they had some scope to take initiative (Bolt 2004, 4).

Within feminist circles, the civilizing mission was promoted in language of global sisterhood. Women's foreign missions and fund-raising organizations constituted an important form of women's activism in the second half of the nineteenth century in Europe and the United States. As Kumari Jayawardena (1995, 24) has pointed out, "a network of Christian women proclaimed 'global sisterhood' and ventured out of their homes and into the male world of work, travel, and adventure in the name of a noble cause to serve God and improve the condition of women." Strong advocates of and pioneers in women's education, missionary women built transnational bridges that were enormously beneficial to some South Asian women. "Many South Asian feminists were products of mission schools and convents" (Jayawardena 1995, 26). With funding from missionary societies some traveled to London and Philadelphia to complete medical degrees and degrees in higher education and then returned to use their education to benefit their home communities.

Incorporating basic elements of Christianity and Western chauvinism, the foreign mission movement was the largest women's organization prior to World War I, attracting over 3 million dues-paying members in the United States alone. Recruiting missionaries to "spread the gospel to the heathens" on Native American reservations and overseas, the foreign mission movement offered women respectable and important work, aimed at benefiting those in "less advanced" civilizations, while also contributing to the missionaries' own salvation. Working in Africa, China, and India as teachers, nurses, and doctors, as well as overt missionaries, women were transmitters of Western culture as well as religion (Giele 1995, 40). Although many missionary workers considered spreading the ideals of Christian civilization to be different from colonialism, racism was integral to the "civilizing project," as cultural emissaries were convinced of the "redeeming power of the Anglo-Saxon race" (Bolt 2004, 12–13).

Through overseas work, European and American women escaped the strictures of the separate spheres doctrine and embraced a "noble calling" that enabled them to come to the aid of women who, according to racist science of the day, sorely needed their assistance. The Women's Christian Temperance Union (WCTU), for example, which was founded in 1874 by Frances Willard, and which launched a world union in 1883, provided a vehicle through which many women escaped the "suffocating protection of white men," while "uplifting primitives" and "emancipating indigenous women from barbaric practices of their cultures" (Newman, 1999, 117). WCTU missionary Mary Clemont Leavitt, for example, traveled to Australia, New Zealand, India, Africa, and Europe between 1883 and 1891, organizing temperance and "social purity" work, including campaigns against the traffic in women as well as the traffic in opiates and stimulants in the communities she visited. Linking the "advance of civilization to women's emancipation within Christian societies," Frances Willard's outline of the "problems" to be remedied by the WCTU indicates the intricate interweaving of imperial and feminist projects in this second strand of transnational feminist activism. According to Willard, the global mission of the WCTU involved liberating "heathen" women from moral enslavement in zenanas or harems and eliminating married women's exploitation by their husbands. Exploitation within marriage took various forms, including deviations from accepted gendered divisions of labor (i.e., failure to enforce separate spheres), nonmonogamous marriages that failed to provide adequate protection for women, and forms of collective property ownership that failed to secure individual property "rights" (Newman 1999, 66, 117; Giele 1995, 100). Working within this frame, proponents of women's rights pressed an assimilationist agenda, which conflated success in "saving primitives" with the adoption of a particular configuration of white, middle-class, Western values and practices. Tied to the imperialist projects of Western nations, the brand of feminism advocated by the WCTU and other versions of missionary feminism recognized that the "miseries produced by slavery, war, intemperance, economic upheaval, and the denial of citizenship to subordinate groups took no account of national borders" (Bolt 2004, 15). Thus they demanded forms of international action that, if successful, would annihilate "barbaric" cultures. With cultural blinders firmly in place, U.S. feminist Elizabeth Cady Stanton could suggest, for example, that in undertaking the Spanish-American War, "the United States was fighting the first disinterested war on earth" (Bolt 2004, 18). Similarly, the British Commonwealth League could promote empire and the ideals of "trusteeship," which brought the "benefits" of Christianity, Western education, engineering, and modern medicine to "backward" peoples in the colonies (Bolt 2004, 84).

Contrary to assumptions concerning age-old "heathen" practices, a good deal of what was taken to be tradition was invented during the colonial period by colonial administrators acting with indigenous male elders. Misinformation and disinformation on both sides contributed to a form of collusion between colonial states and traditional patriarchies that worsened women's conditions and status (Waylen 1996, 46). Many "reforms" were more backward than the traditions they sought to replace. Although these colonial interventions were justified through an ideology of religious and racial superiority, the civilizing mission was routinely characterized in paternalistic language, promising the improvement of everyone's condition (Waylen 1996, 49). Despite claims concerning the beneficence of its civilizing initiatives, colonial policies—aided and abetted by missionary work—altered customary practices and divisions of labor to the detriment of women. In its colonies in Africa, for example, British taxation policies designed to make the colonial administration self-supporting, and land alienation policies, which confiscated certain areas exclusively for white settlement, restricted Africans to rural reserves, created migratory labor systems restricted to male workers, undermined women's customary rights, profoundly altered divisions of labor and power, imposed enormous burdens on African families, and contributed to significant decline in the living standards of rural families (Waylen 1996, 58). Moreover, the British colonial state passed laws criminalizing women's traditional activities, such as the brewing and sale of beer. The British also undercut women's traditional leadership. Enactment of the separate spheres ideology in this context, as in other colonial contexts, was particularly brutal.

Occasionally liberal feminist publications would carry reports that challenged the confident assertions of the civilizing mission. Indeed Leila Rupp (1997, 77) points out that *Jus Suffragii*, the journal of the International Woman Suffrage Alliance, reported that

> women on the Gold Coast of Africa were independent, engaged in trading and sometimes very wealthy; that Islam was not oppressive to women; that projecting concepts and ideas of Western feminists on the lives of women . . . [in Africa and Asia] distorted research findings; and that African women were losing status under European influence as they were

pushed out of agriculture and trade, kept out of local government, and "protected" morally.

Traveling around the world to promote women's suffrage in 1911–1912, Carrie Chapman Catt and Aletta Jacobs sent reports that disrupted established beliefs concerning Western superiority:

> There are millions of women in the Orient who are held in the most pitiful tutelage, and denied every vestige of personal liberty, but we are finding that there are other millions who have always enjoyed more personal freedom than was accorded to most European women a century ago and more than is now permitted to thousands of women under our boasted Western civilization. (Rupp 76–77)

Despite such occasional glimmerings that assimilationist interventions might be wrong-headed and harmful, they were not sufficient to alter the course of missionary liberal feminism.

Anticolonial and Socialist Alternatives

Transnational feminist activism in the late nineteenth century was not univocal. Although missionary liberal feminism constituted a dominant strain, it was not the only form of feminist activism during the period. Colonial practices fueled the emergence of indigenous feminisms across Africa, Asia, and Latin America, which also existed in complex relation to male-dominated nationalist movements (Jayawardena 1986). In addition to fighting against sexist practices within nationalist movements, anticolonial feminist activists mobilized women to protest against taxation, land laws, loss of customary rights, such as the right to refuse a particular suitor in marriage, deteriorating living conditions, and colonial policies that were destroying customary family formations and divisions of power within indigenous communities (Waylen 1996, 62).

Socialist women also continued to espouse feminist principles, fighting for women's right to labor, against humiliating forms of dependency and exclusion, and for full equality in social, economic, and political life (including socialist organizations), as well as the overthrow of capitalism and imperialism (Buhle 1981). Some developed powerful critiques of colonialism as a system of racial, gender, and class oppression and devoted their lives to anticolonial struggles (Jayawardena 1995). Despite steadfast support for sex equality, it became increasingly difficult for socialist women to claim the feminist label, however.

When socialism reemerged in Europe in the late 1850s after a decade of severe political repression, many of the male leaders sought to exclude women from party activities and decision making.[11] When feminist socialists demanded equal participation as a matter of principle, they were attacked for being bourgeois and divisive. Characterizing women's rights as a diversion from the primary goals of the party, socialist women were told that they must put the party agenda first. When socialist women continued to press for women's rights, they faced increasing censure. The Second International (the Socialist International) viewed feminism as a rival enterprise. To counter its attractiveness, the all-male leadership of the Second International launched a smear campaign, denouncing feminism as ineradicably bourgeois. Erasing decades of socialist feminist activism within the party, they forced women socialists to choose between feminism and socialism (Offen 2000, 11; Buhle 1981, 107). While many socialist women continued to work for feminist causes, others, following party dictates, withdrew.

International Women's Organizations

Beyond feminist work carried on within missionary, nationalist, and socialist frameworks, the major form of transnational feminist activism to emerge in the late nineteenth century involved the creation of various international nongovernmental organizations (INGOs) expressly devoted to the advancement of women and to the involvement of women in international decision making. By founding international organizations, feminists sought to build a lasting framework that could strengthen and help expand networks of like-minded women around the globe. Seeking to construct a "collective identity as feminist internationalists" (Miller 1999, 226), the founders of these organizations sought to consolidate an international sisterhood. According to Leila Rupp (1997, 5–6), the "most crucial characteristic of women's movement organizations is their inclination to align with other women's groups . . . attempting to create an international sisterhood out of a multitude of conflicting interests that women from different nations bring into the international arena." Coming together across national borders to create a sense of belonging by working and living together, these transnational feminist activists used the language of sisterhood to forge connections. Although they differed markedly from other women, they began to construct arguments about the characteristics they claimed women shared: the potential for motherhood, disadvantage compared to men in their group, and universal threat of rape in wartime (Rupp 1997, 82–83). And they began to craft a transnational feminist agenda that would shape feminist activism for much of the twentieth century.

Replicating the "dynamics of global power relations" (Rupp 1997, 13), the International Council of Women, launched in 1888, initially brought together women from Europe, Canada, and the United States. Within its first three years, it had expanded its network to include Australia, Argentina, and New Zealand. By 1913, ICW had 6 million members in twenty-three nations (Stienstra 1994, 48). Claiming to represent 35 million women in thirty-five states, ICW declared itself the "Women's League of Nations" in 1935 (Rupp 1997, 19). Conceiving itself as a multipurpose organization that could represent women in the international arena, the ICW sought to build transnational networks among women's religious, literary, and philanthropic organizations, women's social reform movements, women in the arts, and women in education. Trying to forge constructive relations among such diverse interests across many nations involved the art of diplomacy. Thus the ICW sought to preserve a "certain vagueness both in its methods and aims" (Rupp 1997, 19). Seeking to foster international cooperation among women and to expand its membership across the globe, the ICW was careful to avoid controversial issues, such as women's suffrage, about which there was no international consensus. ICW's tactics were decidedly prudent, organizing high-profile meetings, issuing resolutions, engaging in fact gathering concerning various topics of import to women, producing publications to educate its membership as well as world leaders, and encouraging correspondence among the national councils of women it fostered (Bolt 2004, 16). The international meetings provided a venue for the exchange of information and for debates about organizational priorities. They also provided opportunities to build women's solidarity and to promote greater understanding of national cultures and the conditions of women within them. Despite its conservative bent, its aristocratic leadership, and its preference for fostering women's interaction with ruling elites, the ICW organized standing committees to address issues of considerable import, including questions of war and disarmament, equal moral standards for men and women, the traffic in women, women's access to trades and professions, public health and child welfare, and emigration and immigration (Rupp 1997; Stienstra 1994).

Long frustrated by the failure of the ICW to support women's suffrage, proponents of women's suffrage were pushed past the point of endurance when the ICW allowed an antisuffragist to give a plenary address at the 1899 meeting. Using the intervening years to plot their strategy, activists from Australia, Germany, Great Britain, the Netherlands, Sweden, and the United States launched the International Woman Suffrage Alliance (IWSA) at the ICW meeting in Berlin in 1904. The explicit aim of this organization was "to secure enfranchisement of women in all nations and to unite

friends of women's suffrage throughout the world into organized cooperation" (Bolt 2004, 15). Growing rapidly in membership, the IWSA sur-
passed the ICW in number of national affiliates by 1914, when it had active
national organizations operating in twenty-six states (Rupp 1997, 16;
Stienstra 1994, 48). Although its primary focus was the enfranchisement
of women, the IWSA developed a larger women's international agenda, including issues of equal pay, women's right to employment, the nationality
of married women, prostitution, peace, and slavery.

As in the mid-nineteenth century, war posed enormous challenges for
transnational feminist activism. World War I halted the momentum of a
bourgeoning international feminist movement, causing a six-year hiatus in
communication between the International Council of Women and the national councils and severely disrupting IWSA suffrage efforts within and
across national borders (Rupp 1997, 26). Within the nations at war, feminist claims for social justice were made to seem petty and selfish, as women
were once again urged to adopt a demeanor of self-sacrifice essential to
national survival. Noting that hostility to feminism was a deliberate, sustained, and central project of nations involved in war making, Mary
Sargent Florence and C. K. Ogden, two British antiwar suffragists, wrote
in *Jus Suffragii*, the newsletter of the International Woman Suffrage Association, "In war time, only men matter" (Offen 2000, 252). Taking the argument one step further, Irish feminist Francis Sheehy-Skeffington insisted
that "war is necessarily bound up with the destruction of feminism" (Offen
2000, 260). World War I also triggered an impressive counteroffensive by
conservative forces to undermine and erase feminist transformative efforts.
As women were forced out of the lucrative jobs to which they had been
recruited as part of the war effort, pronatalist legislation was passed to enlist women in a new effort to fight the depopulation caused by war. Family
allowances and mothers' pensions were introduced in a number of European states as an incentive for women to bear more children. Abortion and
birth control were criminalized to restrict the options for those uninspired
by the pronatalist incentives.

After the outbreak of World War I, heightened nationalism worked
against internationalism, which was prone to characterization as disloyalty.
Advocates of internationalism were vulnerable to abuse, intimidation, surveillance, government harassment, and imprisonment (Bolt 2004, 29). Despite such pressures, World War I did not bring all transnational feminist
activism to a halt. On the contrary, it provided the motivation for the creation of a new transnational feminist organization devoted to the cause of
peace—the International Committee of Women for Permanent Peace, later

renamed the Women's International League for Peace and Freedom (WILPF).

In February 1915, IWSA activists from the Netherlands, Belgium, Britain, and Germany met in Amsterdam to organize an International Congress of Women to be held in The Hague at the end of April. Issuing a "Call to the Women of All Nations," these feminist activists invited women's organizations in all parts of the world to send delegates to the Congress to consider two major resolutions. The first stipulated that international disputes should be settled by peaceful means; the second called for the enfranchisement of all women. Against the explicit opposition of their governments, feminist activists from neutral and belligerent nations, including Austria, Belgium, Britain, Canada, Denmark, Germany, Hungary, Italy, the Netherlands, Norway, Sweden, and the United States traveled across war-torn Europe to participate in the Hague Conference (Rupp 1997, 27–28; Stienstra 1994, 51). Denied voting rights in their home nations and excluded from institutions of national governance, 1,500 women's rights activists nonetheless tried to insert themselves into the male-controlled world of war and international relations. While their governments pursued a deadly war in which 20 percent of the casualties were women (Turpin 1998, 3) women peace activists devised a plan to end the war, a plan with many similarities to the Fourteen Points, developed by U.S. president Woodrow Wilson two years later. In particular, they urged the end of war making and the creation of an international organization, "a conference of neutral nations," which would remain in permanent session to mediate conflicts and resolve disputes peacefully. In an effort to win support for their plan, thirteen members of the newly formed International Committee of Women for Permanent Peace visited the capitals of fourteen nations to lobby presidents and prime ministers for an end to armed conflict and the adoption of new strategies for peaceful settlement of international disputes. Advancing a profound critique of militarism and imperialism, the feminist peace activists opposed conscription, and urged the creation of mechanisms to provide practical assistance for victims of war, including the provision of war relief work for refugees and internees. They also asked world leaders to allow delegates of the International Committee of Women for Permanent Peace to participate in peace negotiations following the war.

When the Paris Peace Conference convened in 1919, women peace activists were not invited to participate. To protest their exclusion, they convened a parallel conference hosted by the Union Française pour le Suffrage des Femmes (the French Women's Suffrage Union) and invited world leaders to address them. As a result of these meetings, feminist peace activists secured the opportunity to make presentations to two of the Peace Conference's commissions. Making the most of this opportunity, women's rights activists presented a host of proposals to the commission on international labor legislation, including proposals for maximum working hours (forty-four hours in a six-day week), minimum wages, equal pay for women and men, abolition of child labor (for children younger than fifteen years), and paid maternity leave. Their proposals to the commission on the League of Nations were comparably encompassing, recommending that all positions in the League be open to women as well as men, an end to traffic in women and children, support for women's suffrage, an international agreement to protect married women's nationality (which many nations required women but not men to forfeit if they married a foreign national), creation of international bureaus of education and public health, and systematic reduction in armaments (Stienstra 1994, 50–55).

Although these transnational feminist peace activists did not succeed in persuading the official participants in the Paris Peace Conference to adopt all their recommendations, they did secure three notable successes. Three sections of the covenant establishing the League of Nations incorporated their recommendations. The League agreed to bar sex discrimination in employment in all their operations. They made a commitment to endeavor to secure fair and humane conditions of labor for men, women, and children. The League also pledged to supervise the execution of international agreements on the traffic in women and children. Debra Stienstra (1994, 60) has suggested that it would be a mistake to assess the impact of international feminist activism in the aftermath of World War I solely in terms of these three provisions, for their intervention had far more sweeping significance. Women's rights activists succeeded in injecting feminist issues into the international arena; they challenged the male monopoly of the international sphere; and they established the precedent that sex discrimination should not be tolerated in international institutions.

Contrary to the received view, feminism did not grind to a halt after World War I. Leila Rupp (1977, 47) has pointed out that the pattern of growth in the international women's movement challenges what has become "the hegemonic model of first and second feminist waves," which is based on Euro-American women's movements. "The International Women's Movement lurched slowly into motion in the late 19th century and gathered steam at the end of the First World War" (Rupp 1997, 47). The interwar years were a crucial period for transnational feminist activism. In the global South during the 1920s, women's movements emerged in countries newly freed or struggling for economic and political independence.

Indeed the international women's movement crested in the 1920s with new sections emerging in Asia, Latin America, and Africa (Rupp 1997, 47).

International networks grew out of initiatives of various national feminist organizations, and the development of international networks stimulated feminist organizing at local, national, and regional levels. While the growth of the International Women's Suffrage Alliance illustrates the movement from national activism to transnational alliance, WILPF provides an example of institutionalization that moved from the international to the national level. Changing its name to the Women's International League for Peace and Freedom (WILPF) in 1919 and establishing an international headquarters in Geneva, Switzerland, WILPF sought to move from the global to the local. Having been launched as an international venture at the Hague Conference in 1915 and having operated exclusively in the international arena, WILPF launched an effort to build national sections to promote pacifism in all regions of the world. Beginning with fifteen national sections concentrated in Europe and the United States, WILPF expanded its geographic reach throughout the 1920s and 1930s. Conceiving itself as a vanguard organization committed to radical politics, rather than as a mass movement, WILPF brought together bourgeois feminists and socialist feminists in uneasy alliance to campaign against war, militarism, and imperialism. Deeply concerned about the negative consequences of war reparations imposed on defeated nations, it was one of the first international organizations to caution against the dangers of fascism as it was emerging in Italy and Germany. Recognizing that the policies it promoted were impossible to achieve in the "present system of exploitation, privilege, and profits," WILPF also developed a powerful critique of capitalism and imperialism, and urged all national sections to recognize that the "first duty of the organization" was to hasten social transformation (Rupp 1997, 30–33). In keeping with that objective, the French section of WILPF organized a summer school in 1927 on interracial problems of imperialism, which issued a call for an end of military repression in the French colonies and mandates, and for the independence of the colonies. The U.S. section investigated and condemned the U.S. occupation of Haiti in 1926, as well as U.S. interventions in Latin and Central America and Asia (Rupp 1997, 78). WILPF's counterhegemonic discourse was strengthened by the trenchant critiques of feminist imperialism advanced by women from colonized and dependent countries. Indian feminists, for example, notified WILPF that it would be "a great mistake" to allow British women to organize a section of WILPF in India, for British women could not speak for Indian women. They also argued forcefully that imperialism could not continue to be understood as a civilizing project (Rupp 1997, 79–80).

WILPF was not alone in its efforts to contest capitalism and imperialism. Growing out of British Fabian socialism, the International Women's Cooperative Guild was created in 1921 to promote a radical agenda for social transformation that addressed rights of workers and colonized peoples. Within a decade, guilds had been established in thirty-seven nations and were working on various strategies to promote sex equality, the unionization of women, more women in elective offices, maternity allowances, divorce reform, public health, boycotts of non-union-made goods, pure food, disarmament, elimination of all vestiges of militarism from school curricula, and the end of war (Rupp 1997; Stienstra 1994).

Despite enormous differences in size and mission, the international women's organizations made efforts to work together on several issues. In 1925 the Joint Standing Committee on Women's International Organizations was formed to pressure for appointments of women to the League of Nations. The Committee drew upon the assistance of the various women's international organizations in identifying and sending forward the names of women with the requisite expertise to serve on League commissions and offices. The Joint Standing Committee facilitated cooperation among women's international organizations, coordinated work, and began pressuring the League to conduct a worldwide study of the status of women. Although the League agreed to conduct such a study in 1935 and appointed a Committee of Experts on the Status of Women (four of the seven members were women) to organize the research in 1938, World War II delayed the investigation, which was finally conducted under the auspices of the United Nations Commission on the Status of Women (Rupp 1997, 220). In response to pressure from women's organizations, the League of Nations also appointed the Women's Consultative Committee on Nationality, whose membership was drawn from the membership of the international women's organizations, to devise policy recommendations addressing women's loss of citizenship upon marriage to foreign nationals. The various women's international organizations also cooperated under the auspices of the Liaison Committee of Women's International Organizations formed in 1931, concentrating their energies on the issue of disarmament. Working through the dense networks of the various women's international organizations, the Disarmament Committee gathered 8 million signatures for disarmament from women in fifty-six nations, which were delivered to the League in 1932 (Rupp 1997, 42). By 1933, 45 million women around the world belonged to the Disarmament Committee.

While many transnational feminist activists in Europe were focusing on issues of peace and disarmament, Latin American feminists began crafting innovative mechanisms to harness the power of international organizations to pressure individual nations to improve the status of women. Using the Pan-American Union as a site for networking and brainstorming, Latin American feminists organized a Women's International Committee to sponsor a series of conferences on women's rights. This Committee inspired women delegates at the 1928 Conference of American States to propose the creation of an Inter-American Commission on Women (IACW), a recommendation that was approved at the 1933 meeting. With its members appointed by governments, the Inter-American Commission on Women became the first intergovernmental body created to advance women's rights. In the first few years of its existence the IACW prepared an international treaty on the Nationality of Married Women (1933) and crafted the Declaration in Favor of Women's Rights (1938), which was adopted as an official document at the Eighth International Conference of American States in Lima in 1938. This historic declaration set a precedent, which proved enormously important in securing the inclusion of the rights of men and women in the United Nations Charter in 1948, a victory secured by an intensive international lobbying effort led by Latin American women diplomats. In addition to these historic international documents, the Inter-American Commission on Women encouraged member governments to revise discriminatory civil codes and to establish women's bureaus to address various women's issues within the nation-state (Galey 1995; Miller 1999).

Lessons from the Past

Despite the enormity of the challenge, feminists in the nineteenth and early twentieth centuries succeeded in cultivating a new consciousness of a "common situation of women," tied to women's social roles and discriminatory social arrangements that disadvantage women. Challenging forms of biological determinism that constructed women's subordination as "given in nature," feminists drew attention to various cultural practices of separation, exclusion, domestication, containment, and constraint that produced women's "inferiority." Working together across national borders, they forged the political will to investigate structures of disadvantage, politicize them, and build international coalitions to address them. On a number of specific issues, their success was palpable. The enfranchisement of women gained momentum as a direct result of this century of struggle. Although highly controversial, protective labor legislation was passed in many nations and endorsed as a policy objective by the League of Nations. Through sustained work over several decades, transnational feminist activists secured an international treaty on married women's nationality. Fighting assumptions that the situation of women was known, they also won international acknowledgment that the condition of the world's women must be studied as a precondition for problem identification and policy recommendations. Moreover, the Inter-American Commission on Women piloted a strategy for using international organizations to promote change within nations by securing international agreement to a declaration of principle concerning women's rights, then to a convention, and finally to a treaty that, according to international law, would require governments to bring their laws into compliance with treaty provisions upon ratification (Rupp 1997, 145).

Many lessons can be drawn from an examination of the history of women's transnational activism. Perhaps one of the most important lessons is that any account of women's transnational activism must do more than catalogue the victories. As the nineteenth-century feminism clearly demonstrates, victories have costs and victories have unintended consequences at odds with explicit feminist goals and objectives. Minimally, then, assessments of transnational feminist activism require a double narrative. Stories of women's transnational mobilizations for social change must supplement analyses of the creation of international networks and the construction of transnational solidarities with shadow stories that excavate the politics of race and class and explore the consequences of those dynamics in the context of international feminist organizing. Narratives of transnational feminist activism must attempt to trace the intended and unintended consequences of transformative efforts.

Consider, for example, how different the story of the International Women's Suffrage Alliance appears when the narrative of collective struggle across national borders to secure women's votes in all nations of the world is supplemented by the organization's shadow story. Demonstrating the peculiar myopia of privilege, when women in Britain, Canada, and the United States won suffrage in the aftermath of World War I, some newly enfranchised members of the IWSA recommended the abolition of the organization, suggesting that it had "outlived it usefulness." Disenfranchised women in nations across the globe were furious at this act of betrayal by members of the global sisterhood. Because the majority of disenfranchised women were living in Latin America, Asia, and Africa, Leila Rupp (1997, 22) characterized this dispute as transnational feminisms' first "North/South split." Although the rift was eventually overcome by agreement to change the organization's name to International Alliance for Suffrage and Equal Citizenship and to expand its issue agenda, the myopia that generated the rift was emblematic of continuing tensions created by imperial feminism, which played out in multiple venues.

Transnational feminist efforts to fight for women's rights were repeatedly marred by racist and imperial power dynamics. The interactions between feminists in Latin America and those in the United States, for example, were never easy. Letters of leading feminists from Uruguay and Argentina articulate their "discomfort at the missionary attitudes of some U.S. feminists" (Miller 1999, 228). U.S. feminists made little effort to hide the fact that they regarded themselves and their culture as superior. Indeed, when setting out for a tour of Latin America, Carrie Chapman Catt referred to herself as a "missionary," whose explicit objective was to "civilize inferiors." In her interactions with Latin American feminists, Catt made it clear that she did not consider them her equals. On the contrary, she considered it her responsibility to "act as a representative of U.S. policy interests," rather than as an equal participant in women's common struggle (Ehrick 1999, 73–74).

As the examples from the late nineteenth century show, women's internationalism was an expensive undertaking, requiring considerable resources of time and money. As representatives of their governments, unions, or professional organizations, men were often paid for the time devoted to international initiatives, and their travel and living expenses were covered by their sponsoring organizations. Women's international activism seldom had such official sponsorship. Engaging in a voluntary activity, transnational feminist activists had to cover their own costs for transportation and accommodation, and they had to have the wealth to devote their time to unpaid international work. Those who lacked resources to travel to international meetings simply could not participate. From the outset, then, participation in women's international organizations had an exclusive class character, which contributed to a certain amount of cohesiveness among activists (Bolt 2004, 187; Rupp 1997, 6). Cohesiveness of this sort, however, may have contributed to important misunderstandings of the lives of less privileged women and may have constrained the types of activism deemed appropriate for international feminism. Karen Offen (2000, 13) has suggested that economic privilege may have limited affluent feminists' understanding of the tenacity of gender, class, and racial power, leading them to believe that social transformation could be achieved by persuading men in positions of authority that the feminist cause is just. But relying on tactics of persuasion may have unduly restricted the kinds of social change possible. Christine Bolt has suggested that persuasion works best when feminists operate within the parameters set by those in power. "Women's appeals to politicians were most successful when they stressed women's 'special qualities' and roles as wives and mothers" (Bolt 2004, 100). But if the separate spheres ideology was itself implicated in the oppression of women, as suggested above, then advancing arguments within these terms could never adequately address all the dimensions of women's subordination. Moreover, limiting the legitimate tactics for social change to persuasion precludes structural transformation, leaving many dimensions of inequality in tact. Attending to class dynamics within transnational feminism, then, can help explain the choice and important limitations of certain social change tactics.

Replicating geopolitical power dynamics, feminist international organizations were also structured by racial bias both in membership and in toleration of discriminatory practices (Bolt 2004, 186). Few women of color participated in the major international women's organizations, and those involved were subjected to various forms of racism and racial discrimination. In 1921, for example, several German members of the Women's International League for Peace and Freedom (WILPF) proposed that WILPF endorse a call for the withdrawal of African peacekeeping troops from German soil on the grounds that black troops posed a unique threat to the safety of German women. Although African American WILPF member Mary Church Terrell ultimately persuaded the conference delegates to defeat the motion, she had to endure sustained discussion of racist myths concerning the "sexual purity of white women" and black men's "propensity to rape" before she succeeded in defeating the racist proposal (Bolt 2004, 78). When the International Council of Women convened in the United States in 1925, the organizers of the meeting conformed to local custom, segregating black delegates in a particular section of the hall. Narratives of global sisterhood are not only incomplete, but powerfully inaccurate, if they omit these shadow stories.

The effects of feminist activism include both intended and unintended consequences. The power dynamics traced in shadow stories also have effects, often at great remove from the intentions of affluent white feminist activists. One reaction to racism, for example, is withdrawal and creation of alternative spaces from which to work toward transnational goals. To provide a space for international activism and outreach free of racism, African American activists launched the International Council of Women of the Darker Races (ICWDR) in 1920 (Bolt 2004, 82). Although they worked in conjunction with WILPF to mobilize women and men against U.S. intervention in Mexico, Haiti, Nicaragua, Latin America, and Asia, their funds were limited and the organization did not survive the economic crises associated with the Great Depression. During their decade of activism, however, the ICWDR developed a counterdiscourse that helped increase understanding of nationalist struggles in Haiti, Africa, China, and India, demonstrating how nationalism can serve as an antiracist strategy. An unintended consequence of racism within white-dominant feminist organizations, the creation and growth of the International Council of Women of the Darker Races is another important part of the story of transnational feminist activism.

The International Council of Women of the Darker Races was not alone in trying to increase awareness of the pernicious consequences of transnational racism operating in and through colonialism. With the growth of anticolonial nationalist movements in the early twentieth century, women's rights activists in the global South became increasingly vocal about the interference of white Western women in their affairs and about the importance of addressing a particular form of racism, "orientalism." Permeating European and American discourses on the East, orientalism involves the construction of an imagined terrain encompassing North Africa, the Middle East, South Asia, and East Asia in an amorphous undifferentiated whole—the Orient (Said 1978). Manifold differences in language, culture, and history are erased within this composite, as a series of racist stereotypes are superimposed on the inhabitants of the East. Orientalist assumptions were manifested in everyday practices, policy proposals, and the worldview of most early feminist internationalists. At the level of everyday practices, transnational women's organizations incorporated Christian assumptions so systemically that they seemed unaware that the Golden Rule and the celebration of Christmas were not transcultural universals. At the policy level, deeply ingrained orientalism surfaced in a combination of anti-Semitism and pro-Zionism, which generated opposition to Palestinian women's rights and supported a perception that Muslim societies were particularly "backward and degrading to women" (Rupp 1997, 52–58). As a general worldview, feminist orientalism sustained a polarized understanding of West and East that had little to do with geography but much to do with assumptions about the topos of progress, civilization, and emancipation of women (Rupp 1977, 75). Within this orientalist worldview, Northern Europe and the United States were understood as "the core"; Eastern Europe and Southern Europe as "semiperiphery"; and Latin America, the Middle East, Asia, and Africa as "periphery" in a world feminist system. Vindicating imperial feminist interactions and projects, orientalism enabled women of European and American origins to considerate it natural that they lead transnational organizations and ventures, and to assume that their "more oppressed sisters" in the global South would not only willingly follow, but be grateful for their assistance. Understanding the shadow story of racist orientalism is essential to make sense of the practices, priorities, and fundamental worldview of many Western feminists operating on the global scene.

Beyond charting the complex dimensions of analysis required to explain transnational feminist activism, a historical approach also provides some insight into various feminist motivations for going global. The transatlantic alliances forged by feminists since the late eighteenth century involved a search for kindred spirits who affirmed the validity of an emerging analysis of gender injustice. The creation of transnational solidarities was often spurred by developments within particular nations that excluded women from participation in domestic politics. Shut out of participation in national politics by constitutional and statutory provisions, political repression, and changing gender ideology, feminists asserted their freedom by building transnational networks to support the struggle against male domination. International activism offered some women greater opportunity for agency and affirmation than domestic politics, and it provided opportunities for the exchange of ideas and tactics that could reinvigorate struggles within the nation-state.

A long view of women's struggles for social, economic, and political justice also helps demonstrate that capitalism has been transforming women's and men's lives and their social relations for several centuries. Decisions by conservative elites, aided and abetted by male trade unionists, male socialists, and male factory workers, have assisted the market's invisible hand. Impersonal forces governing market competition take on a decidedly human face in the context of men banding together to naturalize the myth of the male breadwinner at a time when women were working in large numbers in industrial factories. Far from being a natural disposition, the "economic maximizing man" was produced by laws denying women an autonomous legal persona, precluding their freedom to contract, and excluding them from various forms of paid employment. These laws, created in conjunction with ideologies of republican motherhood and separate spheres, shed new light on the universalist pretensions of liberal bourgeois encomiums to liberty, equality, and fraternity.

By going global, feminist activists created networks of women whose access to each other and to all sorts of information was not mediated by male-dominant institutions (Wells 2002). The growth of these networks was halted and reversed on multiple occasions, and powerful feminist analyses of prevailing social conditions were largely stricken from the historical record. War, political repression, and economic crises have been powerful agents of backlash, contributing mightily to amnesia. When the rich history of feminist transnational mobilization is stricken from the public memory, each generation of feminist activists has to reinvent itself through struggle, deprived of the rich lessons of experience.

OUTSIDERS, INSIDERS, AND OUTSIDERS WITHIN: FEMINIST STRATEGIES FOR GLOBAL TRANSFORMATION

> Situated both inside and outside the center, yet sometimes pre-
> ferring to negotiate in the interstices, the spaces in-between;
> working outward from the inside, but also influencing the cen-
> ter from the outside; starting from positions of weakness and
> marginality and transforming these into mobility and strength.
>
> —Ping-Chun Hsiung, Maria Jaschok,
> Cecilia Milwertz, and Red Chan (2001, 4)

How do transnational feminist activists produce change? Feminist analyses of globalization identify significant forms of injustice in need of redress. Over the past several centuries, feminist activists have envisioned alternative possibilities for social, economic, and political life. But how are these trenchant critiques and egalitarian alternatives transformed into vibrant social practices within and across the borders of nation-states?

The strategies devised by feminist activists often do not conform to models of social change discussed in mainstream accounts. War has been and continues to be a powerful mechanism for social transformation at the national and international levels, but it is a strategy that feminists have largely eschewed and condemned. Although feminists have participated in revolutionary movements, the revolution feminists envision has not been promoted by violent means. International diplomacy generates conventions and treaties that can profoundly restructure international relations, but women have been largely excluded from diplomatic posts and key decision-making positions within national and international arenas.[1] Banned by law from certain forms of political participation and excluded by tradition from other modes of political and economic life, women historically have been the consummate outsiders. How do outsiders change the institutions that intentionally and effectively exclude them?

This chapter provides an overview of a range of feminist social change strategies, including classic outsider tactics, strategies of engagement that seek to create opportunities for women to become insiders, recent efforts to gender mainstream processes and policies so that women's concerns and perspectives can no longer be excluded, and feminist efforts to create alternative spaces, a feminist civil society or counterpublic from which to challenge dominant institutions. The final section of the chapter assesses the success of these innovative tactics in producing global change.

Outsider Tactics

In *Activists Beyond Borders* (1998), Margaret Keck and Kathryn Sikkink provide a helpful framework for understanding the dimensions of social change sought by transnational feminist activists. Social change includes issue creation and agenda setting, transformation of prevailing discourses, and modification of global conventions, as well as the alteration of the procedures and policies of national governments and international institutions. Particular tactics devised by transnational activists vary depending upon the kind of social change sought. The outcomes of social change initiatives also vary according to activists' success in mobilizing resources, their ability to negotiate the prevailing political opportunity structure, and the extent to which the political and social environments support or inhibit social change efforts.

In the context of transnational feminist activism, issue creation and agenda setting involve daunting challenges. Women are the majority of the world population, but as individuals, they differ from one another on the basis of nationality, class, culture, education, ethnicity, language, worldview, marital status, occupation, parental status, party affiliation, race, region, religion, sexual orientation, personality, personal history, aspiration, capability, and a host of other factors. Women have no natural, given, homogeneous, or self-evident interests that can serve as a basis for a transnational feminist agenda. When feminists seek to speak for women, they confront a host of vexing questions. They have not been elected by a global constituency of women to represent women's interests. There is no meaningful sense in which any particular woman or any group of women can claim to be representative of all women when women do not agree among themselves on any issue. Moreover, given their willingness to challenge prevailing gender relations, feminists are often markedly different from most women. Thus before feminists can hope to engage national and international institutions to press for a social change agenda, they face a prior challenge. Feminists who aspire to represent women in the transnational arena must not only build consensus about what constitutes women's needs and interests but also build global alliances to support an issue agenda. Chapter 4 explores feminist efforts to forge transnational consensus concerning a global women's agenda in the context of four United Nations World Conferences on Women, examining the power relations at play within these arenas, and identifying central contestations that remain unresolved.

This chapter maps a range of tactics used by feminist activists to promote social change. Although the construction of a shared sense of commonalities that can win the allegiance of women across the globe lies at the heart of the diplomatic and political work of transnational feminisms, it is important to remember that feminist efforts to create commonalities are initiated by diverse, self-selected groups of activists. Transnational feminist activists "emphasize solidarity and commonality rather than difference" (Moghadam 2005, 197), but this is a political tactic deployed for multiple purposes. Through repeated invocations of an imagined global feminist community, activists create and maintain bonds, "weaving a cohesive fabric of transnational feminism," bringing together those who share common cause and generating a sense of shared identity (Allen 2001, 47–48). In addition to enacting and fostering transnational solidarity, feminist articulations of shared interests are a means of recognizing differences among women, while suggesting that differences can be surmounted through the very process of negotiating a common agenda for change (Patel 2001, 159). Finally, claiming to represent the interests of women is a tactic designed to heighten feminists' credibility with national and international institutions. Neither male-dominant states nor male-dominant international organizations have been particularly inclined to engage the multiplicity of women's concerns and interests. By engaging in the intricate and time-consuming work of crafting an issue agenda, whether pertaining to women's health, economic well-being, or violence against women, transnational feminist activists step into a breach. Claiming to speak for the world's women, they hope to secure policy ground that otherwise would remain unaddressed or inadequately addressed.

Positioning themselves as a voice for women, transnational feminist activists have mobilized within states for women's economic well-being, physical security, and gender justice, pressuring their governments to raise these issues in international meetings; they have participated in multilateral and intergovernmental arenas to lobby directly for these issues; and they have used international treaties to agitate within states to enhance public awareness of these issues, to pressure governments for change, to monitor government's compliance with international agreements, and to hold governments accountable. Feminists have also mounted protests directed simultaneously to local and international audiences to politicize issues such as the condition of women in regions riven by violent conflict. Moving from local to global, from global to local, and operating in both spheres simultaneously, feminist activists have been remarkably resourceful in developing a complex array of transformative tactics. Shut out of formal decision-making arenas, transnational feminist outsider activists seek to do politics differently, providing opportunities for citizen participation beyond electoral politics and international diplomacy. Transnational feminist activists have actively sought to challenge prevailing understandings of political spaces and political practices. Calling the legitimacy of existing global power relations into question, transnational feminist activists have sought to participate in decision making despite their lack of official credentials, to influence substantive debates, and to create mechanisms that make governments accountable to the world's women. They have also injected new issues, such as violence against women, into international politics, and they have worked to transform the terms of political discourse in areas such as population control and human rights (Stienstra 1999; Petchesky 2003; Weldon 2002). They have also developed a rich array of feminist organizations, which operate individually and collectively to promote change.

Although some long-standing transnational feminist organizations, such as the International Association of University Women and the International Business and Professional Women, are formal membership organizations, many more transnational feminist activist organizations engaged in outsider activism are much looser networks of groups and individuals devoted to particular issues (e.g., economic justice, women's health, violence against women, peacemaking) or coalitions of groups that form alliances to achieve particular objectives (Stienstra 1994). Initially using phone and fax technology and later the Internet to create transnational spaces linking actors across borders, feminist networks were among the first to consciously seek to supersede nationalist orientations, modeling a form of transnational alliance that has become a hallmark of globalization from below. Acknowledging the diversity in forms of transnational feminist organizations, Valentine Moghadam (2005, 80) has noted that feminist organizations have characteristic features that distinguish them from more traditional nonstate transnational actors, such as unions or professional associations. They are largely without formal institutional bases of power; they are segmentary, comprising many, sometimes competing, groups; they are polycentric, having multiple and competing leaders; and they are reticulate (loose, flexible, adaptive, antibureaucratic networks that link to each other on particular actions).

Outsider tactics are in part necessitated by the continuing exclusion and underrepresentation of women in national and international decision making; but some feminist activists have articulated additional reasons for working from the outside to transform the world system. Latin American feminist activists have been at the forefront of efforts to create and sustain autonomous feminist organizations (*autonomas*) free from control by governments and external funding agencies (Mendoza 2000). Reacting against political corruption and in fear of cooptation, many feminist groups prefer to remain outside conventional politics[2] (Waylen 1996, 116). Autonomous feminist organizations enable activists to control their own agendas, avoiding corruption and co-optation in contexts where political parties and governments are hostile to feminist organizations. In nations where conservative parties restrict participation to the most conservative actors, and middle-class groups form pacts with the military, feminists have created alternative political spaces that enable women to develop their political skills and to engage in transformative praxis.

To preserve their distance from the state and to meet pressing needs, autonomous feminist organizations often mobilize around economic survival (Waylen 1996, 20). In Latin America, for example, popular feminism, which emerged in the 1960s and 1970s, encompassed women who constituted 80 percent of the activists in urban popular movements. Organizing at the neighborhood level to meet economic needs, popular feminists, who saw themselves as quite distinct from bourgeois feminists, provided public services unavailable through the state, such as soup kitchens. They also organized craft collectives for economic survival. Because they made problems of hunger and unemployment visible, military rulers considered these organizations subversive and initiated severe measures against them. Confronting increasing levels of state repression, popular feminists continued to press an economic justice agenda, even as they expanded their issue agenda to include sexuality, violence against women, and reproductive rights (Waylen 1996, 110–113). In Bihar, India, feminist activists created a different kind of autonomous organization, Adithi, to address economic survival. Launched as a group savings scheme in 1988, Adithi grew rapidly to involve 40,000 women in agriculture, dairy, forestry, handicrafts, and street vending by 2000. Claiming an explicit feminist identification, Adithi tackles patriarchal taboos along with women's livelihood needs, convinced that "the ability to earn cash income is the most important factor in reducing disadvantages women face as women" (Srinivasan 2001, 91).

In the aftermath of the UN Decade for Women Conferences and in response to the worsening of women's economic situation during the most recent three decades of globalization, many autonomous feminist organizations have created strong global connections, developing communication networks and international issue networks (Stienstra 1994, 92). To mobilize women globally and to coordinate local and national feminist activities via networking and information politics, for example, ISIS (International Women's Information and Communication Service) was launched in 1976. Initially created to publicize the proceedings of the International Tribunal on Crimes Against Women held in Brussels, ISIS became the first global feminist communications network. A North-South collaboration from the outset, ISIS rejected rigid and cumbersome bureaucratic structures in favor of informal, nonhierarchical, open structures and ways of operating. Designed to capture the benefits of flexibility and quick response made possible by the emerging information technology, ISIS piloted the network model, which has become the hallmark of globalization from below (Stienstra 1994, 91–92).

As Keck and Sikkink (1998, 18–22) have pointed out, activists who seek to promote change though information politics require knowledge that can challenge factual claims, issue frames, moral arguments, and perceptions of political significance. Feminist research centers have played a crucial role in transnational activism, producing knowledge that activists can deploy in their work. For example, DAWN (Development Alternatives with Women for a New Era) was launched as a transnational, collaborative feminist research network, involving scholar-activists from twenty-two nations.[3] Working with poor women as coproducers of knowledge, and drawing on subjugated knowledges to identify workable solutions to local problems, DAWN is a transnational alliance of research centers including the Institute of Social Studies Trust in India, Instituto Universitário de Pesquisas do Rio de Janeiro in Brazil, the Women and Development Unit of the University of the West Indies, the Association of African Women for Research and Development, the Christian Michelsen Institute, the Asian and Pacific Development Center, the Pacific and Asian Women's Forum, the Asian Women's Research and Action Network, and El Colegio de Mexico (Sen and Grown 1987; Tinker 1999). Documenting women's invisible labor, calculating its economic value in relation to GDP, demonstrating its importance to national and global economies and to sustainable development, DAWN's work has played a critical role in reshaping development debates and in promoting feminist policies (Sen and Grown 1987, 92; Elman 1996; Gelb 1989; Kabeer 2003; Naples and Desai 2002; Rai 2002).

Symbolic Politics

A classic outsider tactic involves the use of symbolic politics to capture public attention, politicize neglected issues, and dramatize the seriousness of the social justice issues at stake. Feminist activists have been particularly adept in the use of symbolic politics. For example, Women in Black (WIB) draws upon the rich symbolism of the color black—a color of mourning in certain cultures, tragedy in others, a color of married women's attire in some cultures, the hijab, chador, or veil in others—to mobilize women in silent protest against war, militarism, and other forms of violence and injustice. Insistent that they are "not an organization, but a means of mobilization and a formula for action,"[4] Women in Black grew out of a sustained silent protest organized by Israeli and Palestinian women in 1988 in an effort to stop the Israeli occupation of the West Bank and Gaza. Committed to nonviolence, Israeli and Palestinian women chose to stand together at the same hour each week at a major intersection bearing signs saying "stop the occupation." Standing together against the official policies of their governments, these activists sought to demonstrate the possibility of peaceful coexistence and cooperation. Holding a weekly silent vigil, they sought to enter the consciousness of their compatriots as a powerful reminder that "bridges can be built across differences and borders," but not through war. Instantiating an ironic politics, Women in Black sought to educate, inform, and influence public opinion without lengthy arguments, political bombast, or even words. They chose silence as the medium for their message. Claiming a long heritage of women's peace activism, Women in Black sought to refuse the logic of war by manifesting physical solidarity among the citizens of belligerents.

In Belgrade in 1991, feminists formed a group of Women in Black to protest Serbian nationalism and its deployment in ethno-nationalist wars. Organizing weekly vigils of public mourning for all victims of war, they explicitly refused to distinguish between "our" victims and "theirs." Forging ties to women in Sarajevo and Kosovo, WIB sought to challenge the manipulation of ethnic differences to foster hatred. Advocating new forms of "solidarity within our own differences," they conceptualized nonviolent silent protest as a political act of resistance and feminist solidarity (Einhorn and Sever 2003).

Since 1988, Women in Black has evolved into a worldwide feminist network committed to peace with justice and actively opposed to injustice, war, militarism, and other forms of violence, operating in hundreds of cities in forty nations. In addition to the silent vigils conducted by WIB groups in specific locations, WIB is a virtual community, sharing information and action alerts through the Internet. The action alerts mobilize groups across the globe in support of particular actions. For example, when Women in Black in Israel/Palestine called for vigils in June 2001 against the occupation of Palestinian lands, 150 WIB groups across the world responded by organizing vigils. More than 10,000 women in Australia, Austria, Azerbaijan, Belgium, Canada, Denmark, England, France, Germany, India, Israel, Italy, Japan, the Maldive Islands, Mexico, Netherlands, Northern Ireland, Spain, Sweden, Switzerland, Turkey, and the United States participated in silent protests. In the aftermath of the bombings of the World Trade Center and the Pentagon on September 11, 2001, WIB launched a virtual drafting session over e-mail to generate a statement, issued on behalf of its international network, appealing for "justice not vengeance." In 2003, tens of thousands of Women in Black joined millions of antiwar demonstrators across the world in a series of protests against the U.S. invasion of Iraq. Mobilizations against the U.S. war on terror continue.

In the words of WIB-Canberra (Australia),

> Women in Black has become a movement of women of conscience of all denominations and nationalities who hold vigils to protest violence in their part of the world: war, interethnic conflict, militarism, the arms industry, racism, neo-Nazism, violence against women, violence in the neighborhoods, etc. Each vigil is autonomous, setting its own policy and guidelines, though in all the vigils the women dress in black, symbolizing the tragedy of the victims of violence. What unites us all is our commitment to justice and a world free of violence.[5]

"Movement" may not fully capture the fragmentary, intermittent, largely uncoordinated, and leaderless persistence of Women in Black's activism. The difficulty in characterizing WIB is symptomatic of some new forms of transnational feminist activism. Operating globally through virtual exchanges, WIB exemplifies a mode of transnational feminism that creates "spaces to establish connections between women of different nations and cultures, but also of different feminisms . . . and to ponder the possibilities of feminist alliances across discrepant and distinct social conditions and historical axes" (Mendoza 2002). Sharing information and tactics, these computer-assisted networks create circuits of influence or what Joan Scott has called "reverberations." "Reverberation is a good way to think about this global circulation of feminist strategies, of feminism itself. . . . The forms they take and the meanings given them are adapted to local circumstances, which then have international reverberations of their own" (Scott 2002, 12). For Scott, WIB instantiates a new form of feminist activism that recognizes and values diversity.

> What is striking about WIB, in contrast to many earlier peace movements, is that it does not rest on a claim about the sameness of women or the unity of feminists. Instead WIB's existence as a means of mobilization and a formula for action presumes fundamental differences among feminists, differences in context, differences of history, differences of understandings of the feminine and of feminism itself. . . . There is no attempt to elaborate a common platform beyond an opposition to militarism and to violence. (19)

Indeed Scott suggests that WIB also exemplifies how global feminism differs from other forms of globalization. Reverberating across time and space, this mode of transnational feminism offers alternatives to what critics have called "the one-way trajectory of globalization" (12).

Whether understood as a virtual transnational space, a formula for action, a means of mobilization, or a reverberating circuit of influence, Women in Black illuminates the difficulty that nonstate actors have in altering the policies and practices of nation-states and international military alliances. Despite the courage and persistence of WIB in protesting violence and war, their recurrent mobilizations have not dissuaded belligerents from their violent courses of action. The enormous gulf between WIB's tactic of silent witnessing and states' active deployment of the means of coercion marks the limit of the potential impact of WIB's mode of action, as it manifests the paradoxical agency of grassroots activism in an increasingly antidemocratic age of globalization. As Joan Scott (2002, 17) has pointed out, "Standing silently and peacefully in a public place at a regularly scheduled day and time" embodies "paradoxical agency in the face of oppressive power—paradoxical because the mute, non-violent witness signifies powerlessness while it offers a message of peace as the only rational alternative to catastrophe." Outsider tactics remain at a severe disadvantage when confronting the full force of global militarism; nonetheless, the symbolic politics of Women in Black provide a glimpse of a different global order that resists recourse to violence. For marking that alternative and keeping it before the public eye, Women in Black has won international acclaim. Women in Black in Israel won the Aachen Peace Prize in 1991, the peace award of the city of San Giovanni d'Asso in Italy in 1994, and the Jewish Peace Fellowship's Peacemaker Award in 2001. The international Women in Black network was awarded the Millennium Peace Prize for Women by the United Nations Development Fund for Women (UNIFEM) in 2001.

Tribunals on Crimes against Women

In contrast to the silent witnessing formula for action developed by Women in Black, other groups of transnational feminist activists have adopted tactics that emulate war crimes tribunals as a mode of symbolic politics. Drawing upon the moral weight of the War Crimes Tribunals organized in the aftermath of World War II, in 1976 feminists organized an International Tribunal on Crimes against Women.[6] Mobilizing in opposition to the first UN World Conference on Women, the Tribunal on War Crimes Against Women was intended to challenge the "right" of a male-dominant United Nations and its male-dominant member states to claim to speak for women. Proclaiming that "male-dominated organizations do not represent women's interests," transnational feminist activists created an autonomous space for women to articulate their own issue agenda, free of the constraints imposed by an official intergovernmental conference (Stienstra 1994, 104). Enacting the feminist maxim that the "personal is political," the Tribunal recruited women to provide personal testimony of the harms they had experienced under the current male-dominant global order. Attracting 2,000 women from forty countries to participate at the meeting in Brussels, the Tribunal adopted a trial format in which women who had suffered forced motherhood, domestic violence, economic exploitation, and the complex interacting effects of racism, sexism, imperialism, and economic injustice testified before a global jury comprising all who attended the Tribunal. After hearing the testimonies of the injured parties, the jurors deliberated and rendered a verdict, finding the world system guilty of multiple crimes against women.

Although the 1976 Tribunal on Crimes against Women did not produce any immediate palpable results, it was designed to shift the "political register of truth" (Orford 2005). Rather than allowing governments to claim the authority to serve as official sources of truth, controlling the flow of information, and structuring the terms of debate, the Tribunal on Crimes against Women insisted that accounts of injury and injustice offered by the oppressed should trump official governmental accounts. Accrediting women's words and creating an international space in which women's voices could be heard and in which women could render a verdict against existing governments and against the international order, the Tribunal set a precedent for subsequent feminist tribunals and helped legitimate the conception of evidence, that is, testimonies of the oppressed, adopted in a spate of Truth Commissions created in the aftermath of sustained internecine violence.

To give voice to the victims of various forms of gender-based and race-based violence, transnational feminist activists have organized international tribunals at a number of NGO forums held in conjunction with UN conferences, such as the Vienna World Conference on Human Rights (1993), the Fourth UN World Conference on Women in Beijing (1995), and the UN Conference Against Racism, Racial Discrimination, Xenophobia, and Related Intolerance in Durban (2001). Deployed to address egregious issues of discrimination and violence against women in war and on the streets of local communities, international tribunals have been a key organizing strategy in the international campaign against violence against women. The testimonies, providing graphic demonstrations of violations of bodily integrity, physical security, and economic well-being, which remain without redress in the existing international order, are circulated widely in textual, audio, film, and Internet formats, enabling feminist activists around the globe to use the material to raise public awareness of the seriousness of these injustices. Since the early 1990s, the Center for Women's Global Leadership at Rutgers University has become a repository of information about how to conduct tribunals, providing detailed instructions for convening hearings, preparing evidence, and supporting witnesses throughout the traumatic process.

Perhaps the best known of the international tribunals organized by transnational feminist activists is the Women's International War Crimes Tribunal on Japan's Military and Sexual Slavery convened in Tokyo in 2000 (Tokyo Tribunal). More than fifty years after the end of World War II, prosecutors from nine countries colonized or occupied by Japan during the war (North and South Korea, China, the Philippines, Indonesia, Taiwan, Malaysia, East Timor, and the Netherlands[7]) presented evidence of the Japanese Imperial Army's system of sexual enslavement, also known as the "comfort women" system. Feminist activists decided to convene a War Crimes Tribunal after repeated efforts to seek redress in the Japanese courts, the UN Commission on Human Rights, and other UN bodies proved fruitless. Keenly aware that the survivors of these atrocities were growing old, feminist activists across Asia resolved not to allow the male-dominant institutions of international order to continue to "trivialize, excuse, marginalize, and obfuscate crimes, particularly sexual crimes, against women . . . [especially] when committed against non-white women" (Chinkin 2000, 3).

The evidence presented at the Tokyo Tribunal drew upon more than a decade of research conducted by feminist activists from thirteen nations, which carefully documented the experiences of more than 200,000 women from across Asia who were forced into sexual slavery by the Japanese military.[8] In addition to documenting the scope of the abuses, feminist researchers and activists worked with historians to locate recently declassified documents from the various Japanese ministries and other Asian states demonstrating that the institutionalization of the comfort woman system was deemed by the Japanese Imperial Army to be integral to the success of the Japanese war machine. Officers' demands for women to be sent to military garrisons, orders for their shipments, transport details, operational details concerning medical inspections, ticketing systems, and timetables revealed that the unrelenting rape of women in the comfort stations "was not an inevitable consequence of war, nor even an instrument of war but was part of the very engine of war where the sexual enslavement of women was considered necessary to the pursuit of military objectives" (Chinkin 2000, 9).

At the Tokyo Tribunal seventy-five surviving "comfort women" provided testimonies concerning the details of their "recruitment" via force, kidnapping, coercion, and deception, the physical and sexual assaults that continued for the duration of their imprisonment, the brutal deaths of many consigned to the "comfort stations," and the lifelong mental and physical traumas stemming from their violation. Two former soldiers also testified about their participation in these atrocities. Although the Japanese government was invited to participate in the Tribunal, it did not respond to the invitation. To ensure a fair hearing airing all sides of the dispute in the absence of participation by the government of Japan, the Tribunal followed the spirit of Article 53 of the International Court of Justice and retained a firm of Japanese lawyers (Isomi, Suzuki, Koga, and Partners) to prepare an amicus curiae brief enumerating the arguments used by the Japanese government in litigation in the Japanese courts denying responsibility for these practices (Chinkin 2000).

To underscore the fact that rape and sexual enslavement could have been prosecuted at the end of World War II had there been a political will to do so, the prosecutors before this "people's tribunal" opted to apply the international law operative at the time that the post–World War II International Military Tribunals for Nuremburg and the Far East were being conducted. That rape, enslavement, forced labor, and sexual trafficking were all prohibited by international law from the beginning of the twentieth century, and yet the post–World War II war crime tribunals had not prosecuted any of these crimes, highlights how systemically the international community has ignored egregious and widespread violence against women in armed conflict (Spees 2003, 1238–1239).

In a significant break from the practices of other people's tribunals, the Tokyo Tribunal recruited real judges to hear the case against Japan. Judge Gabrielle Kirk McDonald, who had served as the president of the International Criminal Tribunal for the Former Yugoslavia, Judge Carmen Maria

Argibay, president of the International Association of Women Jurists, and Judge Dr. Willy Mutunga, a human rights lawyer and jurist from Kenya, presided over the trial, issuing a preliminary judgment at the end of the hearings in December 2000 and a final decision, Judgment of the Women's International War Crimes Tribunal on Japan's Military and Sexual Slavery, rendered in December 2001 in The Hague. Both the preliminary and the final judgments found Emperor Hirohito guilty of crimes against humanity under the law then applicable and found the State of Japan responsible under the international law applicable at the time for violations of treaty obligations and principles of international law relating to slavery, trafficking, forced labor, and rape, amounting to crimes against humanity. Finding that the evidence showed comfort stations to have been systematically instituted and operated as a matter of military policy, the judges recommended a range of reparations.

As an exercise in symbolic politics, the decision of the judges on the Tokyo Tribunal does not have the force of international law. Nevertheless, it provides a powerful example of how transnational feminist activists have produced social change. The proceedings of the Tokyo Tribunal were broadcast live. Although censured in Japan, live coverage was broadcast across Asia from December 8 through 12, 2000. In addition to the 1,000 people who packed the halls during the hearings, millions of viewers across Asia were stunned by the heart-wrenching testimonies of the surviving "comfort women." In the context of such incontrovertible evidence, violence against women as a crime against humanity gained plausibility. The Women's Caucus for Gender Justice, which devoted several years to preparations of legal evidence and arguments for the Tokyo Tribunal, used this work in support of its advocacy for the creation of the International Criminal Court (ICC), including the prosecution of sexual violence under its mandate (see "Gender Mainstreaming" below). Moreover, by deciding to conduct the Tokyo Tribunal in accordance with the highest standards of international jurisprudence, and recruiting internationally renowned jurists to participate in the trial, feminist activists sought to dissolve typical boundaries between symbolic politics, which aim at moral suasion, and juridical decisions handed down by international courts, which shape international law. In this boundary blurring they succeeded brilliantly.

The Judgment of the Women's International War Crimes Tribunal on Japan's Military and Sexual Slavery was rendered by professional jurists using legal standards drawn from the canons of international law. Their decision set a precedent in that it was the first time that the protracted sexual enslavement of women was recognized as a crime against humanity. As such it was celebrated by feminist activists as a significant symbolic

79

milestone for gender justice and women's rights. But in keeping with the practices of all courts, international courts are guided by legal precedents in their decision making. In March 2001, the International Criminal Tribunal for the Former Yugoslavia (ICTY) drew upon the legal work of the Tokyo Tribunal when they found three Bosnian Serb former military officers guilty of the sexual enslavement, rape, and torture of women in the town of Foca, Bosnia, during 1992. By citing the Judgment of the Women's International War Crimes Tribunal on Japan's Military and Sexual Slavery in its decision, the ICTY gave the precedent set by the Tokyo Tribunal a formal standing in international law. Thus the decision of the Tokyo Tribunal judges has passed from symbolic precedent to legal precedent. Because of the quality of the legal reasoning, the final corrected and edited version of the Tokyo Tribunal judgment, along 1,459 pieces of evidence presented at the Tribunal, have been translated into Korean, Cantonese, Malaysian, Tagalog, Portuguese, Japanese, and Dutch and are being used to train lawyers and jurists specializing in international human rights litigation. With the standing of legal precedent and the heightened prestige of a document used to train international lawyers and jurists, the Tokyo Tribunal judgment has contributed to a significant transformation of international jurisprudence.

Discursive Politics

A second strategy characteristic of outsider politics attempts to disrupt and transform hegemonic discourses, sets of assumptions, and frameworks of analysis and interpretation so thoroughly inured in the dominant worldview that they have been naturalized and taken as given, inevitable, and unalterable.[9] As a social change strategy, discursive politics seeks to disrupt widely accepted understandings of the world by challenging established definitions, categories, and conceptions; demonstrating the shortcomings of the received view; showing that alternative understandings are possible; and mobilizing to win support for significant changes in accepted meanings or discursive regimes. Transnational feminist activism surrounding the concept of human rights provides a powerful example of discursive politics. Operating in a variety of international contexts, transnational feminist activists have tried to rescue the concept of human rights from the narrow confines of liberal and neoliberal discourses. Building upon the rhetorical power of human rights language, feminists have attempted to refigure rights discourses, shedding narrow individualist assumptions, shifting from a natural law framework to an understanding of rights as a product of international consensus building, refiguring the boundaries of the public and private spheres to make violence against women actionable within an international human rights framework, supplementing liberal concerns with civil and political rights with equal attention to social and economic rights, and establishing international recognition of women's rights as human rights.

Like the modern nation-state, human rights discourses emerged in the eighteenth century as part of the republican political struggle against feudalism. To attack the political privilege of the feudal monarchy and aristocracy and legitimate the political enfranchisement of bourgeois men, human rights rhetoric advanced universal claims concerning the "rights of man," the rights to liberty, equality, and fraternity, and the rights to life, liberty, property, and the pursuit of happiness. As we saw in chapter 2, however, these "universal" rights claims coexisted with practices of slavery, colonization, and the exclusion from republican politics of the majority of the population (women, nonpropertied men, indentured servants, indigenous peoples). Enshrined at the heart of liberal and neoliberal understandings of the appropriate relation between citizens and their governments, rights discourses have become embedded in national and international law, treaties, and covenants. Incorporated in a foundational document crafted in conjunction with the inauguration of the United Nations, the Universal Declaration of Human Rights (1948) was meant to introduce a new global order. Despite the consensus hammered out in support of the declaration, ideological differences between liberal support for procedural civil and political rights and socialist support for substantive social and economic rights made the politics of human rights a primary foil in Cold War struggles during the second half of the twentieth century.[10]

Because human rights discourses hold a particular currency in liberal democracies and social democracies, especially in the courts, some feminist activists began using rights claims in the context of supranational activism to improve women's lives. For example, in 1966 women workers in the Herstal arms factory in Belgium went out on strike for equal pay, legitimizing their demand by citing Article 119 of the 1957 Treaty of Rome, which required members states of the European Common Market to "maintain the application of the principle that men and women should receive equal pay for equal work" (Chichowski 2002, 237). While negotiations were going on between Herstal management and 3,000 striking workers, Elaine Vogel-Polsky, a Belgian labor lawyer, decided to try to use litigation to expand women's labor rights, bringing a series of test cases before the European Court of Justice (ECJ) in the late 1960s. After several years of hearings and deliberations, the European Court of Justice began handing down a series of decisions finding that women had "an enforceable right to equal pay," thereby transforming an international treaty into something approximating a supranational constitution (Chichowski 2002, 224). Inspired by these court rulings, feminists working in the European Commission began drafting sex equality legislation and sharing it with feminist activists within the member states, who then proceeded to press their governments for new laws that would bring their nations into compliance with European Union treaties (Chichowski 2002). Over the next few decades, feminists in Europe won some significant gains in formal equality pertaining to discrimination in employment, wages, and social security by using an approach that combined litigation with model legislation crafted by "femocrats" in the European Commission and grassroots lobbying by feminist activists within member states. The limitations of an equal rights strategy began to become apparent, however. Working within the parameters set by liberal discourses, rights claims failed to go beyond a "formal equality" model. They were insensitive to differences among women, and they allowed women to seek only what men have. As such, they could not remedy social inequalities or injustices experienced by women that had no clear parallel to male experiences (Chichowski 2002, 221). Noting the limitations set by the masculinist and individualist assumptions informing liberal conceptions of rights, feminists began to debate whether human rights discourses could be transformed to circumvent these limitations.

Some of the concerns that triggered these discussions stemmed from blatant violations of women's rights associated with racist population control policies enacted under the auspices of development programs across the global South. Incorporating neo-Malthusian notions that poverty was caused by the existence of too many poor people, brutal regimes of sterilization abuse were being imposed on women in poor nations. One UNICEF study, for example, documented an increase in sterilization rates of women in Brazil from 11 percent in the 1960s to 45 percent in the 1990s. Indeed, in one rural area in northeastern Brazil, Maranhao, 79.8 percent of the women had been sterilized (Purewal 2001, 113). Given such egregious abuses, feminist activists working in the fields of women's health, economic development, and violence against women (e.g., DAWN, Women's Global Network for Reproductive Rights, International Women's Tribune Center) initiated a series of debates about how best to introduce a discursive shift in human rights. They were particularly concerned to cultivate an understanding of rights that could encompass an expansive conception of bodily integrity. Within this feminist frame, the right to bodily integrity would include sexual and reproductive rights that could be used to protect women from coerced contraception, forced sterilization, inadequate maternal and child health care, malnutrition, unwanted sexual relations, involuntary maternity, and violence in the home. Seeking to "shed the abstract universality, formalism, individualism, and antagonism encumbering rights language," feminist scholars and activists sought to recast a conception of rights:

> (1) to emphasize the *social*, not just the individual, nature of rights, thus shifting the major burden of correlative duties from individuals to public agencies; (2) acknowledge the *communal* (relational) *contexts* in which individuals act to exercise or pursue their rights; (3) to foreground the *substantive* basis of rights in human needs and a redistribution of resources; and (4) to recognize the bearers of rights in their self-defined, multiple identities, including gender, class, sexual orientation, race, and ethnicity. (Corea and Petchesky 2003, 90; emphasis in original)

In the words of feminist historian Temma Kaplan (2001, 37), feminist activists sought to "redefine human rights as the common good or what socialism once meant: a fulfilling life in which safe housing, proper health, food, education, air and water were assured."

As these debates were continuing, women's rights activists participating in the first Women's Global Leadership Institute (1991) organized by the newly created Center for Women's Global Leadership decided to launch a worldwide petition drive as part of a global mobilization to politicize the issue of violence against women. The petition urged the UN to recognize "women's rights as human rights." Identifying the UN World Conference on Human Rights to be held in Vienna in June of 1993 as the appropriate forum in which to take the campaign for women's rights as human rights to an intergovernmental arena, feminist activists in all regions of the world circulated the petitions through their networks. By the time the Vienna World Conference on Human Rights convened, approximately half a million signatures had been collected from over eighty countries. The petitions were presented to the Human Rights Office of the UN and to the World Conference, as feminist activists lobbied official delegates to support an international declaration recognizing "women's rights are human rights." Securing near unanimous support, the Vienna Declaration (1993) formally recognized women's rights as human rights. A discursive shift in human rights was underway.

Following the Vienna Declaration, feminist activists working within UN networks began developing guides for the use of a human rights framework for feminist ends. These guides emphasize that the human rights framework is particularly powerful because it is rooted in international treaties that have been ratified by the majority of nations around the globe. Drawing upon international agreements such as the Universal Declaration of Human Rights (1948), the International Convention on the Elimination of All Forms of Racial Discrimination (1969), the International Covenant on Economic, Cultural, and Social Rights (1976), the Convention on the Elimination of All Forms of Discrimination Against Women (CEDAW) (1979), and the Declaration on the Elimination of Violence Against Women (1993), the human rights framework enables feminist activists to develop broader and more integrated strategies to advance the full spectrum of women's human rights—civil, political, economic, social, and cultural (Landsberg-Lewis 1998).

When addressing the policies of states that have ratified these treaties, for example, the guides urge women's rights advocates to draw upon the explicit language of the international conventions to draft constitutional amendments or statutory legislation to address issues such as reproductive rights, divorce rights, and women's rights to be free from violence. The guides also cite cases in which feminist activists have succeeded in using a human rights framework to promote constitutional change. In Brazil (1988) and Colombia (1991), for example, feminist activists succeeded in their efforts to use CEDAW language as leverage to shape provisions for new national constitutions that recognized women's equal rights and explicitly prohibited violence against women (Landsberg-Lewis 1998). In the Colombian case, the constitution requires the state to take action to create substantive equality, to eliminate any discrimination, to take affirmative measures to rectify inequities, and to actively promote the conditions to make legal equality real and effective. Thus the Colombian constitution shifts the burden of rights enforcement to the state, just as feminist activists had hoped. The Colombian constitution also creates an enforcement mechanism, the Constitutional Court, to hear citizens' petitions concerning violation of their rights. One of the first cases heard by the Constitutional Court in 1992 established a critical precedent in domestic violence cases, ruling that the state had a positive obligation to secure the protection of women and prevent husbands from violent action.

The Colombian case highlights one of the advantages of using a human rights framework to advance women's rights. International human rights treaties impose specific obligations on states to (1) promote the rights included within the treaty, (2) secure those rights for all by translating them into policies, (3) prevent violations of those rights, and (4) provide remedies to victims should their rights be violated. When feminist activists invoke treaty provisions, they can draw upon more than a global moral consensus to reinforce the legitimacy of their arguments. They can also invoke legal requirements concerning compliance with ratified treaties. Where legislatures are recalcitrant, feminist activists may be able to use the human rights conventions to persuade national courts that national laws must be reinterpreted to conform with these treaties.

In India, for example, women's rights advocates achieved just such a significant victory in the case of *Vishaka v. State of Rajasthan* in 1992. The case involved the brutal gang rape of a woman social worker by her male coworkers during working hours. Local officials refused to investigate the case. A group of feminist NGOs brought a petition to the Supreme Court of India claiming that the absence of sexual harassment laws in India constituted a failure to meet CEDAW's mandate to protect women from sexual harassment. They asked the Court to draft a sexual harassment law to compensate for the Indian parliament's inaction. The Court accepted the NGOs arguments and drew up guidelines for investigating and resolving sexual harassment complaints that would be binding on public and private employees until the government passes suitable legislation (Landsberg-Lewis 1998).

International reporting mechanisms associated with human rights covenants can also assist feminist efforts to advance women's rights. In accordance with UN procedures, governments are asked to complete reports on their efforts to fulfill their obligations under international agreements. These reports are reviewed by international commissions. Each nation's desire for approbation in the court of world opinion can serve as an important stimulus to national efforts to appear to be in compliance with treaty provisions. Eight country reports reviewed by the CEDAW Commission in January 2001, for example, mentioned violence against women as a major problem that the governments were seeking to address. Women's rights activists in those nations are now developing accountability criteria to hold their governments to their expressed intention to find remedies to this problem. In nations that generate overly optimistic accounts of their progress on women's rights, feminist advocacy groups have developed shadow reports to publicize the gap between official statement and actual practice. During the Beijing Plus Five Review, for example, a coalition of twenty feminist advocacy groups in the United States developed a shadow report, *Women's Equality: An Unfinished Agenda* (Women's Environment and Development Organization 2000), which was presented to the U.S. Congress as well as to the United Nations Commission on the Status of Women. The shadow report was also used by grassroots organizations in the United States to mobilize women's activism around the twelve Beijing platform items.

Proponents of feminist appropriations of a human rights framework suggest that this discursive shift can have additional benefits, helping to refigure the relation between private and public spheres. Violence against women committed by a domestic partner is a leading cause of injury and death for women in their child-bearing years in many parts of the world. Feminist campaigns against domestic violence that use a human rights framework demand that rights pertaining to relations in the private sphere be accorded the same legal status as rights operative in the public sphere. Rather than insulating the private sphere from intrusion by the state as liberal discourses would have it, feminist appropriators of human rights rhetoric seek to impose a responsibility on the state to prosecute domestic violence cases, citing the failure to do so as a violation of a human right. By blurring the liberal boundary between public and private to create mechanisms of state accountability, feminist activists would impose an obligation on states to remedy violence in the domestic sphere (Patel 2001, 168). Contesting women's differential access to the courts and the criminal justice system, this deployment of women's rights as human rights insists that women have a "right to justice, to file complaints, to be taken seriously" (Linkogle 2001, 129). Refiguring a notion of women's global citizenship, transnational feminist activists have suggested that an expansion of the UN Declaration of Human Rights to include "gender equality, freedom from violence, free expression of sexuality, reproductive rights including safe and legal abortion, the right and responsibility to raise children, and support them after breakdown of partnership" would be a way to incorporate women's needs and interests into an international rights regime that could be used to foster gender democracy within nation-states (Linkogle 2001, 129).

Despite considerable progress in producing a discursive shift in the human rights framework, some feminists remain suspicious of feminist appropriations of human rights discourses. Some feminist activists in the global South perceive appeals to human rights as a neocolonial ploy that reinscribes the power of the North and West (Cheah 1997). Others suggest that the state-centered focus of human rights strategies should be approached with great caution because the majority of states are far from women-friendly and are unlikely to contribute to the kinds of social transformation feminists envision. Others note that the long liberal tradition of giving priority to civil and political rights, while discounting economic and social rights, is extremely difficult to reverse, especially in a period of neoliberal ascendancy (Butegwa 1995; Basu 2000). Moreover, in the current state of global capitalist power relations, international leverage to hold governments to account to universally agreed upon human rights standards is far more likely to be used to hold Third World governments to account than to hold to account the United States or other Western states responsible for human rights abuses (Naples and Desai 2002, 271–272). This debate about human rights framework is likely to continue.

Creating Spaces for International Feminist Activism on the Inside

From their experiences with the Paris Peace Conference in 1919 and through two decades of efforts to influence the policies and practices of the League of Nations, transnational feminist activists discovered that outsider politics within the international arena have clear limitations. Outsider activists can lobby international organizations and the representatives of member states. They can provide background information, draft proposed declarations and resolutions, serve as consultants, and provide expert advice, but in an important sense they are limited to "statement power" (Stienstra 1994, 96). Reacting to initiatives framed by men and making recommendations to men, feminist statements raise certain concerns, but only within the existing agenda. As outsiders, it is extremely difficult to raise new issues, shape an agenda, or secure the adoption of alternative courses of action. Recognizing limitations of this sort, some transnational feminist activists have long sought means to create spaces for women inside international organizations.

As noted in the last chapter, women's NGOs launched a major effort to secure a guarantee of nondiscrimination in employment at the League of Nations. In pressing for employment opportunities for women, they assumed that women working within international agencies would have access to information, opportunities to inject issues, and the ability to influence outcomes. Rather than simply reacting to agendas set by men, women on the inside could frame a women's agenda and use the power of the international organization to achieve it. They could also air women's concerns and share women's perspectives, demonstrating that all issues are women's issues. Drawing lessons from the frustrated efforts of women's rights activists to effect international policies in the interwar years, in the aftermath of World War II feminist activists sought to place women inside the newly created United Nations and to create "women's machinery" at the international level—the UN Commission on the Status of Women. That struggle illuminates how difficult it is for a small group of women to transform male-dominant institutions.

No women were included in the 1944 Dumbarton Oaks Conference, which produced the initial, gender-blind framework for the United Nations. Concerned that a gender-blind UN would perpetuate male power and privilege, Bertha Lutz of Brazil and Minerva Bernadino of the Dominican Republic, experienced diplomats who had honed their skills in the

Inter-American Commission on the Status of Women, joined with Jessie Street from Australia to spearhead a campaign to inject gender into founding documents of the United Nations. Creating a caucus of the few women included in their nation's official delegations to the 1945 United Nations Conference on International Organization (UNCIO), Lutz, Bernadino, and Street launched an arduous and successful effort to secure an affirmation of the equal rights of women and men in the preamble to the UN Charter. Women diplomats from Brazil, Australia, Canada, China, the Dominican Republic, Mexico, Norway, Uruguay, and Venezuela also succeeded in adding nondiscrimination clauses guaranteeing "fundamental freedoms for all without distinction as to race, sex, language or religion" in four other clauses of the Charter (Stienstra 1994, 78–79). Their effort to include a commitment to equal opportunity in employment at the UN encountered extensive opposition, however. Opponents appealed to a *presumption* of nondiscrimination as justification for omitting any reference to the "eligibility of men and women to participate in any capacity and under conditions of equality in the principal and subsidiary organs" of the UN. Women in the delegations from Brazil, Uruguay, Mexico, and the Dominican Republic countered with a bold observation: The near total absence of women from the delegations of the vast majority of the forty-nine states participating in the conference provided little support for any presumption of nondiscrimination. Combining lucid arguments with sophisticated behind-the-scenes diplomacy, they overcame the opposition, and the equal opportunity article was included in the UN Charter (Stienstra 1994, 80).[11]

Pressing the point that gender neutrality might be insufficient to protect the rights and secure equal treatment of women, the Brazilian delegation also introduced a resolution calling for the creation of a "special commission of women to study the conditions and prepare reports on the political, civil, and economic status and opportunity of women with special reference to discrimination and limitations placed upon them on account of their sex" (Stienstra 1994, 81). Although there was widespread support for this resolution, the U.S. delegation opposed the proposal, arguing that the question of women's rights should be subsumed under the rubric of the Commission on Human Rights (CHR). Transnational feminist activists in the World Women's Party, the International Alliance of Women, and the Six Points Group of England lobbied hard in support of Brazil's proposal to create a Commission on the Status of Women. When the Economic and Social Council (ECOSOC) met in 1946, however, it followed the course recommended by the United States, creating a Sub-Commission on the Status of Women under the auspices of the Commission on Human Rights, which was to be chaired by Eleanor Roosevelt (Galey 1995).

The Sub-Commission on the Status of Women held its first meetings in April 1946. Among its members were experienced international feminist activists such as Bodil Begtrup, chair of Denmark's National Council of Women, Minerva Bernadino, chair of the Inter-American Commission of Women, and Hansa Mehta, president of the All-India Women's Conference. Defining its mission as raising "the status of women to equality with men in all fields of human enterprise," the sub-commission set an expansive agenda, encompassing multiple dimensions of women's existence. The agenda included efforts to promote women's equal participation in governance and full rights of citizenship; equality in marriage; guardianship of children, nationality, and property; equal opportunity in education at all levels; protective labor legislation for women workers; and international policies to address prostitution. The sub-commission also recommended that the UN complete the worldwide study of the status of women that had been commissioned by the League of Nations. They recommended that the UN convene a World Women's Conference to enable women to shape the international agenda. They urged the UN to develop systematic training for international and national leaders in women's affairs. They encouraged the UN to devise strategies to restructure housework, enabling women to take greater part in civic affairs. They also drafted an equal rights resolution to bring to the floor of the UN. Modeled on the Equal Rights Treaty that had been passed by the Pan-American Conference in 1933, the resolution was passed by the General Assembly despite opposition from Eleanor Roosevelt and the U.S. delegation, who argued that the resolution was redundant because the ideas in the resolution were already contained within the UN Charter (Stienstra, 1994, 84).

Having developed an ambitious agenda, followed by an immediate success in the passage of the Equal Rights Resolution, the sub-commission was poised to move forward. Several members of the sub-commission were concerned, however, that Eleanor Roosevelt would continue to use her position as chair of the Commission on Human Rights to obstruct their initiatives. Required to have its recommendations approved by the CHR before they could be taken to the General Assembly or to other UN specialized agencies, the sub-commission knew that Roosevelt's opposition would be fatal. In a shrewd diplomatic maneuver, sub-commission chair Bodil Begtrup decided to report the sub-commission's findings directly to ECOSOC, accompanied by a renewed request to confer full commission status on the sub-commission. After an intensive round of behind-the-scenes diplomacy by members of the sub-commission, augmented by extensive lobbying by the World Women's Party, ECOSOC agreed to create the Commission on the Status of Women (CSW) (Stienstra 1994, 84).

89

Having won an important victory with respect to institutional status, CSW faced enormous opposition to the scope of its proposed mission and agenda. Leading the opposition to the CSW's progressive agenda, the British delegation resurrected a well-honed parliamentary maneuver to undermine the CSW's work. Developing a two-pronged strategy, the spokesperson for the UK delegation argued that much of the CSW's proposed work was *already being done* by specialized UN agencies; hence, the agenda entailed unnecessary duplication of effort. Moreover, before any initiatives could be undertaken to improve the status of women, more *study* was needed of the particular mechanisms that contributed to women's situation. Thus the British delegation persuaded ECOSOC to limit the scope of CSW's work to "examination of existing legal and customary disabilities of women as regards political and social rights, and economic rights (subject to consultation with the International Labor Organization [ILO]), and also of educational opportunities with a view to framing proposals for action" (Stienstra 1994, 86). Through such skilled diplomatic maneuvering, the British delegation convinced ECOSOC to curtail the vibrant action agenda proposed by the CSW, restricting its mission to indefinite further study conducted in consultation with the male-dominant ILO. Authorized only to study and monitor, CSW was stripped of any direct power to change the status of women. This curtailment of the CSW mission and agenda provides a prime example of the perils of insider activism. Feminists working within male-dominant institutions often lack the autonomy needed to accomplish their preferred objectives. Standard institutional operating procedures can be used to undermine the radical potential of feminist efforts. With such dire restrictions imposed on its institutional mandate, it is not surprising that it took CSW almost three decades to move forward with agenda items developed in 1946, such as a UN-sponsored World Conference on Women.

Women's Policy Machinery

As a strategy for social change, the idea of women's machinery envisions separate policy units within national or international agencies, staffed by feminists, to coordinate, evaluate, and implement women's programs or policies targeting women. As noted in chapter 2, the Inter-American Commission on Women was the first intergovernmental women's machinery created at the regional level. Modeled on the Inter-American Commission, the UN Commission on the Status of Women was the first effort to create global women's machinery. Although its own mandate had been severely curtailed, the CSW used its position within the UN to encourage member states to cultivate their own agencies to address women's needs and interests. In the late 1950s the CSW suggested the development of women's policy machineries at the national level to enhance women's social and political status (Stetson and Mazur 1995, 3). In 1960 U.S. president John Kennedy appointed the President's Commission on the Status of Women, which ironically—given her opposition to the creation of the CSW at the UN—was chaired by Eleanor Roosevelt. In addition to conducting a systematic study of sexual inequality in the United States and developing recommendations to remedy these inequities, the President's Commission on the Status of Women created feminist networks across the country that provided the essential infrastructure for the emergence of U.S. women's movements in the 1960s (Freeman 1975; Duerst-Lahti 1989). Similarly, the Royal Commission on the Status of Women (RCSW), appointed by the Canadian government in 1967, conducted a national study culminating in reports and recommendations, which "provided the blueprint for 20 years of subsequent feminist activism" in Canada (Harder 2006). As in the U.S. case, the Royal Commission reinvigorated feminist activism across Canada.

In 1975 the UN passed a resolution calling on member states to "establish the appropriate government machinery to accelerate the integration of women in development and the elimination of discrimination against women on the grounds of sex" (Tripp 2003). Continuing a pattern of policy learning from global to local, many transnational feminist activists involved in UN activities during the Decade for Women (1975–1985) advocated creation of national commissions on the status of women as a means to advance women's interests. In 1995, the Platform for Action developed at the Fourth World Conference on Women in Beijing endorsed creation and strengthening of women's machinery as a means to achieve platform objectives.

The CSW experience at the UN, however, foreshadowed difficulties associated with women's machinery as a tactic for social change. During the UN Decade for Women many countries established women's policy offices, but most remained marginal to overall decision-making processes at national and international levels. By and large, they lacked resources, authority, and expertise to achieve their objectives (Stienstra 1994, 95). By 1990, one hundred nations had created national machineries for the advancement of women. By 1995, 90 percent of UN member states had created various forms of national machinery to promote women's concerns, including ministries of women's affairs, women's bureaus, and women's units within ministries of health, education, and employment, as well as women's wings within political parties (Snyder 1995, 109). Creating women's machinery to conform to international agreements, many nations accorded these units broad mandates but provided them slim means with which to fulfill those mandates. Of the one hundred states that had created machinery for women by 1990, most had insufficient staff and insufficient authority to deal with issues in their remit (Stienstra 1994, 141). In some states, nepotism marred the appointments to professional positions within women's ministries. The wives, daughters, sisters, or nieces of senior elected officials who were appointed to these agencies lacked the professional qualifications and the administrative experience to do the job. In some states, pressure from conservative forces and religious organizations excluded key issues such as divorce or abortion from the jurisdiction of women's units. Limited budgets, unclear briefs, lack of power to monitor other government agencies, and real threats of co-optation have constrained the feminist impact of many of these agencies (Waylen 1996, 129–130). Moreover, at the same time that states have agreed to international standards to promote equality for women and have established national machineries to monitor and promote gender equality, they have simultaneously implemented structural adjustment policies and policies related to the globalization of production and trade, which "have the effect of stifling and reversing many changes that could have helped women" (Stienstra 1994, 118).

Women in Decision Making

Engendering good governance by increasing the numbers of women in elective and appointive public offices is another strategy advanced by transnational feminist activists to move women inside the state, thereby making states more responsive to women's concerns. Research on women officeholders suggests that women are more likely than their male counterparts to include policies for women and families among their top legislative priorities. In contrast to neoliberal concerns with privatization, women are more supportive of government intervention to meet the most basic human needs. Engendering the institutions of governance, then, promises to be a strategy that builds bridges linking elected women officials, NGO activists, and women citizens. Women candidates running on anticorruption platforms and incorporating feminist concerns with transparency and accountability in government develop strong ties to women's organizations supportive of those stances. By supporting women candidates for office and helping to secure their election, women's organizations gain access to decision makers, a critical step in efforts to create a policy agenda for women. Women's groups working outside government to press for feminist agendas can give women in office leverage within their parties that is essential to legislative success. By mobilizing voters around particular women's issues, and helping to turn out voters in elections, grassroots feminist activists can also develop a powerful tool to hold their elective representatives to account. Thus engendering governance contributes to democratic accountability as well as gender equality.

Transnational feminist activists have identified several dramatic means to increase the number of women in elective offices, including the creation of quotas that establish numerical targets for women candidates on political parties' nominating slates, and reservation policies that set aside a number of seats in an elective body specifically for women. Norway was the first nation in which political parties voluntarily set quotas, stipulating that no gender should have more than 60 percent of the slots on a party's nominating slate. Adopted in the 1980s, Norway quickly catapulted to the top rank of nations in terms of the representation of women in parliament, the cabinet, and the office of prime minister. In 1990, India established a reservation policy that set aside 33 percent of the seats on village councils for women. Since then, women who were first elected to reserved seats have successfully run for nonreserved seats with the result that more than 40 percent of local elected officials in India are women, twice the average for nations around the globe. Learning from these impressive accomplishments, feminist activists have mobilized to press for quotas and reservation policies in more nations. By 2003, feminist activists had accrued impressive victories: More than thirty nations have introduced gender quotas for elections to national parliaments by constitutional amendment or electoral law; and major political parties in more than fifty nations have altered their party electoral practices to require that a minimum number of candidates on party electoral lists (often 30 percent) be women (Dahlerup and Freidenvall 2003).

Feminist activism in South Africa during the transition to a postapartheid system of governance provides a powerful example of how feminists have been able to use quotas in conjunction with creation of women's machinery to foster gender equality. Feminists within the African National Congress (ANC) had developed strong ties with progressive transnational feminist organizations during their long struggle against the apartheid regime. Using their position within the ANC and extensive feminist research concerning strategies for social change, ANC activists injected gender issues into discussions about the construction of new democratic institutions.

Women had played vital roles in the ANC since its creation in the early twentieth century. After the organization was banned, women continued to take an active part in the party's underground activities and were subject to arrest, detention, and imprisonment along with their male counterparts (Fester 2001). From a position of equality in struggle, feminist activists within the ANC lobbied their male counterparts for commitments to gender equality in a "new" South Africa. In the late 1980s, ANC slogans began calling for a "nonracial, democratic, nonsexist South Africa" (Seidman 1999, 292). When the ban against the ANC was lifted and preparations began for a transition to a multiracial democracy, feminists in the ANC pressed hard to ensure that race and gender equality were included in all negotiations concerning the new political institutions. Although Nelson Mandela urged the adoption of a gender quota for all ANC official activities, the proposal was voted down at the 1991 national ANC conference. Keenly aware of how quickly their role in the ANC could be diminished if the male party activists closed ranks against gender equality, women in the ANC began to mobilize for full participation of women in national negotiations for democracy and for the development of gender-sensitive democratic practices during and after the transition.

To develop a mechanism for gathering women's views and airing women's voices, feminists in the ANC organized the Women's National Coalition, which brought together seventy women's organizations across the political spectrum. For the first time in South African history, an organization brought people together bridging divisions of race, class, ethnicity, ideology, religion, party, and rural-urban rifts. Rather than assume that it knew what women wanted, the Women's National Coalition launched an eighteen-month campaign to discern what women wanted from the new state. Traveling around the country, they organized 203 focus groups with 1,620 participants and collected 2,973 questionnaires from all regions (Seidman 1999, 298). On the basis of the information gathered in these cross-country discussions and questionnaires, the Women's National Coalition generated the Women's Charter, a set of demands reflecting interests of women across the country, which included equal opportunities in the world of work and sharing burdens equally in the home; equal participation in decision making; reproductive and sexual rights; protection from sexual harassment and violence; parental leaves; access to child care facilities; and creation of health, welfare, and pension benefits that did not discriminate against women whose work was unwaged. Through this prolonged and participatory process, the Women's National Coalition modeled a new form of deliberative democratic practice, forged a public consensus for gender equality,[12] and gave notice to male politicians that women in South Africa would not settle for anything less than a gender-equitable constitutional design.

At the same time that the Women's National Coalition was mobilizing, feminists in the ANC continued to lobby all parties involved in constitutional negotiations to take gender equality seriously. Although all the official negotiators participating in transition talks were male, the ANC feminists persuaded all parties to agree to the creation of a Gender Advisory Board, which would investigate the gender impact of negotiated agreements (Seidman 1999, 293). When the members of the Gender Advisory Board were not allowed to participate actively in negotiations, ANC feminist activists decided more radical tactics were necessary. In 1993, ANC women "stormed the negotiating chamber, blocking talks until women were literally given places at the table" (Seidman 1999, 294). Through this direct action, ANC women convinced all twenty-six parties participating in negotiations to accept a rigorous gender quota for further negotiations: 50 percent of each two-person team had to be women. South Africa's new constitution is the product of this egalitarian structure.

Within the constitutional negotiations, women negotiators formed a caucus and through this innovative collaboration designed the most sophisticated women's machinery in any government in the world. In crafting their own political institutions, South African feminists drew upon feminist research on women's machinery in states ranging from Australia to Nicaragua. They were particularly concerned that women's ministries could ghettoize women's issues, separating them from other political issues on the national agenda, and limiting their scope to issues of domestic relations, child care, nutrition, health, and handicrafts (Seidman 1999, 301). To avoid such marginalization, South African feminists devised a multipronged approach to ensure that gender issues would be mainstreamed in all aspects of governmental work. A national Office on the Status of Women was included among the institutional components of the Office of the President; a Women's Caucus was created within the parliament; gender focus desks were created within all ministries with mandates to complete gender impact audits of all policies. In addition, the 1993 interim constitution and the 1996 democratically approved constitution mandated the creation of a Commission on Gender Equality, charged with the responsibility to oversee the operations of all units of government to ensure their full implementation of the gender equality provisions in the constitution. During their first year of work, the newly appointed members of the Commission on Gender Equality articulated their expansive mission:

> The Commission on Gender Equality will strive for the transformation of society through exposing gender discrimination in the laws, policies, and practices; advocating changes in sexist attitudes and gender stereotypes, in-

stilling respect for women's rights as human rights . . . [through the] transformation of gender relations; redefinition and redistribution of power; and
equal access to and enjoyment of economic, social, and political opportunities. (Seidman 2003, 547)

In preparation for the 1994 elections, the first in which black South
Africans were allowed to participate, ANC women convinced their male
counterparts to create a gender quota in the party's electoral slate: Women
were 30 percent of the ANC candidates nominated for public offices. The
argument that feminists advanced to secure this quota was straightforward.
Women were the majority of citizens in South Africa, and, as such, their
votes were crucial to the outcome of the election. The power of this point
was apparent to politicians outside the ANC. All parties made special efforts to appeal to women voters in the 1994 election (Seidman 2003).
Fielding more women candidates was an important part of those appeals
even in parties that refused to create a specific quota. In the first postapartheid parliament, women constituted 26.5 percent of the members (MPs),
a dramatic change from the nearly all-male, white parliament that preceded
it.

Gender Mainstreaming

The concept of gender mainsteaming, used so adeptly by South African
feminist activists in designing the institutions of the postapartheid state,
is itself the product of transnational feminist activism. First developed by
feminists working in the European Commission in their efforts to promote
gender equality policies among the member states, the call for gender
mainstreaming was included in the Platform for Action created at the
Fourth World Conference on Women in Beijing. The "fundamental prem-
ise of mainstreaming is that gender perspectives are essential to all programs and issues" (West 1999, 191). As a social change strategy, then,
gender mainstreaming requires that all decision-making processes across
all policy domains take gender into account, exploring the implications
of proposed policies for men and women, investigating differential gender
impacts and disparate gender outcomes of existing and proposed programs. In the language developed by the United Nations Economic and
Social Council, gender mainstreaming is

the process of assessing the implications for women and men of any
planned action, including legislation, policies and programs, in all areas
and at all levels. It is a strategy for making women's as well as men's concerns and experiences an integral dimension of the design, implementa-

tion, monitoring and evaluation of policies and programs in all political, economic, and societal spheres so that women and men benefit equally and inequality is not perpetuated. The ultimate goal is the achievement of gender equality. (ECOSOC 1997)

Some transnational feminist activists have been working on gender mainstreaming at the international level, as well as within national institutions of governance. Feminist mobilization around the creation of the International Criminal Court provides a powerful example of this tactic in action. The International Criminal Court (ICC) was created by the Rome Statute, an international treaty approved by 120 nations in 1998 (21 nations abstained; 7, including the United States, China, Iraq, Israel, Libya, Qatar, and Yemen, opposed). By April 11, 2002, the Rome Statute had received the necessary 60 ratifications to go into effect the following July. As noted in the discussion of the war crimes tribunals above, feminist activists working on issues pertaining to women in conflict situations have been particularly concerned that mechanisms be created to hold individuals, partisan groups, and governments to account for egregious crimes against women. As the world's first international criminal tribunal, the ICC was authorized to try individuals, regardless of their official position or status, for genocide, war crimes, crimes against humanity, and aggression. Transnational feminist activists saw the creation of the court as a prime opportunity to mainstream gender issues in the ICC's mandate (Spees 2003).

A transnational group of feminist activists involved in issues pertaining to violence against women launched the Women's Caucus for Gender Justice in the International Criminal Court in 1997. A regionally diverse group of experts with experience at national and international levels, the Women's Caucus for Gender Justice included feminist activists whose expertise had been honed in human rights organizing around the 1993 Vienna Convention on Human Rights, in monitoring the work of the International Criminal Tribunal on the Former Yugoslavia (1993) and the International Criminal Tribunal on Rwanda (1994), and in violence against women activism at the Beijing Conference. They were keenly aware that existing international law provided inadequate protection for women. For example, although Article 27 of the Geneva Convention of 1949 sought to protect women from "any attack on their honor, in particular against rape, enforced prostitution, or any other from of indecent assault,"[13] the convention did not classify violence against women as a grave breach, which states have a duty to investigate and prosecute no matter where they are committed or by whom (Spees 2003, 1239). In practice, Article 27 was largely ignored; and conceptually it was defective, for it failed to acknowledge that men and children were also raped in war. To remedy such defects, members of the Women's Caucus began attending ICC negotiations, providing technical information about defects in existing laws, advocating changes in legal terminology, and mobilizing support for core principles of gender justice. By the time the Rome Diplomatic Conference convened in July 1998, the Women's Caucus had developed a strong network of diplomats and organizations that supported gender mainstreaming the ICC.

The technical expertise provided by the Women's Caucus enabled diplomats participating in the negotiations to illuminate deficiencies of existing humanitarian law with respect to crimes of gender and sexual violence. Materials prepared by the Women's Caucus enabled official negotiators to expand the conceptualization of sexual violence to include rape, sexual slavery, enforced prostitution, forced pregnancy, and enforced sterilization; to affirm the gravity of these forms of violence; and to include these forms of sexual violence as war crimes and crimes against humanity in the Rome Statute. Through the intervention of the Women's Caucus, trafficking and gender-based persecution were also included as crimes against humanity. Feminist advocacy succeeded in severing any connection between sexual crimes against women and crimes against the "honor" of families, an outdated formulation that suggested women were family property. Thanks to the work of the Women's Caucus, the Rome Statute includes a feminist definition of rape (i.e., the coercive invasion of the body of a person by force or threat of force); and the rules of evidence were structured to allow victim and witness testimony, and to avoid attacks on a victim's character or the use of "consent" as a defense in instances of blatant coercion (Spees 2003).

The advocacy work of the Women's Caucus for Gender Justice played a crucial role in shaping the International Criminal Court itself, ensuring its independence from political manipulation by the Security Council. The Women's Caucus lobbied intensively and successfully against proposals that would afford the UN Security Council a veto over the cases the court could prosecute. They worked arduously to ensure that not only state agents but private perpetrators of violence could be prosecuted under the jurisdiction of ICC. Their intervention accorded the ICC power to protect victims and witnesses who testify from retaliation and, where appropriate, to devise broad reparation schemes (Spees 2003).

In addition, the Women's Caucus for Gender Justice scored another impressive victory in their efforts to ensure equitable gender representation on the court and the inclusion of judges with expertise in areas of violence against women and violence against children. Seven of the eighteen judges elected to the ICC in February 2003 are women. By comparison, only one woman has ever served on the fifteen-member International Court of Justice (Spees 2003, 1243).

The Women's Caucus for Gender Justice was committed to a feminist conception of gender, which includes complex issues pertaining to sex, sexed embodiedness, sexuality, sexual identity, gender roles, and gender identity. Seeking to expand the project of gender mainstreaming to encompass the complexity of feminist analysis, they fought for a definition of gender-based crimes in the Rome Statute that could encompass persecution based on sexual orientation or deviation from traditional gender roles and identities. During the 1990s, conservative forces, led by the Roman Catholic Church and an alliance of Arab states, had mobilized to contest feminist activism in UN conferences, and feminist conceptions of gender, in particular. At the International Conference on Population and Development in Cairo (1994) and at the Beijing World Conference on Women (1995), this conservative coalition succeeded in derailing a number of feminist policy initiatives. In the course of these struggles, "the notion of 'gender' in and of itself was passionately contested and constructed as a concept that presented everything illicit, immoral and decadent that is being imported from the West" (Al-Ali 2004). Under the leadership of the Vatican, this coalition mobilized again at the Rome Diplomatic Conference, explicitly seeking to exclude sexual orientation from gender-based crimes. That this effort failed is a testament to the astute diplomatic maneuvering of the Women's Caucus.

Pam Spees (2003, 1246) has pointed out that as an international treaty, the Rome Statute has potential benefits for feminists working on the issues of gender violence within nation-states. The gender-based crimes codified in the treaty are not recognized by all nations. Moreover, the legal definitions of the crimes of sexual and gender violence are more progressive than definitions used in the statutes of many nations. Feminist activists in countries that ratify the Rome Statute can use the treaty provisions "to help strengthen the capacity to address violence against women at the national level via the inclusion of additional crimes of sexual and gender violence, progressive definitions of existing crimes, and more gender-sensitive procedures in the trials for these crimes" (Spees 2003, 1246). The Rome Statute might also help increase recognition of gender-based persecution, creating opportunities for feminist activists within nations to favorably influence asylum policies for women fleeing gender-based violence and for those endangered because of their sexual orientation or gender identity.

Like many of the social change strategies discussed in this chapter, gender mainstreaming has critics as well as supporters. Some feminists have suggested that as an insider tactic used by groups who work for change

99

within the context of existing institutions, gender mainstreaming fosters adaptation—change without transformation (Stienstra 1994, 33). Operating within male-dominant institutions, expansive feminist intentions and objectives are often diluted, as gender mainstreaming becomes indistinguishable from raising women's status via piecemeal reforms (Petchesky 2003, 11). Calls for gender mainstreaming and gender sensitivity may deteriorate into mechanistic quick fixes, which assume that problems of gender inequality can be addressed by redirecting some resources toward women's and girls' education, skills development, access to health services, or improvement of communication between women and men. Offering such superficial solutions, gender mainstreaming may ignore deep-seated imbalances of power, structural inequities, and entrenched practices of subordination characteristic of gender relations in most societies (Petchesky 2003, 11). Lois Harder (2006) and Laura Macdonald (2006) have also pointed out that gender mainstreaming can be co-opted by governments hostile to feminism and used to dismantle sophisticated women's policy machinery that produced important gains for women. In a telling Canadian case study, Harder (2006) demonstrates how the neoliberal government of Brian Mulroney and the Liberal government of Jean Chrétien used gender mainstreaming mandates to dismantle the state agencies that had historically acted as the main voice for women in national-level policy.[14] The diffusion of responsibility for gender equality across all institutions may have the unintended effect of dissipating all responsibility.

Feminist Civil Society

In addition to outsider tactics and insider tactics, some feminist scholars have characterized transnational feminist activism in terms of a third alternative, feminist civil society. Neither fully outside nor fully inside national and international political arenas, feminist activism operates in a new political terrain in which the boundaries between the public and the private, the national and the transnational, and the global and the local blur. Although references to feminist civil society (and civil society more generally) have proliferated in the past fifteen years, the meanings associated with this concept differ depending upon the theoretical framework in which the discussion of civil society is situated.

Within liberal political theory, civil society is a realm of nonstate action, voluntary association, and individual pursuit of private interests. It is the domain of negative liberty, the private sphere, insulated from state intrusion through the establishment and enforcement of civil rights and immunities. As litigation has played out in liberal democratic states, corporations as well as individuals have been declared rights-bearing "persons," protected from unwarranted state intrusions. Thus liberal and neoliberal theorists define civil society capaciously to include the home, the economy, religious institutions, and all forms of voluntary associations and organizations.

While liberal political theorists celebrate the institutions of civil society as a haven from the machinations of bureaucratic state power, disciples of Hegel construct a less idyllic image of civil society. Within a Hegelian frame, civil society is the realm of unmitigated self-interest. Populated by self-serving individualists whose relations are governed solely by contract, civil society is a manipulative world of opposing wills, devoid of moral concerns, much less ethical action. Seeing others as obstacles to the satisfaction of their own selfish desires, amoral individuals seek to manipulate and control one another, refraining from abusive practices only when they fear detection and punishment. Thus civil society is sorely in need of control by the state, as the "embodiment of the Ethical Idea." Marx concurred in Hegel's censorious judgment of civil society, construing it as the "arena where man acts as a private individual, regards other men as means, degrades himself into means, and becomes a plaything of alien powers" (Seligman 2002, 30). Conceiving the bourgeois state as an instrument of capitalist oppression, however, Marx rejected any facile hope that the defects of civil society might be transcended through the redemptive action of the state.

In contrast to liberal and neoliberal theoretical frames, neo-Gramscians reject liberal constructions of the public and private spheres as autonomous domains. In this view, all social relations are politically constituted and ideologically mediated. Thus civil society is construed as a political realm, a site of contestation in which individual identities are formed, hegemonic relations shaped, and ideological struggles played out. Challenging the notion that individuals, interest groups, or corporations operate independent of the state, neo-Gramscians suggest that the state constructs the boundaries of civil society and uses civil society organizations to maintain hegemony, a form of power that has been so thoroughly naturalized that it becomes invisible.

Theorists working within a Habermasian framework conceive civil society in terms of sites that facilitate communicative processes. In contrast to that of neo-Gramscians, Habermasian civil society operates through deliberative mechanisms, through persuasion and agreement, not through coercion. In civil society, groups and individuals appeal to norms, making claims on each other and engaging each other in rational and ethical discussion. Within the Habermasian frame, as a realm of deliberative engagement, civil society stands in opposition to large-scale, rule-following bureaucratic organizations and to the profit-driven logic of markets. "In associations of civil society, people coordinate their actions by discussing and working things out, rather than by checking prices and looking up rules" (Young 2000, 159; Weldon 2004). Thus, civil society is fluid, consisting of those voluntary interactions and associations governed by discussion.

A form of voluntary organization, a kind of self-interested action, a space of contestation, or a process of deliberation, civil society may appear to be all things to all people. Yet the proliferation of discourses on civil society is itself a manifestation of the past two decades of globalization, closely tied to marketization, and to liberal and neoliberal agendas for democratization. Discussions of global civil society emerge in the wake of a bipolar global world order, after the demise of the Soviet system, marking a resurgence of capital flows to an emerging nonstate, voluntary sector. The donors helping to fund civil society organizations include huge foundations such as the Soros Open Society Institute and the Ford Foundation and the governments of Western nations. In the newly independent states created from the former Soviet bloc, 63 percent of the women's organizations receive all of their funding from Western foundations (Hrycak 2002, 71–77). In the late 1990s, as Aili Tripp (2003) has pointed out, 40 percent of USAID funds in Africa were going to civil society organizations. Funders of civil society organizations are explicit about their motivations. They seek to promote organizations that can serve as a counterweight to the state, monitoring and challenging state practices, generating proposals for reform, and pressuring for democratization. Aiding and abetting neoliberal economic restructuring, the promotion of civil society stands in complex relation to the neoliberal ideological agenda, a relation that is not always clearly marked in academic treatments of the subject, as the following definition makes clear. "Global civil society is the sphere of ideas, values, institutions, organizations, networks, and individuals located *between* the family, the state, and the market and operating *beyond* the confines of national societies, politics, and economies" (Anheier, Glasius, and Kaldor 2001, 17). While the nature and scope of civil society is a subject of ongoing contestation, spatial metaphors that portray civil society simply as a location may need to be supplemented with strenuous interrogation of what goes on within civil society spaces.

These various conceptualizations of civil society reverberate in feminist understandings of the nature and possibilities of transnational feminist civil society; but feminist analyses converge on a finding omitted from mainstream accounts: Civil society is a thoroughly gendered space. As Barbara Einhorn and Charlotte Sever (2003, 167) have pointed out, whether construed as "informal political activity," as a "space between state and household," as a "defining characteristic of liberal democracies," as a "third point in society's triangle of state, market, and voluntary, non-profit sector," as "the mobilization of citizens outside governmental arenas," as a space for political resistance," or as an "idealized space for dissident groups," civil society is "structured by gendered relations of unequal power and its institutions—trade unions, religious organizations, dissident political movements—are male dominated." Specifically "feminist civil society," then, refers to those voluntary associational activities aimed at undermining male domination and promoting the empowerment or status of women (Beckwith 2000). As a strategy for social change, feminist civil society involves women's self-organization to undermine social practices and norms that devalue women and keep women subordinate (Weldon 2004, 5). Addressing a wide array of social, political, and economic issues, including many that are not easily resolved via legislation (e.g., gender division of labor in the family or women's triple shift), feminist civil society enables discussion and critique of dominant views and generates ideas and strategies that can lead to social change. As discursive spaces in which marginalized groups organize and express themselves more freely than is possible in the hegemonic public sphere (N. Fraser 1992; Dawson 1994), feminist civil society is characterized by relations of contestation and struggle. As a "counter-public of women" (Weldon 2004), self-organizing to resist domination, feminist civil society facilitates mutual aid and the articulation of group consciousness, as well as the production of "public goods," ranging from new concepts to innovative policy solutions (Young 2000, 166).

The NGO forums organized in conjunction with the four UN-sponsored World Conferences on Women are perhaps the best examples of feminist civil society as a counter-public of women. Running parallel to the official intergovernmental conferences and consisting of those feminist activists who choose (and who can afford) to participate, NGO forums are an "inchoate form of [a] more democratic and participatory global governance" (Petchesky 2003, 24), which gesture toward alternatives to existing hierarchical structures dominated by nation-states and international organizations. While there is no question that NGO forums are exhilarating sites of debate, performance, mobilization, information sharing, petition gathering, brainstorming, and sometimes, solidarity building, they remain at some remove from the Habermasian ideal of rational deliberation, much less consensual decision making. As Rosalind Petchesky has pointed out, they are neither representative nor accountable assemblies.

There is no reliable mechanism for representing the voices of the oppressed; those who claim to speak for them are not "representative" in any
systemic sense. An infinitesimal fragment of the world's women are represented at, much less participate in UN Conferences, and those who do participate are divided by region, class, race/ethnicity, culture, positioning
within global capitalism, and access to power and resources. (Petchesky
2003, 25)

In contrast to these global gatherings of women, a second construction
of transnational feminist civil society focuses on a much narrower framework, nongovernmental organizations (NGOs). The term *nongovernmental
organization* is itself the progeny of the United Nations, adopted by the UN
when it agreed to provide a mechanism for citizen-based organizations to
participate in the Economic and Social Council (ECOSOC). As defined by
the UN, NGO applies only to private, nonprofit groups (Tinker 1999, 89).
Often created to make claims on behalf of those who are excluded from
official institutions of national and transnational governance, however,
"NGOs are a special set of organizations that are private in form, but public
in purpose" (Weiss and Gordenker 1996, 18). Moreover, NGOs include an
enormous array of organizational types and sizes, ranging from grassroots
or community-based organizations to service or advocacy organizations
dependent largely on private donors, to giant nonprofit organizations that
are funded mainly through public resources—some having budgets larger
than those of some poor countries (e.g., International Red Cross, CARE
International) (Petchesky 2003, 28).

By 1945, the international women's movement had created twenty-five
international NGOs (INGOs) that were involved in efforts to shape UN
practices and agendas. By 1975, that number had grown to fifty (Stephenson 1995, 135). Despite claims within the literature on globalization from
below concerning the populist character of NGOs, "most NGOs in membership or headquarters reflect rather than counteract prevailing hegemonic structures of the world system" (Stephenson 1995, 138). Feminist
NGOs also fall under that indictment. Most come from or are funded by
rich Western nations. Carolyn Stephenson has traced the changing character of women's international NGOs over the course of the twentieth century. Prior to 1915, most women's NGOs were religious in origin and
orientation. From 1916 to 1970, the character of women's NGOs shifted
as women's professional organizations came to dominate the field. Prior to
1977, less than 10 percent of women's NGOs were headquartered outside
the United States or Europe. Of the thirty new women's NGOs launched
in the 1980s, however, more than half were headquartered in the global
South (Stephenson 1995, 138).

As noted in the discussion of feminist activism to create spaces for women inside the UN, feminist INGOs have played a number of significant roles in development of a women's rights agenda at the UN. They have organized, educated, and lobbied to ensure that women are included in UN offices and decision-making circles. They also played a central role in the creation of the International Women's Year, the Decade for Women, and the UN World Conferences on Women, which in turn contributed to the formation of a new spate of transnational feminist organizing. In a sense, then, feminist INGOs not only are constitutive of, but also gave birth to increasingly vibrant transnational feminist civil society. INGOs have also played key lobbying and monitoring roles, pressuring for UN conferences, then pressing intergovernmental conference participants to produce concrete Platforms for Action, then using the Platforms for Action to leverage nations to change their laws and structures to conform to the UN platforms (Stephenson 1995, 150). Chapter 4 explores feminist mobilizations around UN conferences and the substance of continuing feminist contestations within those sites in greater detail.

In addition to feminist INGO activism at the United Nations, the UN system (UNDP, UNIFEM, the World Bank) has stimulated the emergence of a new agenda for development that requires a gender perspective. International agencies "exert pressure and provide incentives in favor of gender policies," significantly increasing the demand for "gender experts" (Rios Tobar 2003). To meet this demand, feminist NGOs have proliferated, further populating the sphere of feminist civil society. The new feminist NGOs address myriad issues including women's political and civil rights, reproductive rights, violence against women, women's health, poverty, employment, transportation, access to banks, credit, and finance, legal aid, women's capacity building, education, peacemaking, women's political leadership, civic education, and AIDS education. Over the past fifteen years, the growth of women's NGOs has been exponential. In China, for example, 5,800 new women's NGOs were created in the two years immediately preceding the Beijing World Conference on Women (Howell 2003). Women's organizations now constitute the largest organized sector in many African nations—indeed, the largest proportion of human rights organizations in Africa are women's rights organizations (Tripp 2003). A study conducted by the Chilean Centro de Estudios de la Mujer (Center for the Study of Women) found that 38.4 percent of the feminist activists surveyed were employed in NGOs (Rios Tobar 2003).

The proliferation of feminist NGOs in all regions of the world is intimately connected with the resurgence of capitalism and the ascendancy of the neoliberal agenda. Far from being a "privileged terrain for the construction of liberty, equality, solidarity, ecological care, and cultural tolerance" (Waterman 2000, 138), the emergence of feminist civil society in many regions of the world is directly related to severe cutbacks in state provision. In Eastern and Central Europe, for example, "grassroots groups have stepped in to fill the gap left when welfare and social services previously provided by the state were privatized or ruthlessly culled" by incoming regimes (Einhorn and Sever 2003, 173). Provision of health care services, poverty relief, domestic violence shelters, and hotlines for HIV/AIDS are not an idealized Habermasian communicative space but desperate efforts to take up the slack left by retreat of the state from welfare and social provision (Einhorn and Sever 2003). NGOs pick up problems that states in fiscal crisis or under the mandate of structural adjustment policies disdain. Working on soft money and without job security, NGO staff offer cheaper means to alleviate poverty or provide health care than state employees. Funded by Western foundations, governments, and INGOS, "NGOization" gives rise to "contractual bureaucracies responding to policy directives remote from the people they serve" (Rowbotham and Linkogle 2001, 6). Far from the image of open and participatory democratic spaces, NGOs are small, professionalized organizations that are not subject to democratic control. As a flexible means to overcome gaps in service provision, NGOS are accountable to their funders as much as if not more than to the constituencies they serve. The capital flows to NGOs are subject to the same problems of deterritorialization characteristic of production facilities in an age of globalization. Funding is short-term and subject to movement offshore with little advance warning. Indeed, Marcela Rios Tobar (2003) has noted that as Chile has moved forward with the project of democratization, the withdrawal of funds from Chilean feminist NGOs by Oxfam (UK and Canada), as well as Dutch, German, and French funders, has created a crisis of funding, contributing to the unemployment of feminist policy experts and the demobilization of feminism as a force in some policy debates.

Scholars who study feminist civil society agree that increased funding by international donors helps to sustain autonomous women's organizations free from partisan political networks and co-optation by the national governments. They disagree, however, in their assessments of the implications of NGOization (Lang 1997). Some of this disagreement reflects careful attention to the disparate effects of NGOization in different regions of the world; some reflects widely varying assessments of the connection between NGOization and privatization.

In some nations of the world, states regulate and monitor NGOs, requiring registration or licensing that can be revoked if the government disapproves certain forms of NGO activity. In China, for example, feminist civil society has emerged in the context of marketization, with the assistance of major international donors such as the Ford Foundation; yet, the existence of NGOs is carefully monitored by the state (Howell 2003). All NGOs must register with the government and be sponsored by state apparatus.[15] Negotiating these intricate boundaries of the permissible, the "new women's organizations" in China have nonetheless created a "new public sphere of critical reflection and dialogue about gender issues," and they are addressing an array of issues previously neglected, including exploitive working conditions, the plight of women workers laid off from collective and state-owned enterprises who face sex discrimination in the labor market, growing sex discrimination in employment, sexual harassment, the expansion of the sex industry, violence against women, trafficking in women, lesbian and gay existence, and women's studies (Howell 2003). Facing unique challenges posed by Islamization—the imposition of a particular fundamentalist version of Islam—Women Living Under Muslim Law (WLUML), a transnational feminist activist network, has created a vibrant feminist civil society involving more than 2,000 women across several continents (Moghadam 2005, 95). Grappling with political and legal structures of more than twenty-five nations, WLUML "creates links amongst women and women's groups (including those prevented from organizing or facing repression if they attempt to do so)," mobilizing for women's rights and against changes in personal and family law that violate women's human rights (Farida Shaheed cited in Moghadam 2005, 162, 144). Banned in some nations and subject to licensing requirements in others, WLUML nonetheless takes very public stands on issues such as the continuing rise of fundamentalism, militarization and armed conflict in Muslim countries, and their effects on women's lives.

If feminist civil society has a courageously public character in authoritarian contexts, its character in some democratizing and neoliberal contexts is more ambiguous. Sonia Alvarez (1999), Teresa Caldeira (1998), and Marcela Rios Tobar (2003) have noted the "hybridity" of feminist NGOs in Latin America, juggling the roles of policy entrepreneur, government consultant, fundraiser, service provider, and women's rights advocate. As states cut back social provision under structural adjustment policies and poverty grows, feminist NGOs struggle to promote their own objectives within a changing global economic order in which the World Bank requires cultivation of NGOs as a condition of loans and requires gender perspectives in implementation and assessment of programs yet operates with a degree of rigidity that minimizes NGO influence (Tinker 1999, 93).[16] To paraphrase the astute assessment of Sabine Lang (1997), civil society cannot protect the population from state power when the embodiment of neoliberal state power is a capitalist economy.

With the bulk of funding coming from Western sources, the advocacy strategies, mobilizing tactics, policy models, and substantive agenda of feminist civil society has had a decidedly Western cast. Indeed, women's rights advocates in socialist states and former socialist states have complained that Western biases may distort understandings of the scope of feminist activism and strategies conducive to success in these contexts (Einhorn and Sever 2003; Hrycak 2002; Hsiung and Wong 1999). East-West partnerships created to train feminist activists in the Commonwealth of Newly Independent States, for example, assume the validity of a Western model of feminist activism and promote a Western agenda, providing funding for rape crisis centers, business incubators, microenterprise and microfinance, gender studies centers, and women's leadership training. Established women's councils are largely bypassed in these new partnerships, and a "maternalist orientation," deployed by many women's rights activists negotiating nationalist agendas, is actively repudiated (Hrycak 2002, 71–77). Under such conditions, feminist civil society may seem less open, participatory, and democratic, and more imperialist.

Measuring "Success"

Shirin Rai (2002, 158) has noted that "tensions between feasible politics" and "transformative politics" frame feminist activism in the contemporary world. Within the increasingly conservative political context shaped by neoliberalism and fundamentalism, outsider politics is often marginalized as utopian, while insider politics is often co-opted by state and dominant parties or derailed by the standard operating procedures of gendered institutions. Neither altogether outside nor inside, NGOs are constrained by the privatizing neoliberal agenda and the priorities of Western funding agencies. Transnational feminist activists face powerful challenges and difficult choices as they attempt to promote social change in this period of globalization. Any fair assessment of the success of transnational feminist activism must take the challenges and the constraints imposed by globalization into account.

The analysis of various outsider and insider social change tactics in this chapter suggests that transnational feminist activists face formidable challenges both as outsiders and as insiders. In most national and international organizations, gender discrimination continues to keep women on the outside, cutting them off from power that could facilitate social transformation. Moreover, the few women who succeed in gaining entry to national and international decision-making institutions often experience marginalization and routine operating procedures that make it difficult to articulate and address women's concerns. Even significant feminist victories have been undercut by political maneuvers limiting the available options for implementation of women-friendly policies. Thus feminist activists have learned that neither states nor international organizations are gender-neutral spaces, and the gendered agendas of national, transnational, and international actors constitute systemic obstacles to social change efforts. In a sense, however, unmasking the gendered nature of the global system must count as a feminist "success," for it documents a dimension of global power relations rendered invisible by the universalist rhetoric deployed by national and international institutions and by mainstream academics who investigate them.

Given the tendency of entrenched power structures to perpetuate the status quo, it is not surprising that many feminist victories have been partial, but even partial victories are significant in the continuing struggle against raced and gendered injustices. Transnational feminist activists have succeeded in creating spaces for women in international decision making, opening doors for women as diplomats and professional staff in international agencies, and politicizing the persistent underrepresentation of women in positions of national and international leadership. They have secured a significant shift in discursive politics, adding women's rights to the human rights agenda and crimes against women to the actionable list of crimes against humanity. They have helped shape international declarations, conventions, and treaties, generating new mechanisms with which to pressure nations to improve the conditions of women.

Operating in an increasingly hostile environment, transnational feminist activists have illuminated dangers posed to an egalitarian social change agenda by both fundamentalism and neoliberalism. And despite considerable obstacles, they have built vibrant alliances encompassing grassroots activists, regional women's movements, NGOs, policy networks, feminist academics, gender experts, elected women officials, international agency staff, diplomats, and major foundations. Working from the outside, inside, and in between, transnational feminist activists have built global feminist civil society. And in so doing, they have become major nonstate actors in the international arena, using their liminal position to engage and challenge state and global forces. Given the scope of their aspirations, these successes are partial and contradictory, but they are successes indeed.

GLOBAL FEMINIST CIRCUITS:
CONTEMPORARY CONTESTATIONS

> Though we look at the same things, we see them differently.
>
> —Virginia Woolf (1938, 5)

> Women's movements are far from homogeneous or conflict free. Like all social movements, they are riddled with conflicts that reflect and cut across regional, class, and ideological differences while raising serious issues of ownership and representation.
>
> —Rosalind Petchesky (2003, 2)

Transnational feminism has been characterized as an "imagined community" (Mohanty 1991), but the positive connotations of community often mask the fact that communities are constituted by exclusion, structured by hierarchies, and riddled with political disagreement. Political contestations concerning claims made on behalf of women, the conditions under which such claims are made, who makes the claims, for whom they are made, and whose interests are served by particular articulations of women's needs and interests have been a staple of transnational feminism. The term *transnational* came into general use in the 1920s to describe events and gatherings that bring people together across national borders and to indicate that participants in these gatherings meet as individuals or as representatives of civic organizations, clubs, unions, or other local or regional entities, not as representatives of their governments (Miller 1999, 225). Operating without a mandate from official state institutions or electoral constituencies, and often contesting the explicit laws and policies of their national governments, transnational feminism poses unique challenges for democratic theory. In what sense can unelected, self-selected feminist activists claim to represent women? Which women and which interests tend to be represented in the diverse interactions of global feminist civil society? What cleavages surface in intergovernmental and in transnational sites of feminist activism? In the face of persistent disagreements, whose views and interests prevail? This chapter examines feminist mobilizations in and around the United Nations and the politics of representation within these global feminist circuits.

The UN Commission on the Status of Women as a Free Space of Feminist Activism

The Commission on Status of Women (CSW) did not rest content with its circumscribed mandate to study and to monitor the status of women across the world. From its earliest meetings, CSW also assumed the responsibility of monitoring the UN General Assembly and ECOSOC, pressing for the adoption and implementation of declarations, conventions, and treaties to advance the status of women. Using international instruments such as the guarantee of equality of rights under the Declaration of Human Rights (1948) and the Convention for the Suppression of Traffic in Persons (1949), CSW insisted that the UN had a responsibility to serve the interests of women by promoting compliance among member states. The CSW also forged ties with UN agencies, working with the World Health Organization (WHO) on initiatives to foster women's health, especially in poor nations, and with the International Labor Organization (ILO) to safeguard the interests of women in the waged labor force. As early as 1965, for example, CSW tried to pressure the ILO to reconsider its long-standing support for "protective" labor legislation, arguing that it harmed women more than helped them.

Working within the United Nations, diplomats appointed to the CSW had dual constituencies. They were official representatives of their governments even as they sought to define and represent the interests of women. Arvonne Fraser (1995, 83) has suggested that the members of CSW struggled to find a way to serve a global constituency of women while carrying out their particular responsibilities to their national governments. This was by no means an easy feat, for the nations participating in the UN were at odds for a various reasons, including superpower rivalries, Cold War animosities, and North-South splits concerning colonialism, neocolonialism, and imperialism. To prevent CSW discussions from being derailed by prevailing political alignments within the UN, the commission found a way to operate as a free space in which members could meet, share information, and develop strategy somewhat insulated from the political rifts among their governments. Modeling the principle that feminism is international, the CSW tried to hold national disagreements in abeyance while commission members discussed issues, explored alternative policy options, framed language for resolutions, and negotiated concrete proposals. This free space was created by parliamentary maneuvers governing the rules of debate and voting procedures. Preliminary discussions were conducted off the record. Voting procedures enabled members to express reservations or abstentions on particular subparagraphs while still voting for the document under discussion as a whole. Gathering information in advance of CSW meetings about members' views as well as the formal positions of the members' governments, the CSW chair exercised considerable diplomatic skill in deciding when to hold votes and when to refrain from holding votes on controversial measures. Navigating the obstacles posed by entrenched national objectives and the power dynamics of the world system, the CSW carefully devised institutional mechanisms to carve out a "feminist free space" within the UN, but it was a free space operating within determinate bounds (A. Fraser 1995, 81–83).

The scope and possibilities for such a free space were initially explored in the course of more than four years of CSW deliberations culminating in the UN Declaration on the Elimination of Discrimination Against Women (1967). Contrary to claims that feminism in general, and women's rights in particular, are the exclusive product of Western bourgeois cultures, the first push within the UN for a declaration of women's rights came from the nations in the global South and in Eastern Europe. In 1963, twenty-two developing and Eastern European nations including Afghanistan, Algeria, Argentina, Austria, Cameroon, Chile, Colombia, Czechoslovakia, Gabon, Guinea, Indonesia, Iran, Mali, Mexico, Mongolia, Morocco, Pakistan, Panama, the Philippines, Poland, Togo, and Venezuela introduced a resolution calling for a UN declaration condemning all forms of discrimination against women. The resolution itself was a product of Cold War positioning, introduced as a strategic intervention to demonstrate that (1) legal equality alone could not emancipate women; (2) socialist states were more committed to the promotion of women's rights than were liberal democratic states; and (3) developing nations embraced modern principles of gender equality and were prepared to combat customs and traditions that thwarted the advancement of women. Given the politics inspiring its creation, the declaration could easily have fallen prey to the political posturing of member states. To avoid that likely fate, the CSW launched a campaign to have responsibility for drafting the proposed declaration assigned to it, rather than to ECOSOC or the General Assembly. Once CSW members succeeded in having the development of the draft placed within their remit, they faced the formidable task of creating a declaration that could overcome North-South and East-West antagonisms and win the assent of the General Assembly.

The original women's rights resolution had generated considerable response including a memorandum from the secretary general and replies from thirty-three governments, fourteen NGOs, and four specialized UN agencies. These became the raw materials from which an antidiscrimination declaration was crafted. At a time when no nation did more than pay lip service to women's equality, the CSW faced a daunting task. "Never before had discrimination on the grounds of sex been defined internationally and equality between men and women sanctioned in all areas of life and work" (A. Fraser 1995, 77). The sheer magnitude of the challenge reinforced CSW resolve not to fail, for the members saw this as a historic opportunity to craft universal norms of gender equality. The CSW devoted four years to drafting, debating, negotiating, and redrafting a Declaration on the Elimination of Discrimination Against Women. Asserting that discrimination against women was "incompatible with the dignity of women as human beings, and with the welfare of the family and of society" (A. Fraser 1995, 83), the declaration framed discrimination in relation to political, social, economic, and cultural life, suggesting that discrimination undermined formal equality, hindered development efforts, and enhanced poverty. In taking such an expansive approach, the CSW draft sought to bridge the gulf between civil and political rights and social and economic rights. The eleven articles of the declaration identified the scope of sex discrimination and the kinds of remedies required for its elimination. Declaring sex discrimination "fundamentally unjust" and "an offense against human dignity," the declaration called for measures to abolish discriminatory laws, customs, and practices, create legal protections for equal rights, eradicate sex prejudice, and develop strategies to change public opinion. The provisions of the 1952 Convention on the Political Rights of Women and the 1957 Convention on Women's Nationality were also incorporated into the declaration. In addition, the declaration recognized women's equal legal capacity and demanded that penal codes treat women equally. Recognizing a problem seldom discussed in international arenas, the declaration also called for the prohibition of sexual abuse of women in detention. Moreover, the declaration recognized the critical importance of nondiscrimination in education and health care and endorsed the free choice of professions, equal pay for work of equal value, the right to paid maternity leave, and the provision of social services to enable women to work outside the home. The final article urged all nations of the world to implement the declaration. Following an intensive CSW campaign to mobilize support for the declaration among member states, the UN General Assembly adopted the declaration on November 7, 1967.

A UN declaration is a statement of principle. With the adoption of the Declaration on the Elimination of Discrimination Against Women, the CSW had virtually all the nations of the world on record supporting the substantive equality of men and women. While this was unquestionably an important symbolic achievement, it did not require any states to take any action to bring their laws and practices into conformity with this statement of principle. In contrast to a declaration, a convention is an international legal instrument that includes mechanisms for implementation and monitoring. Moreover a convention has the potential to become a treaty if ratified by an agreed upon number of states. Treaties are legally binding documents, which become fully effective when ratified by two-thirds of the UN member states. To move from symbolic victory to a convention with mechanisms for implementation, CSW began work on the Convention to Eliminate All Forms of Discrimination Against Women (CEDAW). It took twelve additional years of diplomatic work for the CSW to win UN approval of CEDAW.

CEDAW defines discrimination as "any distinction, exclusion or restriction . . . which has the effect or purpose of impairing or nullifying the recognition, enjoyment or exercise of . . . human rights or fundamental freedoms in the political, economic, social, cultural, civil or any other field" (A. Fraser 1995, 92). In the 1970s, virtually every legal system in the world violated provisions of the proposed CEDAW, failing to provide equality under the law, equality in marriage and family matters, access to family planning as a right to be freely exercised, equal education and employment opportunities, equal pay for work of equal value, and paid maternity leaves. Fully aware of the gulf between existing laws and practices and the proposed convention, and reluctant to have national laws, practices, customs, and traditions subject to international monitoring, the UN member states took great care in reviewing every word, concept, and provision of the draft document.

Ideological differences about the meaning and scope of "equality" and global politics played central roles in protracted debates over the proposed convention. For example, during the drafting stage Senegal added a provision stipulating that apartheid and colonialism were fundamentally incompatible with women's equality. The German Democratic Republic added language linking international peace and security to the protection of women's human rights. An observer from the Food and Agriculture Organization added language pertaining to the special needs of the majority of the world's women who lived in rural areas. Another representative added a provision calling for nuclear disarmament as a prerequisite for equality. While these provisions might seem altogether reasonable from a progressive feminist perspective, their introduction aggravated long-established fault lines dividing North and South, as well as socialist and capitalist member states. Quite predictably then, debates on all these provisions were lengthy and intense. Demonstrating extraordinary skill in the continuing negotiations, CSW members succeeded in brokering compromises.

To keep the negotiations moving forward, CSW again followed the practice of allowing governments to note reservations to specific articles or provisions while voting for the document as a whole. When the UN General Assembly took up the draft convention on December 19, 1979, three of the most controversial provisions of the convention were set for separate votes prior to a vote on the convention as a whole. The shifting vote tallies from one provision to the next illuminate how the CSW was able to navigate the objections of particular blocs of member states while insulating the convention from defeat. The paragraphs in the preamble dealing with apartheid, colonialism, and nuclear disarmament were adopted by a vote of 108 to 0, with 26 abstentions cast primarily by the United States and the industrialized countries. The provision granting women equal rights to convey nationality to their children passed, 92 to 13, with 28 abstentions from Muslim countries and Brazil. The provision concerning "equal rights and responsibilities during marriage and in its dissolution" carried by a vote of 104 to 0, with 32 abstentions from Catholic and Muslim countries. The final vote on the convention as a whole passed 130–0, with 11 abstentions (A. Fraser 1995, 88).

By 1981 CEDAW had been ratified by 20 nations, the number specified to bring the convention into force. By 2005, 169 nations had ratified CEDAW, far more than necessary to transform the convention into a legally binding international treaty. In keeping with its provisions, states that have ratified CEDAW submit reports to the UN every four years, providing detailed information about the measures they have taken to promote women's legal equality, eliminate discrimination rooted in customary and traditional practices, promote women's development and empowerment, and protect women's human rights. These reports are reviewed by a special commission elected by representatives of the ratifying nations, which is empowered to make recommendations concerning each nation's implementation efforts. CEDAW monitoring has become an important site of feminist NGO activism, as feminists use governmental reports and CEDAW Commission recommendations to press for additional improvements for women within their nations. For example, eight country reports reviewed by the CEDAW Commission in January 2001 mentioned violence against women as a major problem that the government was seeking to address. Women's rights activists in those nations have developed accountability criteria to hold their governments to their expressed intention to find remedies to this problem. When nations generate overly optimistic accounts of their progress on women's rights, feminist advocacy groups often develop shadow reports documenting the gap between official statements and actual practices. These shadow reports are used by the CEDAW Commission when they meet with national representatives to discuss their compliance reports. They are also used by feminists to publicize the government's inadequate compliance and to mobilize women within the nation to demand change. As noted in chapter 3, feminist activists in many nations have drawn upon the explicit language of CEDAW to secure constitutional recognition of their rights, pass new legislation to protect women's bodily integrity and full citizenship, and to petition the courts in their nations to address continuing discriminatory practices.

Given the absence of opposition in the final vote on CEDAW, quick ratification by many member states and the regular submission of compliance reports by most of the nations of the world, it is possible to say that there is near universal support for CEDAW.[1] Since 1979, the nations of the world have committed themselves to the promotion of sexual equality in all areas of human life. Such an optimistic account of universal support for women's equality, however, masks the host of objections manifested in negative votes and abstentions on particular provisions of the convention. Indeed, as Arvonne Fraser (1995, 91) has pointed out, CEDAW "carries the largest number of reservations of any international human rights instrument. Twenty ratifying countries entered over 80 reservations . . . [concerning] nationality, employment, legal capacity, and family law articles." A near universal commitment by the world's governments to gender equality, then, should not be mistaken for consensus about the meaning of gender equality or agreement about the substantive needs and interests of women. Continuing contestations over both these issues have been a staple of transnational feminist activism, as will be discussed in greater detail below.

UN World Conferences

Conference of International Women's Year in Mexico City (1975)

The product of repeated demands by international women's rights activists over a fifty-year period, the Conference of International Women's Year in Mexico City in 1975 was the first intergovernmental conference on women. The story of the Mexico City conference brings into stark relief the complex forces operating to enable and constrain feminist activism in the international arena. The mobilization of feminist activists around the intergovernmental conference also explicitly politicized the question, Who can legitimately represent the world's women? challenging the assumption that male-dominated governments and international institutions are entitled to speak for women, and questioning the legitimacy of some feminist activists who appointed themselves as the voice of women.

In 1970 the UN General Assembly approved the Long-Term Program for the Advancement of Women, including the designation of 1975 as International Women's Year (IWY). The goal of IWY, according to the UN, was "to define a society in which women participate in a real and full sense in economic, social, and political life, and to devise strategies whereby such societies could develop" (Snyder 1995, 112). In launching a series of initiatives for IWY, CSW sought to focus governments' attention on women's issues and their relation to major world problems such as poverty, underdevelopment, and sterilization abuse. Acting on behalf of the Women's International Democratic Federation (WIDF), Romania proposed that the CSW adopt equality and development as the twin themes of IWY. Greece and the Eastern European nations recommended that women's contributions to peace be added as a third theme. With the approval of the General Assembly and the secretariat, the CSW undertook the task of organizing various programs for IWY that would help shape public opinion on the significance of IWY and contribute to national and international activities to deepen understanding of the relation of gender to equality, development, and peace. The government of the German Democratic Republic volunteered to host a congress on IWY in Berlin in October 1975. As planning began for the Berlin conference, Cold War politics erupted (Allan, Galey, and Persinger 1995).

When the United States realized that the only celebration of IWY was to be held in a communist country, it threw its support behind a proposal to host a world conference in the Western Hemisphere as the focal point of IWY activities.[2] Colombia initially agreed to host the conference, but the venue was shifted to Mexico when political violence led to the fall of the Colombian government. Planning for the Mexico City conference began only a few months before the meeting was to convene. During the planning session in March, geopolitical disagreements framed discussions about the core conference themes, equality, development, and peace. The Group of 77, a coalition of developing countries created in 1964 to promote the economic interests of Third World nations within the UN, made the case that meaningful equality for the majority of the world's women was inseparable from the New International Economic Order (NIEO), a proposal for social and economic justice that would require systemic redistribution of global resources. The Eastern European states argued that equality, development, and peace presupposed decolonization, détente, and disarmament. The United States insisted that references to economic justice, decolonization, détente, and disarmament politicized the agenda and detracted from the goal of equality, which the United States framed narrowly in terms of political and civil rights (Allan, Galey, and Persinger 1995, 32). Such substantive differences about the meaning of equality structured the IWY Intergovernmental Conference in Mexico City and set the terms of debate for subsequent UN world conferences on women.

Five thousand delegates from 138 nations participated in the IWY conference in Mexico City in June 1975. In stark contrast to the sixty-five previous UN conferences, women constituted a majority of delegates, making up 75 percent of the national delegations and 85 percent of the delegation heads. While all the delegations made stirring opening speeches denouncing sex discrimination, they disagreed about the best way to eliminate it and about the substantive meaning of equality. Some governments suggested that "revolutionary change" was necessary to promote the liberation of women and ensure their equal rights; others claimed that incremental changes to existing laws would be adequate to the task (Allan, Galey, and Persinger 1995, 36). Third World nations stressed the importance of the New International Economic Order and the continuing struggle against colonialism, racism, apartheid, and foreign occupation. The United States and other Western delegations rejected NIEO, insisting that alone the NIEO would not change women's status. China added superpower hegemony to the list of institutions that oppressed women, only to be rebuffed by the United States and the Soviet Union. An Australian delegate identified sexism as a profound impediment to women's equality, defining sexism as "artificial ascription of role, behavior, and even personalities to people on the basis of sex alone, occurring in societies ruled by men who colonized women by mute consent" (Allan, Galey, and Persinger 1995, 34). Claiming that the term *sexism* signified an untoward preoccupation with sex, the majority of the conference delegates rejected any use of the term. When the draft Plan of Action referred to women as "a powerful revolutionary force," the United States objected that "no government wanted to invite its own overthrow," and demanded a change in language (Allan, Galey, and Persinger 1995, 36). From this competing array of issues and agendas, the IWY conference delegates had to craft a Platform for Action within a two-week time frame. The resulting draft Declaration of Mexico blended disparate agendas, calling for a New International Economic

Order, condemning apartheid and Zionism as forms of racism, supporting the "maximum participation of women and men necessary to fulfill the complete development of any country," and endorsing equal access to education and decision-making positions in all spheres of activity, equal pay for work of equal value, and joint parental responsibilities. To circumvent the G-77 agenda embedded in the Declaration of Mexico, the Federal Republic of Germany, the United Kingdom, and the United States introduced their own draft declaration. The Western Declaration omitted any reference to racism, apartheid, Zionism, and the NIEO, although it did call for efforts to eliminate race discrimination, imperialism, and colonialism (Allan, Galey, and Persinger 1995, 38). During the final plenary of the conference, the delegates approved the World Plan of Action, an amended version of the Western Declaration, without a vote. In a separate vote, the Declaration of Mexico also won approval 89 to 3 with Denmark, Israel, and the United States voting against and eighteen Western nations abstaining. The first "comprehensive global policy on the status of women" (Allan, Galey, and Persinger 1995, 39), then, was an amalgam of views encompassing radically different conceptions of equality with dramatically differing implications for implementation.

While the official intergovernmental conference conducted its sessions in Mexico City, two unofficial, parallel conferences were held concurrently, the IWY Tribune, and a "countercongress" organized by leftist feminist activists from Mexico. The IWY Tribune was initially designed to provide information about the intergovernmental conference to unofficial observers expected to flock to Mexico City. Toward that end, the planning committee, headed by Rosalind Harris and Mildred Persinger, two long-time NGO leaders based in New York, organized daily morning briefings on official proceedings, 25 workshops on IWY themes, and plenary sessions featuring government officials from various nations playing key roles in the IWY conference. Attracting 6,000 women from 114 organizations—one-third from Latin America, one-third from North America, and one-third from Africa, Asia, and Europe—the tribune took on a life of its own. Participants organized an additional 200 workshops over a ten-day period. A self-appointed "open and representative committee" prepared thirty pages of suggested revisions to the text of the proposed World Plan of Action, which they hoped to present not only to a plenary session of the tribune, but to the intergovernmental conference as well. Although they found an eager audience at the tribune, they were quite astonished to find that they would not be allowed to present their recommendations to the IWY conference (Stienstra 1994, 126; Allan, Galey, and Persinger 1995, 40). A group of unhappy tribune participants stormed the U.S. embassy, protesting U.S. imperialism, as well as the exclusionary practices of the IWY conference (Antrobus 2004, 44).

The tribune allowed women from different regions of the world to begin to come to terms with their different worldviews and priorities. A survey of feminist activists participating in the tribune suggested that national and regional differences were as pronounced among NGO participants as they were among official delegates to the intergovernmental conference. While feminists representing NGOs in Africa and Asia listed development as the top priority for women, feminists from Latin America identified imperialism as the major issue confronting women, and feminists from Western nations indicated that sexism was their primary agenda item (Stephenson 1995, 143). The workshops organized in conjunction with the tribune enabled transnational feminist activists to participate in cross-cultural discussions of feminism, development, and pacifism. In the context of these transnational conversations, feminists were forced to review and assess their national priorities and tactics and to consider how to develop transnational standards of comparison. These were not easy conversations. For example, on behalf of the feminist caucus, Gloria Steinem prepared a feminist manifesto without any consultation with or input from women of the global South. When she presented the manifesto to the tribune, it was denounced by Latin American feminists as an expression of cultural imperialism (Bolt 2004, 172, 186). When the administrator of the U.S. Agency for International Development, a cochair of the U.S. government delegation to the IWY conference, spoke to a session of the tribune, he was pelted with tomatoes by an angry audience insisting that "men had no right to represent women at the Tribune or the Conference" (A. Fraser 1987).

A countercongress organized by Mexican feminist activists illuminates another complex dimension of UN conferences in relation to transnational feminist activism. The countercongress grew out of the concerns of Mexican women on the Left who worried about the national and international legitimacy that the corrupt PRI (Partido Revolucionario Institucional) government could harvest by hosting the conference. Wishing to distance feminist projects from complicity in the actions of a government that had massacred students involved in democratic protests, some progressive Mexican feminists decided to boycott the UN conference to call attention to the Mexican government's record of human rights abuses, sterilization abuse in population control policies, indifference to growing poverty, and general neglect of pressing problems confronting Mexican women. The Mexican feminists organized the countercongress to politicize issues such as voluntary motherhood, reproductive freedom, violence against women, and sexual freedom. The countercongress garnered a good deal of press coverage, which helped the Mexican feminists organize a political wing, the Coalicion de Mujeres Feministas (Coalition of Feminist Women) (V. Rodriguez 2003). Liaising with other feminist activists from Latin America who were participating in the tribune, Mexican feminists raised important questions about the legitimacy of patriarchal governments and the male-dominated UN system itself to represent women's interests, suggesting that the participants in the intergovernmental conference were mere window dressing likely to divert attention from the pressing needs of the majority of the world's women.

The significance of the IWY conference has been variously assessed. Despite competing geopolitical agendas, the intergovernmental conference produced the World Plan of Action, the first international public policy to improve the status of women. With the Western press briefly focused on Mexico City, global feminism announced its presence on the world stage, orchestrating the largest consciousness-raising event on record.[3] Women's entitlement to full citizenship was officially adopted as part of the UN agenda, and energy mobilized in Mexico City played an important role in building momentum in support of CEDAW (Allan, Galey, and Persinger 1995, 29). In addition, both the intergovernmental conference and the tribune initiated debates central to the politics of women's representation, raising questions about the relationship between the complex agendas of states, regions, voting blocs, and the UN itself and women's needs and interests. Intensive conversations about the political dimensions of every definition of women's "needs" or "interests" dispelled naïve assumptions concerning any given or unmediated nature of women. Clashes among feminist priorities and clashes between feminist concerns and the concerns of delegates to the intergovernmental conference shed new light on what it means to politicize women's issues. The refusal of feminists at the tribune and at the countercongress to be passive recipients of official briefings set a precedent for global feminist civil society. Through street protests and demonstrations, as well as unruly behavior in the official briefings and plenary sessions, feminist activists made it clear that they would not be kept to a "male-set agenda" and they would not be contained in marginal sites. Using free media and public demonstrations, tribune and countercongress participants proved remarkably resourceful in finding ways to inject feminist content into the IWY agenda and to push beyond states' definitions of women's interests. Challenging the federative nature of the UN, which as an alliance of states allowed formal input only from member states' appointed delegates to the intergovernmental conference, transnational feminist activists sought to make UN processes more open and accountable.

The fault lines that became apparent among feminist activists from different regions of the world, however, also raised critical questions about the conception of accountability operative in global feminist circuits. To whom should the UN be accountable when feminists disagree among themselves? Are there criteria for feminist democratic accountability that differ from the hegemonic relations structuring the global system?

Continuing Contestations

Since 1975, the United Nations has created multiple sites for transnational feminist organizing including three more World Conferences on Women (Copenhagen 1980, Nairobi 1985, Beijing 1995), as well as the Conference on Human Rights (Vienna 1993), the Conference on Population and Development (Cairo 1994), and the Conference Against Racism, Racial Discrimination, Xenophobia, and Related Intolerance (Durban 2001). The continuing activities of the UN Development Program, UNIFEM, the Commission on the Status of Women, and the Conference of NGOs in Consultative Relationship to the Economic and Social Council of the UN (CONGO) also constitute key venues for feminist mobilization and strategic negotiation. Although the platforms for action produced in these forums suggest a global feminist consensus, as the Mexico City Plan of Action demonstrates, compromise language can mask a host of disagreements. Examining these disagreements can provide insights into the power dynamics within global feminist circuits and their relation to the power dynamics of globalization more generally.

Naila Kabeer (2003, 31) has pointed out that "the dominance of the voices of the First World women in articulating their version of the problems and priorities of Third World women frequently led to acrimonious debates in a number of international forums" (see also A. Fraser 1987).[4] In many instances, the debates intensified in the aftermath of the conferences, although all parties to the debates have not received equal attention. Moreover, the terms of discourse that mark conference outcomes in public memory often skew the historical record toward the views of Western feminists. For example, the 1975 World Plan of Action has been characterized as a "bold women's agenda to achieve equality between the sexes within the context of changed relations between North and South" (Maguire 1984, 12). While the full text of the World Plan reflects multiple compromises among participants at the conference, the privileged place accorded to equality between the sexes indicates the dominance of Western feminist conceptions of women's interests.

Coalitions of feminists from nations of the South took issue with this formulation of priorities. The Association of African Women for Research and Development (AAWORD 1982, 101) "rejected the approach of Western women who insist on prioritizing problems of inequality between the sexes as the fundamental issue facing all women." DAWN (Development Alternatives with Women for a New Era), a network of feminist activists, researchers, and policymakers from African, Asian, Caribbean, and Latin American nations, pointed out that throughout the 1960s and 1970s,

> The dissonant voices of poor women from racially or nationally oppressed groups could be heard stating their priorities—food, housing, jobs, services, and the struggle against racism. Equality with men who themselves suffer unemployment, low wages, poor work conditions and racism within the existing socioeconomic structures did not seem an adequate or worthy goal. (Sen and Grown 1987, 24–25)

The arguments of feminist activists from the South incorporate the central tenets of a postcolonial critique of imperial Western feminism. By focusing on selective commonalities, such as the power differential between men and women, proponents of global sisterhood elide material differences in power, resources, and interests among women within and across nations. As AAWORD (1982, 105) noted,

> While patriarchal views and structures oppress women all over the world, women are also members of classes and countries that dominate others and enjoy privileges in terms of access to resources. Hence, contrary to the best intentions of "sisterhood," not all women share identical interests.

When critical differences among women are not recognized, "the concept of gender equity, which is focused on sex-based or gender-based discrimination, has been used by women's organizations and even governments to avoid issues of racial, environmental, civil, political, economic, and cultural injustices" (Tauli-Corpuz 2001; see also Taylor 2000).

In making claims for and about women, Western feminists have often fallen into the "ventriloquist's fantasy" (John 1996, 22), projecting a white, Western voice and view onto a silenced subaltern subject. Within the context of American feminism, Audre Lorde (1984) pointed out that such silencing of Black women is not just an omission, it is part of the oppression. Similarly, Chandra Mohanty (1991, 52–55) characterized these forms of "ethnocentric universalism" as structural domination that suppresses the heterogeneity of women in the global South.

Consider, for example, how the ventriloquist's fantasy operated in the context of the 1976 Wellesley Seminar on Women in Development. Attracting 500 academics and feminist activists from North and South, this international conference focused on issues confronting women in the South as a result of changing development strategies in the region. The conference organizers characterized the seminar as an opportunity to "craft a global consensus." Toward that end, they established certain ground rules for conference discussions. In particular, certain "political questions" were bracketed as "beyond the scope" of the meeting. Several conference participants from the South, however, contested the conference ground rules. Nawal El Saadawi from Egypt, Fatima Mernissi from Morocco, and Mallica Vajrathon from Thailand delivered an open letter to the conference protesting "the myth that the mere fact of being women will unite us and that women are not political beings; that political discussions at women's meetings mean 'diverting from women's issues'" (Stienstra 1994, 107). Insisting that the politics of multinational corporations, trade, and the global economic order were integrally related to development and its impact on women's lives, these voices from the South sought to make it clear that the international political economy divided rather than united women, indeed that global capital played a central role in oppressing many in the global South. Discontent with the way that U.S. feminists were defining the realities of women in the South, African feminist scholars participating in the conference decided to form their own research network, Association of African Women for Research and Development (AAWORD) (Antrobus 2004, 64).

Similarly, feminists from the South launched a major challenge to the terms of debate operating at the Mid-Decade Conference on Women organized by the UN in Copenhagen in 1980. At the intergovernmental conference, comprising delegations from 145 nations, women diplomats from the South took issue with the efforts by Western states to restrict the discussion of the "factors inhibiting women's full participation in social, economic and political life" to the problem of discrimination. From the Southern perspective, structural factors producing women's oppression— exploitation by multinational corporations, colonialism, and imperialism—had to be on the agenda as well. At the request of the General Assembly, Lucille Mair, a Jamaican historian and diplomat serving as secretary general of the conference, added two agenda items, a discussion of the effects of the Israeli occupation on Palestinian women in the occupied territories and a discussion of the abysmal condition of women refugees, who with their children constituted 80 percent of the world refugee population (Jaquette 1995, 49–50).

With 8,000 women from all regions of the world participating, the NGO forum in Copenhagen also foundered on North-South rifts. Many Northern feminists still assumed that women shared a common situation and that political wrangling over apartheid, colonialism, the New International Economic Order, and the conflict in the Middle East simply diverted attention from "women's issues." Objecting vociferously to charges of imperialism and racism lodged by activists from the South, many feminists from affluent Northern nations seemed unable to grasp that exploitation by multinational corporations, the plight of migrant workers, the devaluation of women's agricultural labor and domestic work by development experts, and nuclear tests in the South Pacific could actually be priorities for feminists from the South (Stienstra 1994, 129). Indeed, some Northern feminists accused women from the South of being pawns in a geopolitical game, "used by male-dominated political and revolutionary movements to further masculinist agendas" (West 1999, 179). The acrimonious debates in Copenhagen had spill-over effects. Upon their return to the United States, some feminist groups lobbied Congress in support of the Reagan administration proposal to cut U.S. funding for the UN Development Fund for Women (UNIFEM) and the International Research and Training Institute for the Advancement of Women (INSTRAW) (Snyder 1995, 103).[5] Halfway through the Decade for Women, the U.S. government, with the support of some feminist organizations, withdrew financial support for the UN-sponsored policy machinery devised to promote global feminism.

Jane Jacquette (1995, 48) has pointed out that feminist activists may share strong commitments "to improve the condition of women," but as the Copenhagen conference demonstrated, "there was no prior epistemic community of agreement" about what such improvement entailed or which strategies were most likely to achieve it. Assuming that they represent women's interests, some Western feminists have replicated patterns of Western hegemony, exercising influence beyond their geographic and national borders, selectively permeating the boundaries of other nation-states and other women's lives (John 1996, 16). Conflating the interests of some North American and European women with the interests of all women, some transnational feminist activists from the North have created and exacerbated inequalities. Applying Western concepts and frameworks to the global South, these imperial feminists seem unaware of how poorly their theories travel and of the dangers of forcing women in the South into these ill-fitting and oppressive molds. This lack of awareness requires interrogation, especially because feminists of the South have been eloquent in their articulation of their critiques of Western feminism and in the development of their own priorities for feminist action.

In addition to the emphasis on gender equality and the apparent indifference to the structural asymmetries within and between nations, many Western feminists have retained a "persistent faith in the reformability of a

126

market-led development process" (Kabeer 2003, 32; Taylor 2000). Despite convincing evidence of the deteriorating conditions of the majority of women in the South after four decades of development, many Western feminists remain convinced that women's liberation remains closely linked to modernization, which they construe in terms of the experiences of Western nations. Thus they assume "that liberation hinges on work outside the home" (Mink 1999, 182), on "opportunities for paid work in the formal sector" (Giele 2001, 181), which will loosen patriarchal strictures and create economic independence. Accepting the economic determinism of the modernization model, they assume that capitalist economic ventures will foster political liberalization and the cultivation of civil society. Thus they advocate women's entry into male spheres from which they have been excluded, whether those spheres are economic, educational, ethnic, national, international, political, professional, religious, or tribal. The individualist bias and elitist implications of such advice is seldom acknowledged. And the potent legacies of colonialism and neocolonialism disappear behind the rhetoric of individual upward mobility.

Views from the South

Feminists of the South have insisted that modernization cannot be understood apart from centuries of colonization, economic exploitation, and environmental degradation, which produce markedly uneven development within the South as well as between North and South. Meaningful liberation, then, must take into account the needs and interests of very different kinds of women marked by membership in particular class, caste, ethnic, national, racial, and religious groups. Once complex social hierarchies are acknowledged, then

> feminism cannot be monolithic in its issues, goals and strategies since it constitutes the expression of the concerns and interests of women from different regions, classes, nationalities and ethnic backgrounds. While gender subordination has universal elements, feminism cannot be based on a rigid concept of universality that negates the wide variation of women's experiences. (Sen and Grown 1987, 18)

Western feminist prescriptions involving the liberatory force of the market, work outside the home, and employment within the formal sector are a form of universalization marred by systemic class and regional biases. Even within nations of the North, "women of color and poor, white women have not usually found work outside the home to be a source of equality. On the contrary, such work has been the site of oppression and a mark of inequality" (Mink 1999, 182). Within many parts of the world, the demarcation of public and private spheres, which informs the notion of work outside the home, is far less clear-cut than Western feminists might presume. In India, for example,

> It is mainly women belonging to upper class and caste who are confined to "private" activities within the domestic sphere, while a large number of women belonging to the poorer section of society, those of lower caste, and members of peasant and tribal communities work outside the house participating extensively in agricultural, animal husbandry, and allied activities. Their work is often seen as the extension of their household activities and no clear demarcation occurs between the private and public realms in such situations. (Chauhan 2001, 74)

Nor does such work provide a clear path to emancipation.

Strategies that emphasize employment in the formal sector also fail to take into account the realities of the majority of women's lives.

> More women and men around the world are in informal employment arrangements than are in formal market jobs. . . . Most of the world's women who are economically active are in the informal economy, frequently working as micro-entrepreneurs. More than half of the economically active women in Sub-Saharan Africa and South Asia are self-employed in the informal economy, as are about a third in Northern Africa and Asia. In Latin American countries, 30–70 percent of women workers are employed in the informal economy. (Esim 2001, 165)

Working in microenterprises or as microentrepreneurs, in sweatshops or home-based units, in the most vulnerable forms of employment exempt or hidden from national employment and labor legislation, the majority of the world's women may see modernization in starkly different terms than do affluent Western women (Taylor 2000).

"In striking contrast to the benign view of modernity held by many Western and Northern feminists, the women from the economic South believe that economic development is by and large destructive" (Giele 2001, 183). Rather than experiencing improvements in health, education, and living standards, women across the South have found their living conditions worsened as they are forced off the land, as they lose space for their subsistence crops to export agriculture, as aggregate food production falls, as malnutrition increases, as structural adjustment policies cut back educational opportunities, health care, and other minimal social services, as growing worldwide militarization diminishes physical security and unleashes powerful social forces such as national chauvinism, racism, and sexism (Sen and Grown 1987; Taylor 2000; Kabeer 2003).

If Western prescriptions for capitalist development conflict with the views of feminists from the South about what is needed to improve their lives, so too does the notion that the North can "save" the South. One of the most consistent themes articulated by feminists from the South over the past forty years is that solutions to development crises in the South require "people-centered approaches: overall policies (monetary, fiscal, agricultural, industrial, employment, and social services) directly oriented to meeting people's basic needs," which presuppose the involvement of local people in project choice, planning, and implementation (Sen and Grown 1987, 40). Insisting that Third World women are "agents of change, not objects or recipients of change" (Denis 2001, 155), feminists in the South have called for open, participatory processes that involve local stakeholders in diagnoses of problems and identification of solutions.

Across the South grassroots feminist activists have advanced strategies for "empowerment from below" (Kabeer 2003, 224) that posit "self-definition as a key ingredient of relevant political action" (Sen and Grown 1987, 80). Invoking long-standing arguments about the benefits of direct democracy, feminist activists suggest that local women's participation in decision making will generate benefits for the individuals involved (self-development), as well as for the community (collective solidarity and improved policies to alleviate poverty).

> Where a space is created for women's own voices to be heard, either through participatory processes of needs identification or by organizational practices that encourage participation in shaping and changing the "decisionable agenda," a different set of needs may come into view. (Kabeer 2003, 230)

In case after case across the global South, the involvement of local women in decision making has helped to "challenge conventional stereotypes about gender needs, make visible hitherto hidden categories of women's needs, and lay bare the interconnections between different aspects of women's lives" (Kabeer 2003, 231). Contrary to stereotypes of illiterate peasant women, feminist activists in the South suggest that "peasant women are fully conscious of the reasons for their poverty and their subordinations" (Mazumdar 1989, 29). They lack information, however, about their "new rights—as human beings, as workers, as citizens, their rights and responsibilities to participate in all decisions within the family, the community, and the state, to influence the process of change and claim a share of state assistance for themselves" (Mazumdar 1989, 29).

Providing women with information about their rights under national constitutions and international treaties, such as CEDAW, has been a continuing focus of grassroots feminist activism. But in contrast to individualist deployments of rights discourses focusing on discrimination, feminist activists in the South have linked rights rhetoric to the building of collective identities for women. Drawing upon Paulo Freire's conception of *conscientization* and feminist notions of consciousness raising, feminist activists in the South have devised strategies to heighten women's understanding that they can stand together and act together, cultivating their strength to resist and transform oppressive practices through collective organization and mobilization.

Enhancing women's capacities to organize, mobilize, build alliances, and form coalitions to demand accountability and to create social change is a staple of the "transversal" politics in the South (Grewal and Kaplan 1994; Yuval-Davis 1997). Deploying these skills at home and abroad, feminist activists from the South have developed vibrant transnational networks, which they use to amplify their voices. At subregional, regional, and global conferences, as well as through websites, listservs, cyberjournals, newsletters, and public reports and books, feminists from the South have articulated strategies to break down structural inequality between the North and South, to redress the depredations of colonial and neocolonial domination, to fight institutional, cultural, and individual racisms, to alleviate poverty through debt forgiveness, land and income redistribution, expanded educational opportunity, and accessible and affordable health care, to foster national self-reliance, to control multinational corporations, and to reduce military expenditures. They have worked with international organizations, transnational NGOs, national, regional, and local governments, and progressive solidarity networks to redefine development as "equitable and sustainable allocation of resources in order to meet the basic needs and strategic interests of all" (Denis 2001, 157). In this view, development is inseparable from the empowerment of local women to determine their own priorities and the means to address them. Aggregating the views of autonomous women's movements across the South, Third World feminist activists identify the most pressing priorities facing women as poverty, racism, unequal trade relations, structural adjustment policies, coercive population control strategies, militarism, and environmental degradation (compare World Women's Congress for a Healthy Planet 1992; Sen and Grown 1987; Taylor 2000; Demos and Segal 2001; Tauli-Corpuz 2001; Kabeer 2003).

Convergence or Continuing Contestation?

With the exponential growth of transnational feminist networks that seek to politicize women's issues beyond the borders of the nation-state, build solidarity among feminists across the globe, and act strategically to influence international agencies and foundations, national governments, and transnational NGOs to improve the conditions of women, questions about what gets said by whom about women's needs and interests and what gets heard have increasing cogency.[6] Many accounts of transnational feminist activism suggest that the intense conflicts surveyed in this chapter represent an early stage in the development of global feminism that has been overcome, giving way to the cultivation of a new consensus on women's needs and interests. Consider, for example, Valentine Moghadam's (2005, 1) optimistic assessment: "Prior to the mid-1980s the world's women had not yet developed a collective identity, a collective sense of injustice, or common forms of organizing. The year 1985 was, in many ways, a watershed" (Moghadam 2005, 1; see also Antrobus 2004; Jaquette 1995; Keck and Sikkink 1998; Patton 1995; Stienstra 1994). According to Moghadam, new economic and political realities led to a convergence of feminist perspectives across the globe, a convergence that first surfaced at the Third UN World Conference on Women in Nairobi, Kenya, in 1985. The economic and political factors contributing to the new feminist consensus included the "transition from Keynesian to neo-liberal economics, along with increasing feminization of international labor force; the decline of the welfare state and the developmental state; and the emergence of various fundamentalist movements" (Moghadam 2005, 6). These seismic transformations enabled feminist activists from North and South to see the merits of each other's arguments. Thus, according to Moghadam, "for many First World women, economic issues and development policy became increasingly important, and for many Third World feminists, increased attention was now directed to women's legal status, autonomy, and rights" (Moghadam 2005, 8). During the 1990s, a broader feminist agenda emerged, encompassing "a critique of neo-liberalism and structural adjustment policies, as well as an insistence on women's reproductive rights, bodily integrity, and autonomy. Eventually that common agenda took the form of the 1995 Beijing Declaration and Platform for Action" (Moghadam 2005, 9). Indeed, Peggy Antrobus (2004, 104) has suggested that the

> analytic framework that formed the basis for approaches to women's rights discourse was based on new understandings of the link between women's social and economic rights and our civil and political rights. . . . This integration of the development paradigm and the rights paradigm can be seen as one of the achievements of the global women's movement.

While these narratives of conflict resolution are heartening, they tend to overestimate the degree of convergence among contemporary feminisms, rendering important continuing contestations invisible. Moreover, they reflect and legitimize a political tactic, "one-voice feminism," which is recurrently asserted by some feminists within UN circuits as essential if feminism is to be taken seriously in male-dominant policy venues—a tactic that has itself been contested by some feminists.

To challenge the sanguine feminist convergence model, consider the contours of conflict that emerged in 2001 at a Preparatory Committee (Prep Com) meeting for the Third World Conference Against Racism, Racial Discrimination, Xenophobia and Related Intolerance (WCAR). Erupting at the Prep Com held during the forty-fifth meeting of the UN Commission on the Status of Women in New York, the conflict arose precisely because some feminist activists were insisting that feminists must speak with one voice if they wished to be heard at the Anti-Racism Conference in Durban. Much to the chagrin of some feminists from the South, the "one-voice" proponents were endorsing seemed not only to speak in English with a decidedly Northern accent, but also to articulate an agenda at some remove from the priorities of Southern feminists. Third World women's frustration with feminists from the North who seemed neither to hear nor heed the voices from the South led to a demand for a South-South Initiative (SSI) from which feminists from the North would be explicitly excluded.[7]

Rather than recognizing the legitimacy of the demand for the creation of a separate political space for discussion of common problems free from the potential interventions or distortions of hegemonic forces, some feminists from the North attacked the idea of the SSI as exclusionary, divisive, and dangerous, arguing that it would undermine the global women's movement, which needed to speak with one voice. Third World feminists noted that a South-South dialogue replicated feminist practices of the early years of second-wave feminism in the North, when feminists devoted considerable efforts to justifying the creation of women-only spaces as a necessary and legitimate tactic in the struggle against oppression. Feminists of the South also noted that the distinctive problems they faced—histories of colonization, impacts of globalization, acute poverty, and the situations of migrants, trafficked women, and indigenous peoples—warranted the creation of special places in which they could assume leadership, demonstrate their competences, and set their own agendas (Jain 2001; Martinez 2001; Wanyeki 2001; Tauli-Corpuz 2001). "Claiming the space, even in the form of SSI, is an important step. And exclusion is an essential strategy, unfortunately, to send a wake-up call to women of the North" (Joseph 2001). Only within a separate space could women of the South address the power imbalances between North and South, the failure of Northern feminists to move beyond token representation in their consultations with Third World women, and Northern feminists' recurrent tendency to dominate the agendas of global feminism (Jain 2001; Muchina 2001). Moreover, feminists of the South urged women in the North to develop their own Northern Initiative addressing the foreign policies and increasing militarization of Western governments (Obando 2001b): "The North should work harder within their countries against the foreign policy of their governments, which are killing the rest of the world. That would be a good help to the South."

An intensive debate over the South-South Initiative has been ongoing since March 2001. Women of the South did meet in special caucus at WCAR and planned to continue meeting as a caucus during the annual meetings of the UN Commission on the Status of Women. Ironically, however, the contents of these discussions and meetings are not shielded from the Western gaze. While feminists in the SSI caucus do meet in closed session, they have also set up a website for the continuation of the South-South dialogue, which is completely open to Western eyes.[8]

Encounters between transnational feminists of the North and South over the past four decades have been marked by recurrent contestation over the politics of representation. Although feminists from the South have been active and vocal in articulating alternative visions of women's needs and feminist priorities, it is not clear that their voices are being heard within Northern feminist circles. Despite intense and explicit discussions concerning racial, ethnic, and class biases at international meetings, the negotiated agendas of transnational feminism continue to manifest the traces of Western feminist hegemony. Indeed, the convergence model, which is fast becoming a stock narrative of transnational feminist activism, replicates the problem of Western hegemony with its confident assertion that all feminists now speak with one voice. It is important to ask, then, whether Third World feminists are suffering the fate of subaltern speakers.

As articulations of those who have been oppressed by racist, colonizing practices, subaltern speech raises questions of power and privilege, inclusion and exclusion of great import for feminist activism and inquiry. According to Gayatri Spivak (1985), one defining characteristic of subaltern speech is that it *has not been heard* by the privileged and the powerful who participate in colonization. Spivak draws explicit attention to theoretical frameworks such as orientalism and colonialism that insulate those in power from hearing by sustaining a conviction that the subaltern have nothing to say. Despite claims of global solidarity, do the views of some Western feminists incorporate tacit assumptions that keep them from hearing voices from the South? If so, can those assumptions be identified and

133

contested? Are there other factors operating in the current era of globalization to drown out subaltern speech?

From Individual to Structural Explanations of Feminist Contestations

Some feminist scholars might point out that the stark North-South binary used in framing this question is problematic, for it contributes to a mistaken view that all feminists in the North hold one set of views and all feminists in the South adhere to another set of views, when the reality is far more complicated than that. Indeed, writing about feminist contestations occurring in the context of the 1994 Cairo Conference on Population and Development, Rosalind Petchesky (2003, 66) has pointed out that

> some of the most vociferous critics of Northern-based women's NGOs for dominating the "inside" process were themselves Northern-based women's NGOs who condemned the process as inherently cooptive and refused involvement in it. Others were prestigious academic feminists based in elite Northern institutions with ample resources to fly around the globe speaking on behalf of subjugated women from the South.

Many feminists in the North insist that they are hearing Third World women. At one level, the past two decades of intensive debate within Western feminist theory and practice might be interpreted as proof of the validity of that claim. "Difference feminism" and "Third Wave feminism" are founded upon an insistence that the differences among women are central to feminism, indeed, that genders are constituted in and through processes of racialization as well as class, ethnic, and national differentiation. Working within these frames, feminists have learned to be wary of "fictitious unities" (Riley 2000, 176) that evoke identification even as they mask hierarchies of difference. "At least since the 1980s, feminists have learned (often quite painfully . . .) to make nuanced distinctions along multiple axes of difference" (Scott 2002, 6). As pointed out in chapter 2, socialist feminists within the North have emphasized critiques of capitalism, colonialism, and imperialism in their discussions of social and economic justice for almost two centuries.

Within the sphere of feminist development studies, for example, critiques of the liberal presuppositions of Women in Development (WID) and Women and Development approaches have generated intensive discussions about holistic approaches to women's oppression that begin with intersectional analyses of women's needs and interests, attuned to the voices of local women. As Jane Parpart (1995, 240) has noted,

Emancipatory development will only occur when development theorists and practitioners adopt a more inclusive approach to knowledge and expertise, a readiness and ability to "hear" different voices and experiences and the humility to recognize that established discourses and practices of development have done more harm than good.

Western feminist activists have acknowledged that "recovering the bases of solidarity" with women in the South after years of destructive development policies requires strategies such as "developing empathy for people who are different and openness to other values," which can "build bridges, resolve conflicts, and foster care for the other" (Giele 2001, 191). Some Western feminists have emphasized that women in the South must debate and decide the strategies applicable to their unique circumstances free from Western influence: "The proper role of feminist organizations in imperialist core countries is to support this local dialogue with resources and respect" (Brenner 2003, 6). Other Western feminist activists hold out more hope that feminists in the North and South can once again develop innovative partnerships: "Respectful listening and exchange will give rise to useful collaboration between North and South in developing and implementing strategies for feminist transformation" (Denis 2001, 159).

It may be too simple, however, to take the discursive shift to difference and Northern feminist professions of empathy, solidarity, and openness as indicative that views from the South have been taken to heart. For there is a great distance between the articulation of theoretical principles and the realization of those principles in social action, political institutions, and global policy. In analyzing the factors that inhibit social transformation, there is far more at stake than individual intentions or feminist good will. Even when the voices of the South are heard clearly, Third World feminist words can be processed in ways that strip them of their emancipatory potential. Structural forces may constrain feminist principles in multiple ways, creating a gulf between feminist intention and real world outcomes. The adoption of women's empowerment by the World Bank (2000) as a core commitment in its development agenda provides a useful example of a Western appropriation of the Third World feminist theory and practice in which the transformative potential is lost in translation (Vas Dev and Schech 2003).

The World Bank's decision to include women's empowerment within its development objectives was the result of years of feminist efforts to influence the Bank's policies (Bedford 2005). After three decades of mobilization by feminist scholars and activists on the outside and by feminist employees on the inside, the World Bank adopted policies requiring gender mainstreaming, gender impact analyses of all its programs, and the promotion of women's economic development, as outlined in *Integrating Gender into the World Bank's Work: A Strategy for Action* (2002b). Examining the gulf between the feminist politics of women's empowerment in the South and the implementation of women's empowerment strategies by the World Bank, then, helps to illuminate some of the institutional and structural factors that operate independent of feminist intentions to drown out subaltern speech.

In many parts of the South, informally employed women have pooled savings to provide a collective resource to assist them in the face of immediate financial necessity.[9] Taking these traditional self-help programs as a model, some feminist organizations designed microcredit programs as an organizing strategy to empower women to improve their lives. Funded by the pooled resources of women's collectives, these programs afford their members decision power in loan approval, hands-on practice in participatory governance, capacity-building opportunities in collective microenterprises, and innovative strategies for political mobilization and electoral accountability. Access to loans also enables members to meet immediate needs.

Under the rubric of the World Bank's development agenda, however, the relationship between microcredit programs and women's empowerment shifts within the larger context of market-based strategies to attack poverty. Despite adoption of the language of women's empowerment, the capacity-building aspects of feminist microcredit programs are supplanted by concerns with fiscal responsibility and the benefits of entrepreneurship for community development. Microcredit programs for women have been demonstrated to be sound capital investments.[10] Multiple studies have shown that women are far better than men at repaying their loans. In advocating microcredit, the World Bank seeks to provide a route for individual women to engage in market competition via microenterprise, thereby fostering economic growth and promoting community development. Lending individual women investment capital that they will repay from their successful economic ventures is a virtually cost-free means to economic development within a market framework. Empowering women then becomes a means to the expansion of capitalist markets, economic growth, and the protection of capital investments.

Feminist critics have pointed out that in co-opting the language of women's empowerment, the World Bank expunges the critique of capitalism at the heart of Third World feminists' alternative vision of development. *Attacking Poverty*, the World Bank (2002) policy research report, appears oblivious to the fact that the present structures of national, political, social, economic, even cultural norms and institutions in the South are also rooted in particular histories and interaction with international capitalist modes of accumulation. Thus the report neither sees nor factors the World Bank's own involvement in the construction . . . or reinforcement of gender inequality in the South. (Asante 2002, 293)

In the absence of any recognition of the role of capitalism in women's growing impoverishment, feminists in the South remain highly critical of World Bank policies that treat women instrumentally and thoroughly skeptical about microcredit as a means to eradicate poverty. Although feminists acknowledge that microcredit programs can assist some women in meeting their most immediate subsistence needs, this falls far short of eliminating poverty. Unlike the loans made within women's informal financial solidarity groups, microloans from capitalist lenders are restricted to profit-generating business ventures and cannot be used to cover other expenses that burden the poor, such as the costs of funerals, health care, food, and fuel. Within the scope of capitalist institutions, microcredit programs focus on individual women, rather than on prevailing gender and class/caste relations. Emphasizing changes in individual attitudes to promote self-confidence and economic achievement, they ignore structural inequalities. In addition, microcredit programs increase the debt of poor women, imposing new levels of stress as well as responsibility on individual women. Moreover, the rhetoric of individual self-help as a means of poverty alleviation helps to legitimate the government's abandonment of collective responsibility to meet the most basic needs of the people at the very moment that structural adjustment policies require governments to cut back on health, education, and welfare provision.

Poverty has consistently been placed at the top of the Third World feminist agenda. The World Bank's prescriptions for the eradication of poverty, however, also lose a great deal in translation. In recent policy papers, the World Bank has emphasized women's employment in the formal sector as the key to poverty reduction. As noted above, however, excessive emphasis on the formal sector misses the centrality of women's roles in the informal and subsistence sectors to the survival of their families and communities. It also ignores women's roles in social reproduction—their unwaged work caring for children, families, and the elderly, providing health care and education, and sustaining the social fabric. Ignoring women's unwaged work, the Bank not only privileges commercial values quantified in calculations of the gross domestic product (GDP), but also endorses solutions that create twinned social reproduction and exhaustion crises (Bedford 2005). If women enter the formal economy in accordance with the World Bank's antipoverty prescription, there is a crisis of childcare, elder care, health care, and community functioning. If women try to maintain a quadruple shift, working in the formal economy, continuing their labor in the informal and subsistence economies, performing their unwaged care work, and contributing to the maintenance of community ties, they face collapse from sheer exhaustion. Moreover, working quadruple shifts does not guarantee eradication of poverty, because wages in the formal economy and profits from microenterprise remain below subsistence levels in many parts of the world.

The World Bank's efforts to engender development pledges to put women at the center of development policy, but it does so in decidedly nonfeminist ways. The World Bank focus on moving women into the formal economy shifts responsibility for household income support from men to women, which has the unintended effect of shifting household labor from women to their daughters, contributing to growing rates of female illiteracy in many parts of the global South. Promoting self-employment as the paradigm for poverty alleviation also shifts responsibility for development from the nation-state to the market, which favors private lending associations over public service agencies (Poster and Salime 2002, 191–192).

The zeal for microcredit and deployment of the language of women's empowerment in the discourses of the World Bank does not constitute evidence that voices from the South are being heard in the North. On the contrary, they seem to make a compelling case for Spivak's account of the fate of subaltern speech. Yet this example demonstrates that far more is at stake than hearing the voices of feminists from the South. The metaphor of subaltern speech may create the mistaken impression that all that is required for social transformation is to hear the voices of the oppressed. By situating social change within a voluntarist framework, metaphors of speech and voice appeal to the individualist premises that undergird liberalism and neoliberalism. They support hypotheses attributing the failure to hear the voices of the South to attitudinal problems (indifference, hostility) or narrow self-interests of white, middle-class, Western feminists, masking the structural forces that constrain feminist activism. Thus they make it appear that poverty could be remedied if Northern feminists set their minds to the task. But even if every feminist in the world willed the end of poverty, structural forces operating beyond the level of individual intention would have far more influence on the fate of poverty than feminist good will. Moreover, willing the end of poverty and agreeing how to achieve that end are quite different things. Some feminists in the North concur in the critique of global capital advanced by feminists in the South.

Others believe that globalization will eventually make good its promise to improve the economic condition of all. Profound disagreement about the relation of capitalism to human well-being and economic prosperity underlies many contemporary feminist contestations, generating markedly different policy recommendations. Ignoring the scope and depth of these disagreements may foster one-voice feminism, but it will do so at the expense of those who bear the brunt of the hardships engendered by globalization.

Feminists from the South and the North who identify poverty, racism, neocolonialism, and imperialism as their social change priorities challenge the fundamental processes of globalization. Offering a powerful critique of capitalism, they question the validity of optimistic claims that marketization, economic efficiency, and neoliberal development strategies tied to individual "self-maximizers" will eradicate poverty. Knowing that the majority of the world population is poorer now than thirty years ago, they argue forcefully that contrary to its promises, unconstrained capitalism fosters growing inequalities. But their message is often mediated by capitalist institutions in disconcerting ways. When the World Bank hears these voices, it translates feminist discourses into its own vernacular. As one of the premier institutions of global capitalism, designed to preserve and strengthen the market, the Bank purges the radical critique of capitalism as it appropriates feminist language. As noted above, the standard operating procedures of the Bank transform the language of women's empowerment into policy prescriptions that subordinate feminist ends to capitalist imperatives. Thus, even when feminists offer critical alternatives to the established global order, their proposals may be co-opted by the powers that be.

Perpetuating Privilege

It seems counterintuitive that activists who share a commitment to equality can inadvertently contribute to the exacerbation of inequalities. Yet just as certain versions of feminism in the nineteenth century replicated the power dynamics of the global system, so too certain versions of feminism in the twenty-first century reproduce global hegemony. Breny Mendoza (2002) has noted that transnational feminism creates "spaces to establish connections between women of different nations and cultures, but also of different feminisms." Sharing spaces, networking, and building alliances, however, need not imply a total convergence of views or the eradication of fundamental differences.

Calls for feminists to speak with one voice are strategic, designed to heighten the power of feminism by portraying a united front. The strategic call for one-voice feminism recognizes a constraint imposed by many male-dominant institutions. Decision makers busy with national and world affairs have little time to truck with the squabbles and disagreements of women. Only if women present a unified front, articulating a clear and manageable set of priorities, will male decision makers deign to countenance their claims. In demanding that women speak with one voice, however, male elites are imposing a constraint on feminist activists that they would never tolerate for themselves. Accustomed to being taken as they are, male leaders and activists would never consent to having to waive their nationality, race, religion, ethnicity, class, profession, or ideology as a condition for advancing their claims. But this is a condition they willfully impose on feminists. When some feminists endorse a one-voice strategy, they may construe their motives as merely pragmatic. But pragmatic strategies may work precisely because they replicate privilege (Higer 1999). In the current global system, there are good reasons to believe that pragmatic strategies reproduce male privilege and Western power.

A number of recent studies have investigated the effects of transnational activism in an effort to identify the factors conducive to success. Analyzing contestations central to transnational feminist activism in the context of these studies may help to illuminate how privilege is reproduced within the politics of social transformation.

Feminists who seek to place poverty and antiracism at the top of the transnational feminist agenda hope to shift the dominant discourses away from liberal individualism and neoliberal globalism and to transform the procedures and the substance of development policies toward a social justice agenda. Toward those ends, they have engaged in information politics, contesting Western accounts of the benefits of marketization and circulating alternative views of the impact of globalization on the lives and livelihoods of women and communities in the global South. From their investigations of a variety of transnational advocacy networks, Keck and Sikkink (1998) conclude that campaigns relying on information politics are most likely to succeed in cases that involve issues such as torture, bodily harm to innocent people, or a demand for equal opportunities for excluded groups; where these harms can be traced to intentional actions of identifiable individuals; where the targeted agent is vulnerable to international pressure; and where advocacy networks can enlist the aid of powerful international actors to leverage moral and material pressure on the target agent. Indeed Keck and Sikkink note that "problems whose causes are irredeemably structural" are far less amenable to advocacy network strategies (1998, 27). Feminist critiques of globalization seem to run afoul of each of these conditions for success. They seek to address issues of

140

structural inequalities; they are campaigning against global hegemony; and they are targeting activists, who are largely excluded from the key decision-making positions responsible for procedural and policy changes, and who lack the means of moral and material suasion to pressure decision makers to change. Operating outside the parameters of success for information politics, only the most moderate claims of transnational feminist activists are likely to be processed by established institutions within the global system. Thus although feminist activists explicitly include social and economic rights within their human rights framework, neoliberalism filters out the radical content. Within this ideological context, then, the merger of development and human rights agendas within one-voice feminism may work to the disadvantage of the social justice objectives of the development agenda. Wholly independent of feminist intentions, neoliberal bias within the global order privileges rights discourses that conform to individualist conceptions of civil and political rights.

Empirical research supports this conclusion. Studying four decades of transnational feminist activism using international conventions to leverage political change within particular states, Amrita Basu (1995, 2000) found that feminists have been far more successful in securing civil and political rights than in attaining social and economic rights, suggesting that Western feminist agendas reap benefits from the hegemonic force of liberalism and neoliberalism. Regardless of their rhetorical power, depictions of the dire economic consequences of structural adjustment policies and devastating environmental consequences of nonsustainable development have not yet pierced the ideological immunity afforded by capitalist convictions.

In contrast to strategies of information politics that explicitly target a transnational audience, the antipoverty and antiracism activism of Third World women has also been characterized in terms of the weapons of the weak: "Conscientization and organization mobilize the only resources the poor have—the capacity to resist and transform through collective strength" (Kabeer 2003, 251). Yet these tactics have produced their greatest successes when deployed at the local level in combination with partisan political campaigns to win power within the state. In South Africa and India, for example, feminists have worked with parties of the Left to press for increased political representation and redistributive policies. They have formed cross-race, cross-class, and cross-caste coalitions to pressure their governments to change constitutions and statutes to promote gender equality and to develop women's machinery within the state. While engaging in intensive debates about the diverse interests of women arising from intersections of race, class, caste, ethnic, and religious inequalities, they have also done the political work to build women as a constituency that

141

will have political leverage through the ballot box (Hassim 2003). Feminist efficacy in such transformative efforts is measured in terms of conventional politics within particular nations, achieving voluntary, statutory, or constitutionally mandated quotas for women in electoral institutions, increasing numbers of women in political office, passing legislation that ends discrimination and redistributes resources, establishing women's machinery within bureaucracies that can implement gender equity legislation, and winning court battles that secure women's rights. These feminist successes have been tied to mobilizing women as a voting force in electoral politics, electing officials, and holding them to account. Yet even these democratic tactics chafe against structural constraints.

Investigating feminist political engagements within nation-states in comparative context, Anne Marie Goetz (2003) has noted that systematic policy changes remain an elusive goal for feminist activists. In most nations, feminists have been far more successful in articulating a women's agenda than in gaining political representation within the institutions of the state, influencing political decision making, or changing public policies.[11] Feminists have achieved their most dramatic successes in relation to access, representation, and influence, however, in countries that have a tradition of socialist or social democratic parties in government, where women are well organized and exercise political leverage within the dominant political parties, and where a strong women's movement within civil society can mobilize women as a voting constituency and thereby hold governments to account (Goetz and Hassim 2003; Leijenaar 2003, Weldon 2002). Within the nation-state, neoliberalism expressly targets socialist and social democratic parties and the legitimacy of state interventions to promote social justice and gender justice, as noted in chapter 1. Moreover, the "democracy deficit" at the global level precludes such mobilizing tactics. There are no elections to international institutions. Global policy makers are accountable to states, not to the world population. Nations are not equal in these international forums. The one-nation, one-vote principle operating in the UN General Assembly is routinely trumped by decisions of the UN Security Council, where the five permanent members have far more power than the ten rotating members.[12] Decision power in the international financial institutions is tied to wealth, as the nations contributing the bulk of funding control major appointments and policy directions.[13] The United Nations also lacks power to implement and enforce its decisions, which further complicates any meaningful accountability. As the U.S. invasion of Iraq in 2003 made clear, the United States is quite content to adopt unilateralism when the majority of nations in the world object to its proposals.

In seeking to promote global social change, then, antiglobalism feminists face two distinct problems. The first is ideological—how to pierce the ideological immunity afforded by neoliberalism. In this domain, the politics of information is at a distinct disadvantage for it presupposes the efficacy of fact gathering and truth telling. Contestations on an ideological terrain, however, are confronted with a political register of truth. What counts as fact, what constitutes evidence, and what is recognized as truth are issues structured by ideological presuppositions. Efforts to promote change by reporting facts can be foiled by ideological convictions contributing to evidence blindness.

In addition to problems of ideological distortion, antiglobalism feminists confront structural obstacles that are intensifying in a neoliberal era. Transnational feminist activists operating in UN circuits are constrained by frameworks and agendas set by the male-dominant United Nations and its male-dominant member states (Petchesky 2003, 64). Within UN circuits, feminist contestations are necessarily reactive, responding to priorities, programs, and practices determined by men, rather than shaping agendas on the basis of their own principles and priorities.

The sites of major UN agencies (New York, Paris, Geneva) skew power toward the North. Feminists in the North have easier access to these sites, simply because they have shorter distances to travel to reach them. Moreover, feminists in the North often have access to the funding needed to travel to planning meetings and to engage and monitor UN bureaucracies. Feminists from the South who wish to participate in these Northern venues often have to seek funding from foundations located in the North to support their participation, creating various pressures that could curb radical critiques.

In the twenty-first century, feminists who have the financial resources to participate in UN circuits are encountering a global environment that is growing more conservative and far less receptive to social justice activism. In 2000, for example, UN Secretary General Kofi Annan collaborated with the Organization for Economic Cooperation and Development (OECD), the World Bank, and IMF to produce a report that situated social justice squarely within the framework of neoliberal capitalism. *2000—A Better World for All* acknowledges and documents that poverty, social inequality, gender inequality, infant and maternal mortality, and environmental devastation all increased during the last five years of the twentieth century; yet, the report resoundingly reaffirms capitalist and neoliberal strategies to remedy these grave ills. As Rosalind Petchesky has noted, the message to social justice activists is unmistakable.

Goals and targets to reduce poverty "cannot be imposed—they must be embraced" through voluntary measures, not regulations and timetables. So women's and anti-poverty NGOs intending to use this General Assembly process as a forum to demand strong measures to regulate global capital flows, cancel debt, redistribute wealth, and promote gender and economic justice should be forewarned: your efforts will be of little consequence in the eyes of the world's opinion leaders. (Petchesky 2003, 58)

Petchesky has also pointed out that the global circuits to which transnational feminist activists have gained the greatest access tend to be those with the least power within the UN system. Feminist activists have succeeded in gaining some access to the General Assembly, to sympathetic agencies like UNDP, UNIFEM, and the ILO, and to NGO forums and Prep Coms where "soft issues," such as poverty, health, social and gender justice, labor, racism, and xenophobia, are debated endlessly (Petchesky 2003, 68–69). Yet these relatively open sites lack the power and financial resources to enact policies and develop enforcement machinery. Meanwhile the key power sites addressing the "hard issues of globalization—including issues of resource allocation, finance, trade, and security" remain remarkably impenetrable to feminist activism. The closed-door meetings among G7 nations conducted in consultation with the WTO, the World Bank, the IMF, and the Security Council, as well as occasional ad hoc ministerial meetings like the 2000 Millennium forum, operate entirely outside the sphere of democratic accountability. "Women's and human rights groups were not invited to the table" (Petchesky 2003, 69).

Completely independent of feminist intentions and objectives, power in the global system operates to shore up neoliberalism and capitalism. Voices of procapitalist feminists are somewhat more likely to gain a hearing, and voices of anticapitalist feminists are likely to be translated into neoliberal vernaculars. Under these conditions, one-voice feminism can only redound to the benefit of the procapitalist camp. When international agreements "allow nations to appear as if they are addressing concerns of women without really taking action" and women's conditions are deteriorating even as international agreements are signed (Karides 2002, 170), there are very good reasons for resisting one-voice feminism. When states agree to international standards to promote equality for women, establishing national and international machineries to monitor and promote equality as they are simultaneously implementing structural adjustment policies that reverse many changes that could have helped women (Stienstra 1994, 118), there are good reasons to promote polyvocal feminism. Contesting the power ploys of the global system may not be sufficient to change global power arrangements, but it certainly must be a necessary first step to transforming them. Accepting the terms of debate structured by those in power simply perpetuates prevailing patterns of privilege and disadvantage.

Given the enormous diversity of women in the world, no one represents the needs and interests of women. No person, group, or institution can do more than offer a partial and incomplete women's agenda. As a self-selected group, feminists differ from the majority of women in various and manifold ways. Transnational feminist activists bring multiple views and voices to global circuits. These views often differ significantly from the official stances of governments and international institutions precisely because feminists place women at the center of their analyses and use the complex dimensions of women's lives and livelihoods to frame new questions and bring new issues into the global arena. But starting from women's lives does not imply convergence on a single view. Contrary to calls for one-voice feminism, intense, prolonged, and amplified feminist contestations may be the best way to challenge the monotony of the growing neoliberal consensus. By disagreeing openly and giving voice to multiplicity and difference, transnational feminist activists can model a different mode of democratic practice as they struggle against global hegemony.

GLOBAL FEMINIST FUTURES: THE STRUGGLE CONTINUES

> [Neo]liberalism bears the distinctively bourgeois trait of promising freedom while prohibiting it.
>
> —Theodor Adorno (1997, 206)

> The odds against success seem insuperable. Yet a multitude of autonomous feminist groups, working locally, networking transnationally, pooling ideas and strategic resources, may achieve the critical mass needed to transform women's struggles into workable strategies for bringing about gender-equitable society.
>
> —Farida Shaheed (1995)

Male theorists critical of globalization have advanced diametrically opposed forecasts for the future. As Manfred Steger (2002) has pointed out, the pessimists suggest that globalization is inevitable and irreversible. Thus progressives must resign themselves to the fact that nothing can be done. The optimists, on the other hand, suggest that for the first time in history, capitalism has attained global scale, creating the conditions of possibility for the formation of a global revolutionary class that can at long last expropriate the expropriators. In this view, progressives should actively aid and abet the multitude rising (Hardt and Negri, 2000, 2004). Like their nineteenth-century counterparts, however, theorists projecting the mobilization of revolutionary forces have been critical of feminist activism, denouncing its "divisive" effects, and counseling progressive feminists to defer their agenda and devote their energies to the immediate struggle against global capital (Hardt and Negri 2000, 56). Neither of these options is acceptable to feminist activists, who are unwilling to resign themselves to suffering injustice in perpetuity and are equally unwilling to have their principles written out of ongoing struggles for social justice.

The gulf between feminist, pessimist, and progressive assessments of what is to be done in the current period of globalization stems in part from the gendered effects of globalization itself and in part from unique obstacles to social transformation that feminists face. While all progressive social change activists face enormous hurtles in the current era, gendered power structures—on the Left as well as on the Right—raise specific challenges for transnational feminist activism. This chapter sketches alternative futures, identifies challenges to feminist activism posed by alternative scenarios, and maps the probable contours of continuing transnational feminist struggles in the early twenty-first century.

Alternative Futures: Global Feminism and Neoliberal Globalism

If we trace the emergence of neoliberalism as a transformative force to the Washington Consensus developed in the early 1970s, then there is a striking parallel between the decades of neoliberal and feminist ascendance. Neoliberalism was birthed as a top-down policy strategy, which relied upon the policy-making power of nation-states and international financial institutions such as the World Bank and the IMF for its materializations. As we have seen, feminisms erupted both within international organizations and institutions and as bottom-up mobilizations of women engaged in grassroot struggles in communities around the globe. Yet both envision a future and combine activism, political interventions, and policy transformations to bring that future into being. One could also argue that neoliberal globalism[1] and global feminism have devised similar multilevel formulae for success in achieving systemic changes, targeting transnational organizations, national governments, and individual consciousness as sites of transformation. At a rudimentary level, implementation of both transformative visions has required that activists, pressing for change from the outside, work with key government insiders to secure changes in law and policy, and the development of appropriate state and international policy machinery, to achieve desired policy outcomes. Both have relied on transnational covenants and conventions to leverage change within particular nations. Both neoliberalism and global feminism have also sought profound changes in consciousness, attitudes, mentalities, and expectations, not just of institutions and agencies of governance, but of individuals in their daily lives. Over the past three decades, both have wrought profound changes in the world.

What distinguishes neoliberal globalism and global feminism most starkly is the concrete vision of the future that each seeks to produce. Global feminism in its various instantiations seeks to reduce and ultimately eliminate the complex inequities and inequalities characteristic of race- and gender-based oppression (Basu 1995). Toward that end, it envisions an expanded state provision to create adequate health care, education, welfare, employment, personal security, and a range of equity policies that redress gender- and race-based injustices. Suspicious of the continuing depredations of male-dominant states, global feminism has sought to engender states and their policies, seeking gender parity and gender quotas in elective and appointive offices, constitutional guarantees of equal citizenship, and equal protection of the law; policy changes to require gender mainstreaming, gender-impact analyses, gender-equitable budgets, and monitoring to ensure compliance with equality objectives across all policy domains. In the spheres of reproductive and domestic labor, feminist activists have sought to reduce the burden of women's triple shift, redistributing subsistence, childcare, and community-building labor more equitably across genders. Global feminism envisions transformations in consciousness that would make visible, actionable, and intolerable gender- and race-based inequities that permeate interpersonal relations, social organizations, economic and political structures, and symbol systems.

Neoliberal globalism seeks to cut back the very aspects of the state that feminist activists seek to build up. Structural adjustment policies mandated by international financial institutions as a condition for loans necessitate severe funding cuts in state provision in the areas of health, education, and welfare, shifting responsibility for the private provision of these services largely onto women (Waring 1988; Bakker and Gill 2003). State strategies to produce marketization and privatization seek to winnow down the state, reducing expenditures on education and welfare, eliminating civil service positions in social welfare agencies that have been a route to economic security for many women, deregulating the corporate sector, devolving power in export processing zones, and outsourcing a range of military support and domestic security operations. Embracing the economic determinism of modernization theory, neoliberal activists within international financial institutions seek to transform women into *homo economicus*, promoting the incorporation of women into the formal sector of the economy as the panacea for economic development, family well-being, and profit maximization (World Bank 2000). Toward this end, World Bank policy papers identify transformation of consciousness as a goal and train field workers to cultivate "export mentality" and "market mentality," while whittling away "protest mentalities" among the poor in developing nations (Bedford 2005).

In the last three decades of the twentieth century, activists promoting both visions for the future have been vying for popular allegiance, enacting systematic transformations, and permeating the consciousness of supporters and detractors alike. The growth of neoliberalism has been carefully tracked in the press and in academic and policy circles—by proponents and opponents alike. Feminist activism, on the other hand, has received markedly different treatment.

As documented in the previous chapters, feminism experienced unprecedented growth during the last decades of the twentieth century. In the words of Sonia Alvarez (1998, 4),

> The sites where women, who declare themselves feminists, act or may act have multiplied. It is no longer only in the streets, in autonomous or consciousness-raising groups, in workshops for popular education, etc. Although feminists continue to be in those spaces today, they are also in a wide range of other cultural, social, and political arenas: the corridors of the UN, the academy, state institutions, media, NGOs, among others.

Through the far too invisible labor of feminist activists around the world, feminism has surfaced in manifold global struggles that seldom garner the attention of the press or of mainstream academics.

Within the official institutions of state in Africa, Asia, Australia, Europe, Latin America, and North America, feminist projects are ongoing through gender mainstreaming and the creation of national machinery for women, such as ministries for women, women's bureaus, gender equality commissions. The feminist arm of the United Nations, UNIFEM, is working with indigenous women's organizations on all continents to safeguard women's lives and livelihoods, to secure their economic, political, and civil rights. Several states, such as Sweden, Norway, and the Netherlands, have included gender equity efforts among their major foreign policy initiatives. Femocrats work within public agencies in all but one or two nations to structure policy initiatives that address women's needs, concerns, and interests, however contested these concepts may be. In the aftermath of four UN-sponsored world conferences on women, 169 nations have ratified CEDAW, the Convention to Eliminate All Forms of Discrimination Against Women, and women's rights activists in all those nations are working to pressure their governments to change constitutions, laws, and customary practices in accordance with CEDAW provisions. A near universal consensus among nations supports the Beijing Platform for Action, and feminist activists work locally as well as through the UN monitoring processes to press for implementation of the Beijing Platform.

Feminist nongovernmental organizations (NGO's) have proliferated, creating a vibrant feminist civil society. Tens of thousands of organizations around the globe created by women and for women seek to develop women's political agendas, conduct gender audits and gender impact analyses of government policies, build progressive coalitions among women, deepen the meaning of democracy and democratization, deliver much-needed services to women, and pressure public and private sectors to include more women and respond better to women's concerns. The substantive scope of such feminist work includes subsistence struggles; the politics of food, fuel, and firewood; women's health and reproductive freedom; education for women and girls; employment opportunity, equal pay, safe working conditions, and protection against sexual harassment; rape and domestic violence; sexual trafficking; women's rights as human rights; militarization; peacemaking; environmentalism; sustainable development; democratization; welfare rights; AIDS; parity in public office; women's e-news; feminist journals and presses; and curriculum revision, feminist pedagogy, and feminist scholarship.

In contrast to the sustained scholarly and media attention documenting and assessing the growth of neoliberalism, a markedly different phenomenon has accompanied the unprecedented growth of feminist activism around the globe: the recurrent pronouncement of feminism's death. From the 1970s through the new millennium, journalists, academics, and even some feminist scholars have declared the demise of feminism and hailed the advent of the postfeminist age. Between 1989 and 2001, for example, during a period in which the number of feminist organizations grew exponentially, a Lexis-Nexus search of English-language newspapers turned up eighty-six articles referring to the death of feminism and an additional seventy-four articles referring to the postfeminist era. How are we to make sense of such proclamations of the death of feminism? Given the vibrancy and the variety of proliferating forms of feminist theory and practice, why the premature burial of feminism?

Sarah Webster Goodwin and Elisabeth Bronfen (1993, 20) have characterized texts of death as forms of meaning making particularly ripe for semiotic analysis, for "every representation of death is a misrepresentation." In cases of literal death, words seek to make present that which death has made radically absent and thereby misrepresent their subject. But the death proclamations concerning feminism involve a very different kind of misrepresentation. These textual accounts of death serve as allegorical signs for something else, a means of identifying a perceived danger in need of elimination, a way for a community to define itself through those it symbolically chooses to kill. The premature burial of feminism, then, stands in need of further examination.

To unearth the tacit values of feminism's morticians, the next section investigates two mechanisms by which feminism's death has been produced, the obituary, and narrative accounts of evolutionary extinction. Given the particular kind of distortion involved in the premature burial of a thriving global feminism, the following section also explores the semiotics of premature burial, linking the proclamations of feminism's death to ongoing efforts to undermine feminist struggles for social justice.

Mechanics of Death

The Obituary

In November 1976 *Harpers* published as its cover story "Requiem for the Women's Movement" (Geng 1976), the first of many media pronouncements that second-wave feminism was dead.[2] Nothing particular happened in November 1976 to signal the death of feminism—no cataclysmic event, no tragic accident, no death thrall, no bedside drama—simply a messenger with the news. As in the conventions of Greek tragedy in classical antiquity, the death of feminism "comes to us through words. Nothing is seen by the audience in the first instance. Everything starts by being spoken, by being heard, by being imagined" (Loraux 1987, vii).

The *Harpers* essay by Veronica Geng fixed a frame for ensuing obituaries of feminism, chronicling the rise of the movement, tracing the emergence of debilitating disease, assuring the reader that there was no foul play, no external intervention, simply death by natural causes, or perhaps self-inflicted wounds. According to Geng's account the causes of death were numerous and varied. The women's movement had lost its bearings, cut itself off from American women, and abandoned its original purpose: consciousness raising, confrontational politics, and organizing women in accordance with "the belief that change could be had if people got together and declared they wanted it" (Geng 1976, 52). Rather than acting in concert to produce social change, the feminist movement factionalized, devolving into "highly specialized individuals and cliques, each cultivating its arcane little patch of ground in such depth as to mystify and rebuff any interested generalists who wander by in search of a way to aid the larger goals of the women's liberation" (Geng 1976, 53). Factionalism gave way to internecine warfare. The National Organization for Women (NOW) faction became obsessed with image making, generating claims about a unified women's movement even as it purged lesbians and radicals whose very existence seemed incompatible with the politics of respectability that NOW embraced. In Geng's view, the radicals self-destructed by advocating "pseudolesbian separatism, not only from men but from 'patriarchal culture'—thus abandoning most of the ground on which male power can be fought. They congealed the rush of ideas and emotional truth that had given life to their organizations" (Geng 1976, 55). The realist clique that emerged within Democratic and Republican party politics initially demanded equal representation in party forums, including the national conventions, but gradually compromised itself out of existence, toning down its demands on the grounds of political realism until it no longer bore any recognizable relation to feminism, while the social justice clique squandered its energy on too broad an array of causes (racism, discrimination against gays and lesbians, poverty, war, imperialism), leaving them without the time, strength, or concentrated resources to press for "feminist self-interest" (Geng, 1976, 64).

Geng's postmortem offers a narrative of dissolution that may seem markedly familiar perhaps because it has been repeated so often. (For the most recent replay, see Hymowitz 2002.) In these secondhand accounts we are invited not only to imagine feminism dead but to understand that its demise was caused by processes internal to feminism. Colloquialisms used to describe the death of feminism are wholly self-referential invoking metaphors of suicide ("died by its own hand") or old age ("its time was simply up"). Perhaps what is most interesting in Geng's dirge is the invocation of an idealized univocal feminism fostering an abstract women's emancipation even as it denies legitimacy to multivocal feminisms and castigates concrete strategies to foster social change. What social scientists characterize as division of labor and specialization essential to the long-term growth of organizations, Geng depicts as fragmentation and dissolution. What many feminists perceive as a hard-learned lesson (that decentering white, middle-class Western women, acknowledging the multiple voices within the movement, supporting the priorities of women of color and women of the global South, and fighting racism, homophobia, heteronormativity, and cultural imperialism were crucial to the cultivation of an inclusive international feminism), Geng constructs as a lethal dose of difference. This familiar frame for the demise of feminism, then, carries a clear moral. Modes of feminist activism that challenge boundaries fixed by the dominant culture in the United States must be banished from the land of the living.

Evolutionary Extinction

Some accounts of feminism's passing suggest vague evolutionary processes through which feminism has been transformed into some more advanced stage of existence. In the words of Ann Brooks (1997, 1), "postfeminism" is the "expression of a stage in the constant evolutionary movement of feminism."[3] But as the problematic history of social Darwinism and sociobiology make clear, evolutionary metaphors of natural selection and the survival of the fittest are seldom feminist friendly.

While the exact nature of postfeminism has been a subject of considerable controversy, some applications of the term are consistent with a strong conviction that feminism has become or soon will be extinct. In 1988 Nicholas Davidson hailed the advent of postfeminism as a "new consensus on gender," which involved a reclaiming of traditional masculinity and femininity, a retreat from the politicization of personal life, the retrieval and preservation of "women's rights as homemakers," and the restoration of the male breadwinner model of the family (Davidson 1988, 335–340). According to Davidson (1988, 336), the postfeminist era emerges as a revolt against feminists "as they struggle to prop up the dead hand of the past." Indeed, in Davidson's view, postfeminism involves a broad coalition that unifies diverse groups:

> The Postfeminist Era will also involve millions of young single women, in revolt against the unisexist expectations they encounter. But unlike the Feminist Era, it will involve the cooperative participation of all social groups. Indeed it is hard to think of a single major group whose interests do not oppose it to the feminist orthodoxy: feminine women demeaned by the feminist devaluation of the feminine; ambitious women hampered by the feminist politicization of personal achievement; all men; children—in sum, the vast majority of people; so that the early demise of the feminist perspective as a significant social force begins to seem not just possible but likely.[4] (Davidson 1988, 337)

Although his "new consensus" appears to be indistinguishable from appeals to return to traditional family values circulating in Christian fundamentalist circles, Davidson insists that

> American women are not regressing back from feminism but progressing beyond it. They are moving beyond feminism to a world in which their hopes, fears, desires, and instincts are no longer distrusted or rejected as the destructive shreds of "conditioning" but welcomed and accepted as the positive, life-giving, inherent womanly attributes which they are. (Davidson 1988, 339–340)

In contrast to Davidson's invocation of natural instincts and traditional gender relations as the ground of postfeminism, in *Feminism without Women*, Tania Modleski (1991) traces the emergence of postfeminism to the works of a variety of self-proclaimed (often male) feminists in acade-

154

mia. While appropriating terms of feminist analysis, these scholars "negate the critiques and undermine the goals of feminism—in effect delivering us back to a pre-feminist world" (Modleski 1991, 3). Under the guise of studying gender relations, these academics subtly return men to the center of analysis and suggest that women are subjects of scholarly interest only in relation to men. Within such discourses, lesbians and gay men are once again rendered invisible, as heterosexist presuppositions structure the frames of inquiry. In addition, these texts tacitly invoke liberal conceptions of politics, which posit equality before the law as the limit of the feminist project, thereby eliding questions of power asymmetry that permeate social relations. Dubbing these academics "gynocidal feminists," Modleski argues that they use feminism as a "conduit to the more comprehensive field of gender studies [which is] no longer judged . . . as it ought to be, according to the contributions it can make to the feminist project and the aid it can give us in illuminating the causes, effects, scope, and limits of male dominance" (1991, 5). According to Modleski, then, postfeminism involves a mode of intellectual analysis or critique that subverts feminism and as such should be understood as decidedly antifeminist. Despite the co-optation of feminist terms, Modleski suggests that this mode of academic analysis has profoundly conservative implications.

Shifting focus from academia to modes of consciousness, Judith Stacey (1992, 322) characterizes postfeminism as the "simultaneous incorporation, revision, and depoliticization of many of the central goals of second-wave feminism." Stacey describes postfeminism as "the consciousness and strategies increasing numbers of women have developed in response to the new difficulties and opportunities of postindustrial society" (1992, 323). Stacey agrees with Davidson that postfeminism has a mass base, particularly among women, but she argues that the factors contributing to the growth of postfeminism are quite distinct from antifeminism, sexism, and conservatism. Stacey advances a materialist analysis that emphasizes systemic changes introduced by "postindustrial family and work life" (1992, 323). Over the past thirty-five years as the real value of wages has fallen, more and more women have entered the labor force. Divorce rates have risen, as have the numbers of out-of-wedlock births, generating increasing numbers of single women heads of household. These changing material relations, far more than feminist demands for equality, have transformed the conditions of women's lives, leading many women to seek an ideology that can help them cope. Stacey construes postfeminism as just such a coping mechanism, one that depoliticizes feminism, removing its public agenda and situating it squarely within the home. According to Stacey, postfeminist women long for an egalitarian home life in which communicative and supportive men willingly assume their fair share of housework and child rearing.

Frances Mascia-Lees and Patricia Sharp (2000) shift the site of postfeminism from the consciousness and desires of contemporary women to the terrain of contemporary culture. They deploy postfeminism to describe our current cultural context, "a context in which the feminism of the 1970s is problematized, splintered, considered suspect" (Mascia-Lees and Sharpe 2000, 3). According to Mascia-Lees and Sharpe, dynamics within feminism, women's studies, postmodern discourses, and popular culture have contributed to postfeminism. As feminism empowered more and different women to give voice to their concerns, "feminism lost its separate, if illusory, singular identity" (Mascia-Lees and Sharpe 2000, 5). As feminisms proliferated and feminists began to occupy increasingly diverse and contradictory sites, it was no longer possible to identify any particular stance as feminist. Indeed, according to Mascia-Lees and Sharpe (2000, 3), "it is no longer easy, fun, empowering, or even possible to take a feminist position." As women's studies scholars became increasingly absorbed in internal debates cut off from feminist mobilizations outside the academy, feminist theory began to emphasize the paradoxical nature of the feminist endeavor. In the words of Joanne Frye (1987, 2), "Feminism aims for individual freedoms by mobilizing sex solidarity. Feminism acknowledges diversity among women while positing that women recognize their unity. Feminism requires gender consciousness for its basis yet it calls for the elimination of prescribed gender roles." With "only paradoxes to offer" (Scott 1996), feminism seemed to hold little of interest for a public clamoring for the innovative and exciting. As postmodernist discourses gained ground in the academy, contestations over conceptions of identities and differences "radically called into question the authority to speak. . . . [Thus] in the current courtroom of ideas, no one has clear standing to make a claim" (Mascia-Lees and Sharpe 2000, 9). Further complicating postmodernism's synthesizing allegory of fragmentation and helplessness, according to Mascia-Lees and Sharpe (2000, 93), is the prevalence of the self-help ideology in popular culture, which collapses the political into the therapeutic. Those feminists who try to swim against the postmodern tide, pressing their critiques of male power, are "almost drowned out by the ever proliferating discourse of self-help" (Mascia-Lees and Sharpe 2000, 95). Within the frame advanced by the men's movement, what feminists denounce as male domination is redescribed as "bad behavior," which is itself the result of a male's victimization as a defenseless child. Feminist prescriptions to restructure public and private domains are thus supplanted by therapeutic interventions designed to reclaim and treat the hapless child within. Intellectually untenable, politically unfeasible, therapeutically outmatched, feminism languishes. Any misguided attempt to recuperate feminism must be recognized as "nostalgic and naïve, a remnant of a yearning for a lost Eden" (Mascia-Lees and Sharpe 2000, 59).

Whether located in putative popular revolts against feminism, academic criticism, women's consciousness in postindustrial society, or contemporary culture, postfeminism involves a mapping of social space that renders feminism homeless and groundless. The boundaries of the viable are redrawn to exclude any feminist presence. Within the narrative frame of evolutionary extinction, postfeminism is a marker of time as well as space, implying a temporal sequence in which feminism has been transcended, occluded, overcome. Invocations of postfeminism, then, could be read as banishments, commanding us to imagine gender relations, higher education, individual psyches, and contemporary culture at large as spatial and temporal zones in which feminism has been eclipsed. Much like the obituaries in the popular media, assertions about postfeminism proclaim that feminism is gone, departed, dead.

Perhaps it is no accident that feminism's death notice was first published in the United States, a liberal democracy, which professes to hold equality among its most cherished ideals. For the purported death of feminism affirms the self-evidence of the truths proclaimed by the founders of the American republic in the Declaration of Independence (1776), "that all *men* are created equal and . . . endowed by their creator with unalienable rights" (emphasis added). Now, as then, the ideal exists at great remove from the lived experiences of women and people of color. Yet when feminists try to realize the promise of equality, the project is deemed nonviable. The live burial of feminism serves at once to "de-realize" women's aspirations to equality and to disempower women, while affirming the wisdom of the status quo. Many who construct feminism temporally as a transitional moment between a prefeminist and a postfeminist world instrumentalize the feminist project, casting it as a failed experiment in service to a larger truth: the truth of women's "natural role," the truth of "traditional masculinity and femininity." Feminism's function, then, is to demonstrate the impossibility of meaningful equality between men and women, a function served by the advent of postfeminism. In this sense the invitation to imagine feminism dead is an invitation to repudiate sexual equality and gender justice, to accept asymmetrical power relations between men and women as the natural order of things, to accept an unbridgeable gap between our putative ideals and lived reality.

The emergence of feminism as a global phenomenon coincided with the end of the Cold War and the resurgence of capitalism under the sign of globalization. At the same time that the West was declaring victory over the Soviet system and equating democratization with neoliberal economic reforms and liberal democratic political reforms, feminists were documenting pervasive and growing inequality within capitalist states and between the North and South. The feminization of poverty, which feminists have demonstrated to be a growing global phenomenon, bears potent witness to the limitations of neoliberal prescriptions for sustainable development. The vibrant activism of feminists in the global South against structural adjustment policies and around the politics of subsistence makes a mockery of claims that capitalism remedies poverty. The ongoing struggle of feminists for gender balance in governance and for women's equal participation in public and private decision making constitutes a formidable challenge to liberal democratic regimes in which women are woefully underrepresented, holding less than 20 percent of the seats in national decision-making bodies. In their various manifestations, feminist mobilizations seek to subvert the dominant political and economic systems.

Recurrent assertions of feminism's death remove feminist activism from the sensory perception of the living. Subtly transforming the active into the inert in the public mind, proclamations of feminism's death erase the activism of millions of women around the globe who are currently struggling for social justice. That erasure contains any threat that feminist activism poses to the prevailing system even as it helps sustain a myth of universal support for the neoliberal agenda. It underscores the hegemonic notion that the American way is the best way for the world. It relegates to the silence of the grave the voices of those who oppose U.S. efforts to remake the world in its own image. Removal of global feminism from the consciousness of the living by death proclamation fosters social amnesia, eliminating the threat to the values of the dominant regime with the mere application of a balm of forgetfulness.

In declaring themselves women identified, in crafting modes of gender analysis that place women at the center, in developing agendas for political action according to their context-specific articulations of women's needs and interests, in insisting that women's subordination is an intolerable injustice, feminists promote numerous causes deemed illegitimate by male-dominant national and international regimes. The premature burial of contemporary feminism might then be read as a particularly heinous fate, designed to inflict maximum pain on women who seek to enact their freedom. Burial is the ultimate privatization for feminist political strategies intended to make public hitherto private experiences of domesticity, intimacy, sexuality, consciousness. Feminism's live burial then coincides nicely with neoliberalism's curtailment of the political agenda, constricting public spaces, restoring the veil of privacy. In limiting feminists' sphere of action as well as public understanding of the politically actionable, neoliberalism's live immurement of feminism regenders feminists as well as feminist projects, returning feminists to a coerced inertia while reasserting the sanctity of private relations beyond public scrutiny or political action.

The recurrent obituaries of feminist activism can also be interpreted as a redrawing of community boundaries designed to accomplish far more than the exile of feminism, designed, in fact, to annihilate it. Distanciation is a rhetorical device designed to separate an "us" from a "them." For mortals there is no greater distance than between the living and the dead. To declare feminism dead, then, is to characterize autonomous women's activism as altogether foreign to the living, to depict it as a mode of existence so alien that it cannot be tolerated within "our" communities. By ritually reinscribing the death of feminism with each invocation of postfeminism, those who would expel feminism from the contemporary world inflict damage while masking their own culpability. Jean-François Lyotard (1990, 5) has defined damage as a wrong accompanied by the loss of means to prove the injury. The premature burial of feminism constitutes just such damage. With no corpse, no proof of demise, just vague hints of self-inflicted wounds and natural causes, feminism's death by report erases the social justice activism of women around the globe while covering the traces of the erasure. Proclamations of feminism's death invite the public to participate in this damage: to ritually bury those whose cause is race/gender/economic justice while placing injustice beyond remedy. Those who would expunge feminist activism from public perception and memory seek to construct fictive versions of the present and past that will become embedded in culture as shared memory. In so doing, they also shape the future by producing new generations who assent to these cultural fictions.

War Logics: Neoliberalism and Feminization

While the primary focus of globalization scholars remains the interrelated economic, political, cultural, technological, and ideological transformations that are reshaping the contemporary world, the specter of war continues to haunt the global community. Extrapolating from an empirical claim that democracies do not go to war against each other, proponents of globalization optimistically predict the gradual elimination of war as marketization produces democratization in nations around the globe. Yet these confident forecasts coexist uneasily with increasing national preoccupations with security, as securitization becomes the new vernacular of liberal democratic and social democratic states (Waever, Buzan, Kelstrup, and

Lemaitre 1993; Chang 2002). Rather than treating the expansion of the national security state as an aberration stemming from the trauma of the September 11 attacks upon the World Trade Center and the Pentagon, some scholars have begun to explore the intricate connections between the proliferation of security discourses and transformations in international laws governing military engagement as one more manifestation of "Empire" (Enloe 2004; Hardt and Negri 2004). As a blanket prohibition of military aggression has given way to toleration of military intervention for humanitarian purposes, the once inviolable boundaries of the nation-state have become permeable to transnational policing and international peacekeeping forces. Tallying some "two thousand sustained armed conflicts on the face of the earth at the beginning of the new millennium," Hardt and Negri (2004, 31) suggest that far from being an aberration, war has become the "general condition" of the world in the twenty-first century. Because lethal violence is present as a "constant potentiality," war

> becomes the general matrix for all relations of power and techniques of domination, whether or not bloodshed is involved. War has become a regime of biopower, that is, a form of rule aimed not only at controlling the population but producing and reproducing all aspects of social life. This war brings death but also, paradoxically, must produce life. (Hardt and Negri 2004, 13)

Chapter 2 identifies several historical moments when war seriously derailed transnational feminist activism. How is the heightened militarism of the twenty-first century affecting feminist projects? If the strategic deployment of lethal force is also a mode of production and reproduction, then what discursive and material regimes are being created, nurtured, and sustained by war? And which are being expunged from the historical record by the preemptive military operations launched by the George W. Bush administration?

Any thorough assessment of the future of feminism must consider discursive changes aided and abetted by two Bush wars: the war against terror/terrorism, a war that is not between states, but pits a coalition of Western military forces operating under executive order against a nonstate actor, the Al Qaeda network, which moves clandestinely within and across national boundaries of some sixty states; and the equally unconventional war against Iraq, in which the United States broke with international law and its own conventions for the deployment of military force and unilaterally launched a preemptive war against the regime of Saddam Hussein, which quickly morphed into an exercise in occupation/peacekeeping/nation building/insurrection quelling.

To suggest that war creates as well as destroys is not to claim that it creates ex nihilo. On the contrary, in the discursive realm as in so many others, production and reproduction begin with the materials at hand, crafting new forms from contending possibilities, shoring up certain discursive formations while undercutting others. Thus to investigate how the Bush wars are shaping the dominant discursive regime, the next two sections of this chapter explore their effects in relation to the alternative visions of the future crafted by neoliberal globalism and global feminism. Although unevenly matched in every conceivable way, global feminism and neoliberal globalism have vied for popular allegiance and policy influence for more than thirty-five years. One consequence of current war making is the further occlusion of the feminist alternative. The space of social justice carved out in the public imagination by feminist activism, which was already under threat from repeated proclamations of feminism's death, becomes occupied territory, taken over by war logics that reinscribe traditional gender symbolisms to naturalize hierarchical relations and legitimate racist, neocolonial interventions.

War and the Negative Logic of Feminization

Since September 11, 2001, there has been a profound shift in the discursive regime of the Anglo-American world. Gender symbolism is invoked in very old and familiar ways, anathema to feminist values and objectives. Discourses of women fighting for rights have been supplanted by discussions of feminizing processes that trade on a notion of the feminine as weak, vulnerable, and at risk, in need of rescue and protection. As Ann Orford (2005) has pointed out, the rhetoric of rescue cries out for "muscular interventions." Thus it is little surprise that multiple modes of heroic masculinity have been resurrected. Whether in New York City or at the Pentagon, in Afghanistan or Iraq, in Madrid or London, working-class blokes rise to the challenge: Firefighters, police, soldiers, security personnel respond to the call to protect and defend; and the media celebrates their valor, front page above the fold in the print media, 24/7 on the airwaves.

Helen Kinsella (2005) has suggested that such gendered appeals to male protectors do far more than mobilize young men willing to come to the aid of women in distress. The mythos of the male protector, defender of home and hearth, sustains the psyches of men who are compelled by their states to kill. Masking the harm that war does to women, warriors, and other living things, the mythos of the male protector affords soldiers an uplifting balm that instrumentalizes wartime atrocities, linking the abyss of death and destruction to the demands of civilization, and to chivalrous codes of conduct, which undergird the rightness of their cause. Within this mythic frame, the definition of a war of self-defense can subtly expand to encompass preemptive military action, which "defends" against hypothetical future attacks.

In the immediate aftermath of September 11, gendered images and narratives migrated from embodied subjects to discursive constructions of the nation. The United States was stripped of its sense of invulnerability. The impregnable fortress was breached. America joined the ranks of the violated, its borders penetrated by foreign terrorists. Security forces were mobilized and the military put on alert to prevent the further feminization of the United States. Speaking for and to a grieving nation, the president promised retaliation in a place and at a time of his choosing. Echoing honor codes with ancient roots, the president characterized deployment of American military might as the appropriate means to redress the violation. An assertion of force would redress the nation's feminization. Demonstrating the depths of our potency, a show of American military might would performatively restore American virility.

In the months that elapsed between the terrorist attacks and the U.S. retaliation, perhaps because questions were raised concerning the efficacy of a violent response and the ethical propriety of punishing others for a crime they had not committed, and for which the terrorists had already paid with their lives, the president developed a second rationale for the deployment of the "coalition of the willing" in Afghanistan: to save Afghani women from the Taliban. In so doing, he not only invoked the mythos of the male protector, but he also embraced the gendered logic of neocolonialism, which Gayatri Spivak (1985) has documented time and again: Heroic white men set out to "rescue" brown women from "barbaric" brown men. At the very moment that Afghani spokeswomen argued forcefully against invasion, cataloging the disproportionate harms that would befall women and children by additional recourse to military force, the Bush administration feminized them, rejecting their articulate assessment of their own situation and subjecting them to a form of paternalist intervention premised on the assumption that the coalition of Western forces knew what was good for Afghani women better than they knew themselves.

Iris Young (2003) has suggested that the gendered logic of the national security state feminizes the American citizenry. Recirculating the patriarchal rationale first vindicated by Thomas Hobbes, which posits threat and fear as endemic and the need for protection as dire, the national security state promises protection of the "homeland." Within this discursive frame, the home is reterritorialized. Lifted from the private sphere and given geographic purchase, the home qua women's domain is refigured as homeland with borders in need of policing. The private becomes public, but not in the democratic sense envisioned by feminist campaigns for the "personal as political." At one level of public (mis)appropriations of the private, thousands of vigilantes converge on ranches spanning the Mexican border, pledging their guns and their lives to protect the United States from the "security threats" lurking south of the border. At a second level, the state withdraws constitutional protections of the private sphere. The Patriot Act authorizes securitization measures that suspend the right of habeas corpus, as well as Fourth Amendment guarantees against unwarranted searches and seizures. According to the logic of the national security state, the provision of protection necessitates critical trade-offs: Civil liberties are eroded; racial and ethnic profiling are legitimated; surveillance is heightened; detention absent due process of law is routinized; foreign nationals passing through American airports are "rendered" to Egypt, Syria, Poland, or Romania for torture and confinement; and the citizenry is reduced to a subordinate position of dependence and obedience. Rather than enacting their democratic rights through protests against such constitutional violations, citizens of the national security state are expected to be grateful for the protection provided. Some preliminary evidence suggests that this fear-induced feminization of the citizenry is generating the desired effects. Indeed, so grateful are the docile citizens to the valor of their self-sacrificing protectors that they willingly overlook rape within the military and against women in occupied areas and exponential increases in domestic violence on military bases by soldiers returning from war zones. Inured to the demands of homeland security, the feminized citizenry grow increasingly insensitive to heightened control tactics that secure gendered subordination.

But citizens at home are not the only ones who experience feminization at the hands of the national security state. Paradoxically, feminization is part of the basic training of soldiers who must be transformed into a cohesive fighting force. Judith Stiehm (2005; see also Burke 2004) suggests that tactics of feminization, such as insulting and humiliating recruits by calling them "girls," has been a standard practice in basic training as the military simultaneously seek to break down individuality and produce order-obeying soldiers, while turning boys into men. Beyond basic training, the logic of feminization also structures military interrogation techniques. Tim Kaufman-Osborn (2005, 5) has pointed out that the CIA's *Counterintelligence Interrogation Manual* endorses "scripted practices of subordination" with marked gendered associations as strategies to produce helplessness, dependence, and compliance among "resistant sources." Depicting feminization as a "strategy of power deployed by masculinized nationalism,"

Kaufman-Osborne suggests that the modes of torture enacted at Abu Ghraib and Guantánamo and in Afghanistan bear striking similarities to the logic of feminization incorporated in established military interrogation practices.

Long ago, Edward Said (1978) pointed out that orientalism has pronounced gendering effects. Under the orientalist spell, Westerners construe the Middle East and the Far East as an eroticized, feminized Other and act in accordance with that racist construction. U.S. military personnel serving in Iraq have made manifest the behavioral implications of the orientalist gaze. Perhaps no image captures orientalism's feminizing effects more powerfully than the snapshots from Abu Ghraib, in which American soldiers coerce Iraqi detainees to feign homosexual relations. As Jonathan Goldberg (1992) has demonstrated, enacting torture in the form of sexual subordination in general, and allegations of sodomy in particular, is part of the arsenal of violent colonization. During the European conquest of the Americas the conquistadors repeatedly sent home reports that the indigenous peoples "were all sodomites." In Goldberg's view, the colonizers used the accusation of sodomy to rationalize their slaughter of the accused. Applying a particular calculus of biblical culpability, the colonizers could reckon that those who have "perverted nature" "deserve" to be exterminated. The coerced simulation of sodomy among imprisoned Iraqis resonates the same self-vindicating rationale. By forcing prisoners to assume formations that represent homosexual acts, American soldiers—male and female—reap the surge of superiority and the psychic distance that enables them to perform the daily tasks of humiliating and torturing human beings under the ruse that such treatment is warranted. By circulating the images among troops, these perverse colonizing effects are generalized. The construction of the Iraqis as feminized men who enjoy penetration legitimates the U.S. presence, as the Christian civilizing mission once again transforms unlawful invasion into righteous occupation.

Underlying the logic of feminization in each of these instances is a vindictive construction of femininity. Those who are discursively produced as "feminine" are weak, violated, silenced, docile, obedient, humiliated, and craven. The solution to their existential situation is invariably a masculine assertion of power for which the appropriate feminine response is gratitude. This is the discursive gender regime produced and reproduced by the Bush war machine.

Within this discursive formation, feminizing processes simultaneously produce and justify profound inequalities. Trading on forms of gender symbolism that naturalize hierarchies of dominance and subordination, the gendered discourses of war make scenarios of rescue, retaliation, and retribution appear matters of necessity. Fear and angst are cultivated to vindicate patriarchal values. Long-discredited norms of secrecy and paternalism are proffered as sound public policy within a security state in which access to intelligence is restricted, circulating only on a need to know basis. Struggles for sexual equality, for racial and gender justice, for fair and open democratic practices, seem hopelessly naïve within the realpolitik of a state conducting a war against terror.

Calculating the Costs of the New Discursive Regime

The 2004 presidential election in the United States manifested the far from subtle effects of the shift in discursive regime. Myths of heroic men who serve, protect, and defend dominated campaign discourses. Military valor became the mark of character and leadership, as principled critics of war and militarization were ridiculed as "girlie men." Simulations of valor were sufficient to trump actual war records as Bush campaign ads celebrated the commander-in-chief in "top-gun" attire, while Swift Boat Veterans for Truth indulged in levels of historical revisionism only dreamt of by Stalin's propaganda machine. The decorum of political wives and daughters supplanted any discussion of women as running mates, as President Bush and Vice-President Cheney entertained their hawkish following with jibes that vice-presidential contender John Edwards was just "a pretty face" (Eisenstein 2004b).

Although the United States lags behind fifty-seven nations in proportion of women in elected offices,[5] concern for women's political representation receded from the public political imagination at the very moment that women were losing ground in state legislatures. In the first study of the effects of the war on terrorism on voter attitudes, Jennifer Lawless (2004) found that the sustained gender-stereotyping in the post–September 11 era was providing clear electoral benefits for men.

> Citizens prefer men's leadership traits and characteristics, deem men more competent at legislating around issues of national security and military crises, and contend that men are superior to women at addressing new obstacles generated by the events of September 11, 2001. As a result of this stereotyping, levels of willingness to support a qualified woman presidential candidate are lower than they have been in decades. (Lawless 2004, 480)

As we see in chapter 2, war has demobilized feminism on more than one occasion. World War I, for example, slowed the momentum of a bourgeoning international feminist movement and triggered an impressive counteroffensive by conservative forces to undermine and erase feminist transformative efforts. As women were forced out of the lucrative jobs to which they had been recruited as part of the war effort, pronatalist legislation was passed to enlist women in a new effort to fight the depopulation caused by war. Family allowances and mothers' pensions were introduced in a number of European states as an incentive for women to bear more children. Abortion and birth control were criminalized to restrict the options for those uninspired by the pronatalist incentives. Similarly, World War II halted virtually all the transnational feminist activity that had been re-created in the interwar years. And within the nations at war, feminist claims for social justice were made to seem petty and selfish, as women were once again urged to sacrifice for the sake of their nations and for their men at war.

If the form of life being created and nurtured by the Bush wars is governed by a negative logic of feminization, at odds with and inherently destructive of feminism, the collateral damage of this war making involves more than the 27,477 to 30,989 civilian and 2,357 combatant deaths (U.S. and allies) currently estimated in the Iraq body count. Feminist struggles against violence, militarization, and war—and feminist activism itself—are at risk. Despite feminism's vibrant presence around the globe, the new discursive regime would "disappear" feminism and replace it with the realpolitik of evangelical masculinity, crusading against a feminized perversity of its own making, to protect paternalism at home and abroad.

Feminist Futures

The paternalist future envisioned and the feminist future put at risk in the Bush wars place the challenges confronting contemporary transnational feminist activism in stark relief. Despite invocations of freedom and democracy, the neoliberal agenda of the Bush administration is permeated by patriarchal policies that subordinate women to men, restrict women's reproductive freedom, undermine their bodily integrity, and preclude their achievement of meaningful equality. Consider, for example, the gulf between U.S. support for UN Security Council Resolution 1325, which requires that women and women's concerns play an integral role in every new security institution and in every decision-making stage in peacekeeping and national reconstruction in the aftermath of armed conflict, and the practices of the United States in the national reconstruction of Afghanistan and Iraq. Rather than using its power to promote equitable inclusion of women in transitional governments and commissions empowered to draft new constitutions, the United States has forged alliances with traditional male elites. In 2003 the Afghanistan constitution-drafting commission included twenty-eight men and seven women (Enloe 2004, 287). Three women were appointed to the twenty-five-member Iraqi Governing Council (one of whom, Alkila al-Hashimi, was assassinated on September 20, 2003). None of the women appointed to the Iraqi Governing Council had "access to the four bargaining chips crucial to effective political influence. . . . Each entered the Governing Council without her own political party, militia, treasury, and without direct lines of communication to Washington" (Enloe 2004, 293). Despite major mobilization of women in Iraq to press for the establishment of a gender quota in the new system of governance, when the twenty-five-member committee was appointed to draft the constitution, all were men.

Despite such pronounced barriers to their participation, women in Afghanistan and Iraq have not resigned themselves to perpetual exclusion. On the contrary, the Afghan Women Lawyers Association based in Kabul mobilized to monitor the deliberations of the commission drafting the constitution and to lobby them for equitable provisions for women citizens. Indeed, after organizing a series of hearings on systemic violations of women's human rights, the Women Lawyers Association drafted proposed constitutional provisions to promote women's equality. To ensure Afghani women's participation in public life as fully autonomous and effective citizens, they recommended the following:

> (1) Mandatory education for girls through secondary school, (2) guaranteed freedom of speech for women, (3) insurance that every woman would be free to cast her own ballot and to run for elected office, (4) insurance that women would have equal representation with men in the new government's legislature, (5) the appointment of an equal number of women and men to judgeships, (6) entitlement of women to pay rates equal to those of men, (7) guarantee that women would have the right to exert control over their own finances and to inherit property, (8) permission for women to bring criminal charges against men for domestic violence and sexual harassment, whether those violations occurred in a public place or at home, (9) a ban on the common practice of family members handing over girls and women to another family as compensation for crimes committed by the former against the latter, (10) raising the legal age of marriage from sixteen to eighteen years, (11) the right of women to marry and divorce "in accordance with Islam," and (12) a reduction of the amount of time that women would have to wait to remarry if their husbands abandoned them or disappeared. (Enloe 2004, 288)

This lobbying effort produced a partial victory. The Afghan constitution includes a provision guaranteeing the equality of men and women—a provision that coexists in tension with another constitutional provision mandating that all laws be "informed by the principles of Islam," which conservatives claim precludes gender equality (Enloe 2004, 289).

In Iraq, as in Afghanistan, women have mobilized, reinvigorating long-standing organizations such as the Iraqi Women's League, and creating new organizations, such as the Organization of Women's Freedom in Iraq (OWFI), to protest the American occupation, to demonstrate against growing violence against women, to protest the remasculinization of Iraqi politics and public life, and to demand equal constitutional and political rights (Ferguson 2005).

The courageous struggle for inclusion, empowerment, and justice that Afghani and Iraqi women are waging at considerable personal cost is emblematic of feminist struggles that continue all around the globe. Despite the fact that "international and regional organizations such as the UN, the EU, the Southern African Development Community, the Summit of the Americas, and the Association of Southeast Asian Nations, have declared that growth in women's leadership contributes to democratic consolidation and economic and social progress" (Htun 2004, 444), the obstacles to success that national and transnational feminist activists confront are monumental. Within the current global system, most governments are unwilling or unable to seek the fundamental transformation of existing economic and political systems necessary to improve women's lives (Stienstra 1994, 141). Increasing recognition of women as actors at the international level has not been accompanied by concomitant change in numbers of women participating in decision making within national and international elites. Despite growing attention to women's issues at the global level, gender inequalities within and across nations, and inequalities among women within and across nations, are greater now than in 1970.[6] Despite arduous efforts to transform the discursive politics of human rights, feminist strategies that foreground equality and rights tend to be curtailed by neoliberal presumptions, which limit their transformative agenda to the sphere of civil and political rights. Moreover, difference discourses are often co-opted by conservative forces and tied to long-standing gender stereotypes that reinscribe women's double duty and triple shifts, while perpetuating women's marginal status.

In the face of such momentous obstacles, twenty-first-century transnational feminist activists, like their forebears in the nineteenth and twentieth centuries, remain resolute. Keenly aware of the challenges they face, and chafing against the limits of these constraints, feminist activists continue to push the boundaries of the possible, making some gains against the odds. Fueled by their commitment to social justice and buoyed by solidarity generated through collective struggle against injustice, feminist activists continue their transformative efforts.

In contrast to pessimists who advocate resignation to the growing inequities of globalization on the grounds that there is no alternative (Giddens 1998), transnational feminist activists continue to craft alternative possibilities. In the words of veteran transnational feminist activist and cofounder of DAWN, Peggy Antrobus,

> Feminism offers the only politics that can transform the world into a more human place and deal with global issues like equality, development, peace, because it asks the right questions about power, about links between personal and political and because it cuts through race and class. Feminism implies consciousness of all the sources of oppression: race, class, gender, homophobia, and it resists them all. Feminism is a call to action. (Cited in Moghadam 2005, 88)

In contrast to optimists who dream of a revolution miraculously transforming all dimensions of social life, feminist activists construe their transformative praxis more along the lines of a slow boring of hard boards. Mobilizing in response to specific problems, crafting policies to mitigate pressing abuses, cracking open closed spaces to inject feminist content, envisioning and voicing concrete alternatives, transnational feminist activists practice a diplomacy from below when all other options remain closed to them. Starting from the terms dictated by global capitalism and male-dominant politics, they seek to transform the parameters of debate and the processes by which such parameters are set.

The amendments proposed by the Women's Caucus to the Copenhagen Declaration and Program of Action (1995) provide a powerful example of this engaged transnational feminist praxis, an example that maps the contours of an alternative to the global future prized by neoliberalism. The World Summit for Social Development, which took place in Copenhagen in March 1995, attracted the largest number of world leaders to date to deliberate on the issue of sustainable development. The Copenhagen Declaration pledged to make the conquest of poverty, the goal of full employment, and the fostering of social integration the overriding objectives of development. Despite these worthy objectives, the strategies endorsed in the Program of Action were largely neoliberal. Noting that neoliberalism was increasing rather than decreasing global poverty, transnational feminist activists proposed critical changes to neoliberal policy directions, which would enable world leaders to achieve the goals they had agreed upon in principle.

The proposed Women's Caucus Amendments were multiple and concrete. They urged that the program of action shift emphasis away from "promoting dynamic, open free markets" to an emphasis on "regulating markets in the public interest with a view to reducing inequality, preventing instability, expanding employment, and establishing a socially acceptable minimum wage" (Petchesky 2003, 55). They urged that international trade equity be established though effective regulation of the trade and investment activities of transnational corporations. They recommended the creation of "a global fund for human security," funded by a tax on global finance, which could compensate those subjected to social insecurity caused by the instability and recurrent crises of the international market. They endorsed the creation of an enforceable global Code of Conduct for transnational corporations, including provisions guaranteeing labor rights, safe working conditions, and community and environmental protection clauses. They proposed a cap of 1 percent GDP on military spending; and until that cap became effective, annual reductions in military spending equivalent to 5 percent of GDP. The funds reclaimed from military uses should be dedicated to programs designed to meet pressing social needs. In keeping with existing international agreements, they recommended that gender equality be fully integrated into all relevant policy areas and budgetary decisions, and that additional resources be devoted to women's empowerment in all spheres of social life. Finally, the Women's Caucus identified new mechanisms to generate financial resources to promote sustainable social and economic development, such as taxes on resource use and the commodification of common resources, taxes to discourage the production of toxic products, and taxes on international financial speculative transactions (Petchesky 2003, 55–56).

Generating a vision of an alternative, more equitable future—albeit one that continues to operate within the confines of global capitalism—remains at great remove from the realization of that vision. As noted in chapter 4, the Millennium Objectives devised by the UN in collaboration with the major international financial institutions fall far short of the recommendations by the Women's Caucus. Recognizing the gulf between rhetorical commitments to and achievable policies for gender and racial equality, social justice, and sustainable development, transnational feminist activists continue to produce trenchant critiques of the defects of national and international initiatives. At the Beijing +5 (2000) and Beijing +10 (2005) meetings at the UN, feminist activists produced detailed reports on every nation in the world, documenting their failure to fulfill their constitutional commitments and their commitments under international treaties to racial and gender equality. These documents are rich in policy proposals designed to address the specific needs of women in particular nations.

Despite pervasive efforts to bury feminism alive, prevailing global economic and political conditions committed to the perpetuation of male dominance, and the brutal enactment of war logics designed to feminize women, men, citizens, and certain states, feminist activists remain undeterred in their transformative projects. Echoing the words of freedom fighters in the African National Congress, Angola, Mozambique, and Guinea Bissau, global feminists participating in the UN NGO Caucus have issued recurrent statements under the title "La Lutta Continua" (The Struggle Continues). Indicating their profound disappointment in the lack of progress on gender equality and the lack of political will on the part of the United Nations and its member states to make good on their commitments to promote social justice, these statements also assert transnational feminists' unswerving commitment to stay the course and to seize whatever opportunities present themselves to push for a more equitable and just world. This determination provides the best guide to the future of feminist activism in the twenty-first century. The struggle continues. Far more than the fate of women is at stake in the outcome of this long-term engagement.

NOTES

Chapter 1: Engendering Globalization

1. The literature on globalization is now extensive, yet mainstream sources remain markedly silent on the topic of women. Consider, for example, the book that James Rosenau has proclaimed "the definitive work on globalization," Held, McGrew, Goldblatt, and Perraton (1999) *Global Transformations: Politics, Economics and Culture*. In nearly 500 pages of analysis, the authors refer to the women's movement twice, in both cases as an example of a larger phenomenon. In one instance, the women's movement is cited as an example of a "cross-boundary or global cultural network" (371), in the other, as a "new voice in transnational civil society" (452). In neither instance is the women's movement given any substantive analysis. Other leading treatments of globalization are similarly silent on "the woman question." Compare Albrow 1995; Amin 1997; Appadurai 1996; Barber 1996; Bamyeh 2000; Giddens 1998; Hardt and Negri 2000; Hirst and Thompson 1999; Mandle 2003; Robertson 1992. Catherine Eschle (2005, 1745) has pointed out that feminism is "largely absent from the authoritative texts on the anti-globalization movement" as well.

2. It is important to note that neoliberals appropriate only certain arguments of Adam Smith's economic theory. Smith insisted that there were important roles for the government in areas pertaining to the common good that should not be left to the private market. These insights have been eclipsed by neoliberal zeal for privatization.

3. Simel Esim (2001) provides an overview of these "informal financial solidarity groups," including *roscas* in Latin America, *tontines* and *oususs* in West Africa, and *gamayes* in the Middle East. The most widely discussed of these efforts, however, is that developed by the Self-Employed Women's Association (SEWA), which was founded in Ahmedabad, Gujarat, India, in 1972 and which culminated in the

creation of SEWA Bank using the deposits and share capital of its members to give women access to small loans.

4. For detailed discussions of the specific provisions of these contracts in various nations, see Bakan and Stasiulis 1997; Campani and Ling 2000, 27–58; Constable 1997; Daenzer1997; Gonzalez and Holmes 1996; Hogsholm 2000; Parrenas 2000; Parrenas 2001a; Parrenas 2001b.

5. According to Parrenas, most Filipina overseas contract workers are married and are mothers of children whom they leave in the care of relatives for the duration of their overseas domestic contracts (2001a).

Chapter 2: Feminists Go Global

1. Karen Offen (2000) has traced the earliest use of the term *feminism* to mid-nineteenth-century France. Virginia Woolf suggested in *Three Guineas* (1938) that *feminism* gained popularity as a term of derision, introduced by journalists in late nineteenth-century France to caricature and demean women engaged in the struggle for "Justice, Equality, and Liberty."

2. For information about Margaret Brent, see Ann Baker, *Maryland History Leaflet No. 1*. Prepared for the use of Government House. Maryland State Archives, 1997 (rev. 1998).

3. In *Emile* (1762 [1955, 332]), Rousseau envisioned an educational program to train women "to bear the yoke from the first, so that they may not feel it, to master their own caprices and to submit themselves to the will of others." Indeed he insists that "The education of women should be always relative to the men. To please, to be useful to us, to make us love and esteem them, to educate us when young, and take care of us when grown up, to advise, to console us, to render our lives easy and agreeable; these are the duties of women at all times, and what they should be taught in their infancy" (328). Rousseau's educational prescriptions are instructive because they ingeniously display the means by which gender differences can be created and inculcated in a species in which individuals have unlimited potential and malleable characters. Perhaps what is most remarkable about Rousseau's recommendations for the training of women are the precise mechanics he identifies for the production of docile, good-natured, self-sacrificing creatures: "Girls must be subjected all their lives to the most constant and severe restraint, which is that of decorum: it is therefore necessary to accustom them early to such confinement, that it may not afterwards cost them too dear; and to the suppression of their caprices, that they may the more readily submit to the will of others. If, indeed, they are fond of being always at work, they should be sometimes compelled to lay it aside. . . . Deny them not the indulgence of their innocent mirth, their sports and pastimes; but ever prevent their sating themselves with one to run to another; permit them not for a moment to perceive themselves entirely freed from restraint. Use them to be interrupted in the midst of their play, and sent to

work, without murmuring. Habit alone is sufficient to inure them to this, because it is only affirming the operations of nature" (333). Surveillance, discipline to ensure conformity, continual interruptions and distractions, frivolous commands, and rigid control are the key to women's successful socialization. When indulged systematically, they will produce a woman of excellent character. For a discussion of the rise of republican motherhood in the United States following the American Revolution, see Kerber 1980.

4. Reflecting Quaker influence, New Jersey's first constitution awarded voting rights to single women who owned property. This right was rescinded in 1807. For a discussion of the politics behind women's enfranchisement and subsequent disenfranchisement, see Apter Klinghoffer and Elkis 1992.

5. The text of the Declaration of the Rights of Woman is readily available online. See, for example, the *Modern History Sourcebook*, http://www.fordham.edu/halsall/mod/1791degouge1.html.

6. Bonnie Anderson (2000, 136) points out that the twenty-five Fourierist settlements created in the United States before 1848 fell far short of their egalitarian ideals. Women were typically given subordinate roles within the communities, and even when performing identical work, women were paid only 50 percent of the wages men received.

7. The sole vote in support of women's suffrage was cast by the bill's sponsor, Victor Considerant, the only Fourierist elected to the Assembly in the election of April 23, 1848 (Anderson 2000, 165).

8. Upon their release from prison, Deroin and Roland continued their feminist work. In 1852, Roland was rearrested and convicted of fomenting an insurrection. She died in prison later that year. Deroin launched a new publication, *Women's Almanack*, which continued to press for women's equality and liberty, socialism, and the end to the death penalty. The police raided the journal office, seized the material, and shut down the publication. Deroin was forced into permanent exile.

9. Despite their origin at a suffrage meeting, the International Council of Women decided to drop women's suffrage from their agenda because it was "too controversial," and as such, might deter women of some nations from joining the organization. For a full account of this decision, see Rupp 1997.

10. As one indication of the power of the separate spheres ideology, it is interesting to note that by the mid-1870s, leaders of German American Socialists in the United States had incorporated separate spheres doctrines into their party agenda. "In 1875 Socialists moved to amend the party platform to include a statutory restriction of women's labor, demanding the elimination of all work by mothers with children under fourteen, banning of women workers from night work, overtime, and Sunday employment" (Buhle 1983, 12).

11. In *De la Justice dans la Révolution et dans l'église* (*On Justice in the Revolution and in the Church*, 1858) Proudhon, a leader of the socialist movement in Europe, launched a virulent attack against women's emancipation, equating it with prosti-

tution, and against women's rights activists: "Feminine indiscretion has caught fire; a half dozen inky fingered insurgents obstinately try to make women into something we do not want, reclaim their rights with insults, defy us to bring the question out into the light of day." Echoing Aristotle, Proudhon insisted that

> Genius is . . . the virility of spirit and its accompanying powers of abstraction, generalization, invention, conceptualization, which are lacking in equal measure in children, eunuchs, and women. . . . To the generation of ideas as to the generation of children, woman brings nothing of her own; she is a passive, enervating being, whose conversation exhausts you as much as her embraces.

For a fuller elaboration of Proudhon's antiwomen diatribes and their refutation by feminists of his generation, such as Jenny P. d'Héricourt, see Offen 2000, chapter 5.

Chapter 3: Outsiders, Insiders, and Outsiders Within

1. In 2005, women hold less than 1 percent of the positions of president or prime minister of nations. They are equally scarce as foreign ministers or secretaries of state. Women hold more than 15 percent of the ministerial posts in fewer than a dozen countries. Women remain less than a quarter of the delegates to the United Nations. The delegations with the highest percentage of women members represent the Caribbean (29 percent) and Latin America (23 percent). Women reached the goal of 30 percent of professional staff within UN agencies only in 1991. The website of the Interparliamentary Union provides up-to-date statistics on women's political representation at the nation-state level (see also Neft and Levine 1997; Seager 2003).

2. Many governments, on the Right and on the Left, have tried to put a stop to feminist aspirations and channel women's movements to their own ends. Hostility to feminism has been deliberate, sustained, and central to their projects (Offen 2000, 311). Feminists in Spain and Sweden, for example, confronted opposition and co-optation by communist and social democratic party activists. The 1937 Irish constitution took away women's rights as a media blackout kept the public from reading about feminist protests (Offen 2000, 319). Latin American governments in Brazil and Chile created women's organizations to provide alternatives to feminism (Alvarez 1990; Baldez 2002; Caldeira 1998). For an account of the ruthless suppression of feminism and creation of a party-controlled women's organization in Indonesia, see Wieringa 2001.

3. DAWN's founding collective included Neuma Aguiar (Brazil), Zubeida Ahmad (Pakistan), Peggy Antrobus (Barbados), Lourdes Arizpe (Mexico), Nirmala Banerjee (India), Carmen Barroso (Brazil), Ela Bhatt (India), Tone Bleie (Norway), Noeleen Heyzer (Malaysia), Hameeda Hosein (Bangladesh), Devaki Jain (India), Kumari Jayawardene (Sri Lanka), Isabel Larguia (Cuba), Ragnhild Lund (Norway), Geertje Lycklama (Netherlands), Lucille Mair (Jamaica), Katherine McKee (USA),

Fatima Mrenissi (Morocco), Achola Pala Okeyo (Kenya), Marie-Angélique Savane (Senegal), Gita Sen (India), and Claire Slater (Fiji).

4. This language appears in all WIB websites. See, for example, http://www .womeninblack.org.uk or http://www.womeninblack.net.

5. Women in Black-Canberra, http://www.sshub.com/wibabout.htm.

6. Feminist activists were also following in the tradition of People's Tribunals such as that organized by Bertrand Russell in 1966–1967 to consider United States' responsibility for war crimes and genocide in Vietnam (Duffett 1970).

7. Dutch civilians in Java (Dutch East Indies) were interned during the war. Some of the youngest girls in the internment camps were forcibly assigned to comfort stations in Java.

8. This research was initiated by Professor Yun Chung-Ok, who painstakingly documented the abuses of Korean women who had been kidnapped and imprisoned in comfort stations within Korea, in Japan, and across Japanese-occupied territories. Prior to Professor Yun Chung-Ok's path-breaking research, shame and fear had kept survivors from discussing their abuses publicly. Feminists in Korea began mobilizing to challenge the stigma associated with this brutal violation, and their activism triggered feminist investigations of Japanese abuses of women in other occupied territories.

9. Developed in the context of poststructuralist understandings of the constitutive power of language, which challenges the idea that language merely describes or represents what exists, suggesting instead that language is constitutive of reality, discourse encompasses structures of statements, concepts, categories, and beliefs that are specific to particular sociohistorical formations, which constitute us as subjects in a determinate order of things (Derrida 1979, 1980, 1981a, 1981b; Foucault 1973, 1977, 1980; Scott 1988).

10. Although the United States has frequently challenged the human rights practices of communist nations, it has simultaneously acted to shield itself from accountability to international human rights agreements.

> In 1947, for example, the National Association for the Advancement of Colored People called on the United Nations to study racial discrimination in the United States and to insure U.S. compliance with international standards. And in 1966, the National Organization for Women's founding charter explicitly identified it with the "worldwide revolution in human rights taking place within and beyond our borders." Such actions fueled the U.S. government's fear that powerful local constituencies would use international standards and scrutiny to expose and challenge domestic abuses. Its systematic effort over the past fifty years to forestall such action, in particular by never or only nominally ratifying key human rights treaties, has effectively shut down the human rights dimension of U.S. rights advocacy. (Thomas 2000, 1121–1122)

11. Any presumption of nondiscrimination was also belied by the persistent underrepresentation of women on the professional staff in UN agencies. Despite re-

peated affirmative action plans that set targets and goals, women constituted only 26 percent (679 out of 2,523) of the professional staff in 1989, and most of these women were concentrated at the lower professional ranks. Nine women, compared to 126 men, held senior management positions in 1989. Feminists at the UN continued to press for more serious affirmative action. In 1990 Javier Pérez de Cuéllar adopted a more strenuous plan to overcome obstacles to gender equality in the secretariat: "Where the percentage of women is less than 35% overall and less than 25% at P5 level, vacancies must be filled by a woman if there is at least one woman whose qualifications match job requirements. Positions will remain vacant until all efforts have been made to hire a suitable woman" (Timothy 1995, 127–128).

12. Gay Seidman (1999) has suggested that the National Women's Coalition succeeded in generating the appearance of consensus more than actual consensus. In a later article, Seidman (2003) suggests that the absence of widespread support for feminism has created major challenges for the work of the South African Commission on Gender Equality.

13. This provision was included in the Geneva Convention as a result of intensive advocacy work done by the International Council of Women.

14. Harder (2006, 71) points out that

the Secretary of State Women's Program, which had been so instrumental in funding feminist advocacy saw its budget fall from $12.7 million in 1987 to $9 million in 1990. In 1995, the Women's Program and Status of Women Canada were amalgamated, and the Canadian Advisory Council on the Status of Women (CACSW) was eliminated. In addition, the cabinet position of Minister Responsible for the Status of Women was downgraded to the lower rank of Secretary of State Responsible for Status of Women.

15. The All China Women's Federation (ACWF), the state apparatus developed by the Chinese Communist Party to mobilize women to meet the needs of the revolution, not only sponsors 50,000 women's organizations across China, but since the UN World Conference on Women in Beijing has also taken to calling itself and sometimes acting like an NGO. For differing accounts of the ACWF as an NGO, see Howell 2003 and Hsiung and Wong 1999.

16. With 8,000 NGOs in its database, the World Bank now includes NGOs in 50 percent of its projects (Tinker 1999, 93).

Chapter 4: Global Feminist Circuits

1. As of 2005, the United States and twenty other nations have not ratified CEDAW.

2. The Berlin conference did go forward as planned, attracting 2,000 delegates from 141 nations. As the United States had hoped, however, it was eclipsed by the Mexico City conference.

3. In this instance, as in many others, feminists could attract media attention,

but they could not control the content of media accounts. Peggy Antrobus (2004, 45) notes that "the events in Mexico City tended to be misrepresented by the press in North America; the mainstream press in other parts of the world largely ignored them."

4. Within feminist scholarship, there is continuing contestation over the use of the terms *First World women* and *Third World women*. The depiction of Third World women as a "singular monolithic subject" by Western feminist scholars has been problematized by postcolonial feminist theorists who rightly point out that the Third World includes more than one hundred nations with very different histories, traditions, languages, and cultures (e.g., Mohanty 1990; Grewel and Kaplan 1994; John 1996). Concern with accuracy and analytic rigor, then, would seem to warrant the abandonment of such a vague and homogenizing rubric for the majority of the world's population. Other scholars, particularly in the social sciences, have also argued for the abandonment of references to the Third World, but for very different reasons. In the aftermath of the Cold War and the end of a clear demarcation between capitalist (First World) and socialist (Second World) spheres of influence, the nonaligned movement of nations advocating a third alternative has lost its geographic and ideological purchase. Alternative efforts to classify significant differences among nations have generated distinctions between North and South, minority world and majority world, and West and LACAAP countries (Latin America, Caribbean, Africa, Asia, and the Pacific). While some categories are needed to capture important regional economic and political differences, these scholars suggest that the category Third World no longer serves a useful analytical purpose. Fully cognizant of these two sets of critiques, some feminist scholars have attempted to defend the category Third World women, however. The term has been embraced by some feminist scholars and activists as their preferred descriptor for an imagined community, comprising women of color in the global South, as well as internally colonized women of color within the North (Sandoval 2000; Corradi 2001; Kabeer 2003). As a self-chosen identification then, *Third World women* can imply both postcolonial politics and transnational solidarity. Indeed, some scholars have argued that "the use of the term Third World women helps Westerners to recognize the nature of women's struggle against poverty and oppression and stimulates efforts to theorize pernicious social processes that differentiate women" (Chapoval 2001, 148). Whether feminist scholars abandon or reclaim the category Third World women, their choices reflect political decisions. Each of the descriptive locutions noted above is enmeshed in a politics of representation of enormous import to knowledge production. The discursive choices made by particular scholars encompass complex political issues about how to demarcate diversity and commonality, how to circumscribe center and periphery, and how to make certain power relations visible, while rendering other power relations invisible. Far from a neutral description, differently constructed categories lie at the heart of the politics of knowledge. Fully aware of how unsatisfactory these locutions are, in this

chapter, I use the term *Third World women* to capture a sense of shared solidarity among women of the South and low-income women of color in the North. I also use both *Western* and *North* to signify women in affluent nations in Europe and North America, recognizing the huge range of differences that these terms occlude.

5. Both UNIFEM and INSTRAW were created in the aftermath of the IWY Conference in Mexico City as the UN's women' s policy machinery. Both are funded entirely by the voluntary contributions of UN member states. Sweden, the first nation to pass legislation mandating funding for women's initiatives as part of its foreign policy, along with other Nordic states have been primary funders of UNIFEM and INSTRAW. In 1980, the Reagan administration proposed that the U.S. contribution to UNIFEM be cut in half, from $1 million to $500,000 per year. Exceeding the administration's request, Congressman William Lehman of Florida led a successful campaign to cut all funding for 1982 and 1983. In 1984, half the funding was restored with allocations increasing gradually thereafter. Only in 1994 did the Clinton administration restore funding to the $1 million per year level.

6. In 1995, 50,000 women representing more than 3,000 women's organizations participated in the NGO Forum in Hairou held in conjunction with the UN's Fourth World Conference on Women in Beijing, compared to 6,000 women representing 114 women's organizations participating in the tribune in Mexico City in 1975 (Basu 2000). As in former UN conferences the politics of needs interpretation was a subject of intense contestation.

7. Feminists from the South have traced the eruption of similar tensions to the DAWN meeting in Rio in 1985, discussions of the South Commission between 1987 and 1990 (Jain 2001), and to the Cairo Conference on Population and Development in 1994 (Day 2001).

8. A web dialogue on the South-South Initiative was published in a special issue of *Women in Action*, a publication of ISIS, and can be found on the ISIS Manila website: www.isiswomen.org/pub/wia/wia301/index.html. ISIS/WIICS, the Women's International Information and Communication Service, was created in 1974 and has at different times been headquartered in Switzerland, Uganda, Italy, Chile, and the Philippines. Focusing on violence against women and economic development policies that marginalize and exploit women workers, ISIS links over 10,000 women's groups in 130 nations. Its reports on the SSI are part of a long-standing effort to address tensions between feminist activists in the South and North. See A. Fraser 1987.

9. Simel Esim (2001) provides an overview of these "informal financial solidarity groups," including *roscas* in Latin America, *tontines* and *oususus* in West Africa, and *gamayes* in the Middle East. The most widely discussed of these efforts, however, is that developed by the Self-Employed Women's Association (SEWA), which was founded in Ahmedabad, Gujarat, India in 1972 and which culminated in the creation of SEWA Bank using the deposits and shared capital of its members to give women access to small loans.

10. Repayment rates for SEWA bank are over 90 percent.

11. In 2004, women held 15 percent of the seats in national legislatures on average and less than 1 percent of the positions of president or prime minister. The website of the Interparliamentary Union provides up-to-date statistics on women's political representation.

12. The five permanent members of the Security Council are China, France, Russia, the United Kingdom, and the United States. The rotating members are elected by the General Assembly for two-year terms. In 2005, these elected members were Algeria, Argentina, Benin, Brazil, Denmark, Greece, Japan, the Philippines, Romania, and Tanzania.

13. The World Bank and the IMF have a

> strange "one dollar one vote system" such that voting rights are proportional to monetary contributions. In 2003, for example, the United States controlled more than 17 percent of the total votes in the IMF, which has 183 member countries, and the other G7 countries together a total of more than 46 percent. The proportion of votes in the World Bank are [sic] roughly the same. (Hardt and Negri, 2004, 172)

Chapter 5: Global Feminist Futures

1. Manfred Steger (2002, x) conceives globalism as the "dominant ideology of our time. It is an Anglo-American free-market doctrine that endows the relatively new concept of globalization with neoliberal norms, values, and meanings—all of which are produced and reproduced within the media and popular culture for public consumption." In a sense, then, the locution *neoliberal globalism* is redundant. Nonetheless, I have chosen to include the neoliberal referent to help keep the contours of this ideology clearly fixed in the public eye.

2. Geng's analysis focused exclusively on U.S. feminism, reflecting a level of ethnocentrism characteristic of a good deal of American journalism.

3. Although Brooks acknowledges that in popular discourses postfeminism has been linked to the politics of backlash, she argues that the term *postfeminism* has a very different meaning in feminist theory and does not in any way imply antifeminism, a view that I contest below.

4. Unlike many accounts of the death of feminism, which posit a fait accompli, Davidson suggests that a final battle may be required to secure feminism in its grave:

> But feminism will not crumple of its own accord. Entrenched in the most powerful centers of influence in our culture, from academia and journalism to Hollywood and the publishing industry, feminists today are positioned to wield a massive long-term influence on our culture, regardless of their success or failure in the market of ideas or at the ballot box. They must be fought every step of the way, from our political parties to our cocktail parties, if they are not to

prevail though the sheer lack of resistance that has often been their greatest asset. (Davidson 1988, 337)

5. Inter-Parliamentary Union, *Women in National Parliaments* (2005), http://www.ipu.org/wmn-e/classif.htm.

6. The small decreases in gender inequality that have occurred in some nations over the past thirty years is due to the worsening economic condition of men rather than the improvement of the economic condition of women. For a fuller discussion of this problem, see Bayes, Begné, Gonzalez, Harder, Hawkesworth, and MacDonald 2006.

REFERENCES

WORD. 1982. "The Experience of the Association of African Women for Research and Development (AAWORD)." *Development Dialogue* 1–2: 101–113.

ramovitz, Mimi. 1996. *Regulating the Lives of Women: Social Welfare Policy from Colonial Times to the Present*. Boston: South End Press.

——. 1999. "Toward a Framework for Understanding Activism among Poor and Working-Class Women in Twentieth-Century America." In Gwendolyn Mink, ed., *Whose Welfare?* 214–248. Ithaca, NY: Cornell University Press.

orno, Theodor. 1997. *Aesthetic Theory*. Robert Hullot-Kentor, trans. and ed. Minneapolis: University of Minnesota Press.

athangelou, Anna. 2004. *The Global Political Economy of Sex*. New York: Palgrave Macmillan.

Ali, Nadje. 2003. "Gender and Civil Society in the Middle East." *International Feminist Journal of Politics* 5(2): 216–232.

row, Martin. 1995. *Globalization*. London: Routledge.

xander, M. Jacqui, and Chandra Talpade Mohanty. 1997. *Feminist Genealogies, Colonial Legacies, Democratic Futures*. New York: Routledge.

an, Virginia, Margaret Galey, and Mildred Persinger. 1995. "World Conference of the International Women's Year." In Ann Winslow, ed., *Women Politics and the United Nations*, 29–44. Westport, CT: Greenwood Press.

en, Meg. 2001. "Women, Community and the British Miner's Strike of 1984–1985." In Sheila Rowbotham and Stephanie Linkogle, eds., *Women Resist Globalization: Mobilizing for Livelihood and Rights*, 46–69. London: Zed Press.

varez, Sonia. 1990. *Engendering Democracy in Brazil: Women's Movements in Transition Politics*. Princeton, NJ: Princeton University Press.

——. 1998. "Feminismos Latinamericanos: Reflexiones teóricas y perspectivas comparativas." In Marcela Rios, ed., *Reflexiones teóricas y comparativas sobre los feminismos en Chile y America Latina*, 4–22. Santiago: Nostas del Conversatorio.

————. 1999. "Advocating Feminism: The Latin American Feminist NGO 'Boom.'" *International Feminist Journal of Politics* 1(2): 181–209.

Ames, Azel. 1875. *Sex in Industry: A Plea for the Working Girl*. Boston: J. R. Osgood.

Amin, Samir. 1997. *Capitalism in the Age of Globalization: The Management of Contemporary Society*. London: Zed Books.

Amos, Valerie, and Pratibha Parmar. 2001. "Challenging Imperial Feminism." In Kum Kum Bhavnani, ed., *Feminism and "Race."* 19–35. Oxford: Oxford University Press.

Anderson, Bonnie. 2000. *Joyous Greetings: The First International Women's Movement, 1830–1860*. New York: Oxford University Press.

Anheier, Helmut, Malies Glasius, and Mary Kaldor. 2001. *Global Civil Society*. Oxford: Oxford University Press.

Antrobus, Peggy. 2004. *The Global Women's Movement: Origins, Issues, and Strategies*. New York and London: Zed Books.

Appadurai, Arjun. 1996. *Modernity at Large: Cultural Dimensions of Globalization*. Minneapolis: University of Minnesota Press.

Apter Klinghoffer, Judith, and Lois Elkis. 1992. "The 'Petticoat Electors': Women's Suffrage in New Jersey, 1776–1807." *Journal of the Early Republic* 12(2): 159–193.

Asante, E. 2002. "Review: Engendering Development through Gender Equality in Rights and Resources, A World Bank Policy Research Report." *Canadian Journal of Sociology* 27(2): 293.

Astell, Mary. 1694. *Serious Proposal to the Ladies*. Reprinted in Bridget Hill, ed., *The First English Feminist: Reflections on Marriage and Other Writings by Mary Astell*. New York: St. Martin's Press, 1986.

Bakan, Abigail, and Daiva Stasiulis. 1997. *Not One of the Family: Foreign Domestic Workers in Canada*. Toronto: University of Toronto Press.

Bakker, Isabella. 1994. *The Strategic Silence: Gender and Economic Policy*. London: Zed Books.

Bakker, Isabella, and Stephen Gill. 2003. *Power, Production, and Social Reproduction: Human In/security in the Global Political Economy*. Basingstoke, UK: Palgrave Macmillan.

Baldez, Lisa. 2002. *Why Women Protest: Women's Movements in Chile*. Cambridge, UK: Cambridge University Press.

Bales, Kevin. 2002. "Because She Looks Like A Child." In Barbara Ehrenreich and Arlie Hochschild, eds., *Global Woman*, 207–229. New York: Metropolitan Books.

Bamyeh, Mohammed. 2000. *The Ends of Globalization*. Minneapolis: University of Minnesota Press.

Barker, Isabelle V. 2003. "The Privatization of Citizenship." Unpublished manuscript.

Basu, Amrita. 2000. "Globalization of the Local/Localization of the Global: Mapping Transnational Women's Movements." *Meridians: Feminism, Race, Transnationalism* 1(1): 73–88.

———, ed. 1995. *The Challenge of Local Feminisms: Women's Movements in Global Perspective.* Boulder, CO: Westview Press.

Bayes, Jane. 2004. "The Political Economy of Prisons in a Neoliberal World." Paper presented at the Annual Meeting of the Western Political Science Association, Portland, OR, March 19–21.

Bayes, Jane, Patricia Begné, Laura Gonzalez, Lois Harder, Mary Hawkesworth, and Laura MacDonald. 2006. *Women, Democracy, and Globalization in North America: A Comparative Study.* New York: Palgrave.

Beckwith, Karen. 2000. "Beyond Compare? Women's Movements in Comparative Perspective." *European Journal of Political Research* 37: 431–468.

Bedford, Katherine. 2005. "The World Bank's Employment Programs in Ecuador and Beyond: Empowering Women, Domesticating Men, and Resolving the Social Reproduction Dilemma." Rutgers University, PhD Dissertation.

Bolt, Christine. 2004. *Sisterhood Questioned? Race, Class and Internationalism in the American and British Women's Movements, c. 1880s–1970s.* New York: Routledge.

Boxer, Marilyn, and Jean Quataert. 2000. *Connecting Spheres: European Women in a Globalizing World, 1500 to the Present,* 2nd ed. New York: Oxford University Press.

Brennan, Denise. 2002. "Selling Sex for Visas: Sex Tourism as a Stepping Stone to International Migration." In Barbara Ehrenreich and Arlie Hochschild, eds., *Global Woman,* 154–168. New York: Metropolitan Books.

Brenner, Johanna. 2003. "Transnational Feminism and the Struggle for Global Justice." *New Politics* 9(3): 1–20.

Brooks, Ann. 1997. *Postfeminisms: Feminism, Cultural Theory, and Cultural Forms.* London and New York: Routledge.

Brooks, Ethel. Forthcoming. *The Empire's New Clothes.* Minneapolis: University of Minnesota Press.

Buhle, Mari Jo. 1981. *Women and American Socialism, 1870–1920.* Urbana: University of Illinois Press.

Burke, Carol. 2004. *Camp All-American, Hanoi Jane, and the High and the Tight: Gender, Folklore, and Changing Military Culture.* Boston: Beacon Press.

Burton, Antoinette. 1994. *Burdens of History: British Feminists, Indian Women, and Imperial Culture.* Chapel Hill: University of North Carolina Press.

———. 1999. "Some Trajectories of 'Feminism' and 'Imperialism.'" In Mrinalini Sinha, Donna Guy, and Angela Woollacott, eds., *Feminisms and Internationalism,* 214–224. Oxford: Blackwell.

Butegwa, Florence. 1995. "International Human Rights Law and Practice: Implications for Women." In M. Schuler, ed., *From Basic Needs to Basic Rights: Women's*

Claim to Human Rights, 27–39. Washington, DC: Women, Law, and Development International.

Buvinic, Mayra. 1999. *Promoting Gender Equality*. Oxford: Blackwell/UNESCO.

Cairncross, Frances. 1997. *The Death of Distance*. Cambridge, MA: Harvard Business School Press.

Caldeira, Teresa. 1998. "Justice and Individual Rights: Challenges for Women's Movements and Democratization in Brazil." In Jane Jaquette and Sharon Wolchik, eds., *Women and Democracy: Latin America and Central and Eastern Europe*, 75–103. Baltimore: Johns Hopkins University Press.

Campani, Kimberly Chang, and L. H. M. Ling. 2000. "Globalization and Its Intimate Other: Filipina Domestic Workers in Hong Kong." In Marianne Marchand and Ann Runyon, eds., *Gender and Global Restructuring*, 27–58. London: Routledge.

Castles, Stephen, and Mark Miller. 1998. *The Age of Migration*. New York and London: Guilford.

Center for American Women and Politics [CAWP]. 2001. *Women State Legislators: Past, Present and Future*. New Brunswick, NJ: Center for American Women and Politics.

Cerrutti, Marcela. 2000. "Economic Reform, Structural Adjustment and Female Labor Force Participation in Buenos Aires, Argentina." *World Development* 28(5): 879–891.

Chang, Grace. 2000. *Disposable Domestics*. Boston: South End Press.

Chang, Nancy. 2002. *Silencing Political Dissent: How Post–September 11 Anti-Terrorism Measures Threaten Our Civil Liberties*. New York: Seven Stories Press.

Chapoval, Ieda. 2001. "The Devolution of Women as a Category in Development Theorizing." In Vasilikie Demos and Marcia Texler Segal, eds., *An International Feminist Challenge to Theory*, 138–150. Amsterdam: Elsevier Science Ltd.

Chauhan, Abha. 2001. "The Nature/Culture Dualism in the Indian Context." In Vasilikie Demos and Marcia Texler Segal, eds., *An International Feminist Challenge to Theory*, 72–89. Amsterdam: Elsevier Science Ltd.

Cheah, Pheng. 1997. "Posit(ion)ing Human Rights in the Current Global Conjuncture." *Public Culture* 9: 245–265.

Chen, M. Alter. 1996. "Engendering World Conferences: The International Women's Movement and the UN." In Thomas Weiss and Leon Gordenker, eds., *NGOs, the UN, and Global Governance*, 143–156. Boulder, CO: Lynne Rienner.

Chichowski, Rachel. 2002. "No Discrimination Whatsoever: Women's Transnational Activism and the Evolution of EU Sex Equality Policy." In Nancy Naples and Manisha Desai, eds., *Women's Activism and Globalization: Linking Local Struggles and Transnational Politics*, 220–238. New York: Routledge.

Chinkin, Christine. 2000. "Toward the Tokyo Tribunal: A Brief History." Women's Caucus for Gender Justice. Online at http://www.iccwomen.org/archive/tokyo/chinkin.htm (July 7, 2005).

Constable, Nicole. 1997. *Maid to Order in Hong Kong*. Ithaca, NY: Cornell University Press.

Correa, Sonia, and Rosalind Petchesky. 2003. "Reproductive and Sexual Rights: A Feminist Perspective." In Carol McCann and Seung-Kyung Kim, eds., *Feminist Theory Reader: Local and Global Perspectives*, 88–102. New York and London: Routledge.

Corradi, Laura. 2001. "Feminism of Color Challenges White Sociological Theory and Color-Blind Eco-Feminism." In Vasilikie Demos and Marcia Texler Segal, eds., *An International Feminist Challenge to Theory*, 41–62. Amsterdam: Elsevier Science Ltd.

Cruz-Malavé, Arnaldo, and Martin Manalansan. 2002. *Queer Globalizations: Citizenship and the Afterlife of Colonialism*. New York: New York University Press.

Daenzer, Patricia. 1997. "An Affair Between Nations: International Relations and the Movement of Household Service Workers." In Abigail Bakan and Daiva Stasiulis, eds., *Not One of the Family*, 81–118. Toronto: University of Toronto Press.

Dahlerup, Drude, and Lenita Freidenvall. 2003. "Quotas as a 'Fast Track' to Equal Political Representation for Women." Paper presented at the World Congress of the International Political Science Association, Durban, South Africa, June 29–July 4.

Davidson, Nicholas. 1988. *The Failure of Feminism*. Buffalo, NY: Prometheus Books.

Dawson, Michael. 1994. "A Black Counterpublic? Economic Earthquakes, Racial Agenda(s), and Black Politics." *Public Culture* 7: 195–224.

Day, Sheenagh. 2001. "Partners in Population and Development: A South-South Initiative," *Women in Action*. Available at http://www.isiswomen.org/pub/wia/wia301/sheenagh.htm.

Declaration of Mexico. 1975. UN World Conference on International Women's Year. E/CONF.66/C.1/L.37, June 28.

Deem, Melissa. 1999. "Scandal, Heteronormative Culture and the Disciplining of Feminism." *Critical Studies in Mass Communication* 16(1): 86–94.

Delphy, Christine. 1984. *Close to Home*. Amherst: University of Massachusetts Press.

Demos, Vasilikie, and Marcia Texler Segal. 2001. *An International Feminist Challenge to Theory*. Amsterdam: Elsevier Science Ltd.

Denis, Ann. 2001. "Rethinking Development from a Feminist Perspective." In Vasilikie Demos and Marcia Texler Segal, eds., *An International Feminist Challenge to Theory*, 151–162. Amsterdam: Elsevier Science Ltd.

Derrida, Jacques. 1979. *Spurs/Eperons*. Chicago: University of Chicago Press.

———. 1980. *The Archaeology of the Frivolous*. Pittsburgh: Duquesne University Press.

———. 1981a. *Dissemination*. Chicago: University of Chicago Press.

———. 1981b. *Positions*. Chicago: University of Chicago Press.

Desai, Manisha. 2002. "Transnational Solidarity: Women's Agency, Structural Adjustment, and Globalization." In Nancy Naples and Manisha Desai, eds., *Women's Activism and Globalization: Linking Local Struggles and Transnational Politics*, 15–33. New York: Routledge.

Dhruvarajan, Vanaja. 2002. "Feminism and Social Transformation." In Vanaja Dhruvarajan and Jill Vickers, eds., *Gender, Race, and Nation: A Global Perspective*, 295–310. Toronto: University of Toronto Press.

Diamond, Timothy. 1992. *Making Gray Gold: Narratives of Nursing Home Care.* Chicago: University of Chicago Press.

Donaldson, Laura. 1992. *Decolonizing Feminisms: Race, Gender and Empire Building.* Chapel Hill: University of North Carolina Press.

Duerst-Lahti, Georgia. 1989. "The Government's Role in Building the Women's Movement." *Political Science Quarterly* 104(2): 249–268.

Duerst-Lahti, Georgia, and Rita Mae Kelly. 1995. *Gender Power, Leadership and Governance.* Ann Arbor: University of Michigan Press.

Duffett, John. 1970. *Against the Crime of Silence: Proceedings of the International War Crimes Tribunal.* New York: Simon & Schuster.

Economic and Social Council. 1997. *Agreed Conclusions.* United Nations Document E/1997/2.

Edelman, Marc, and Angelique Haugerud. 2005. *The Anthropology of Development and Globalization: From Classical Political Economy to Contemporary Neoliberalism.* Oxford: Blackwell.

Engels, Friedrich. 1958. *The Condition of the Working Class in England.* Stanford, CA: Stanford University Press.

Ehrenreich, Barbara, and Arlie Russell Hochschild. 2002. *Global Woman: Nannies, Maids, and Sex Workers in the New Economy.* New York: Metropolitan Books/Henry Holt.

Ehrick, Christine. 1999. "Madrinas and Missionaries: Uruguay and the Pan-American Women's Movement." In Mrinalini Sinha, Donna Guy, and Angela Woollacott, eds., *Feminisms and Internationalism*, 62–80. Oxford: Blackwell.

Einhorn, Barbara, and Charlotte Sever. 2003. "Gender and Civil Society in East Central Europe." *International Feminist Journal of Politics* 5(2):163–190.

Eisenstein, Zillah. 2004a. *Against Empire: Feminisms, Racism, and the West.* London: Zed Books.

———. 2004b. "Is 'W' for Women?" Mock Election Debates. Ithaca, NY: Cornell University, September 22. Reprinted on SMTP:moderator@portside.org.

Elman, Amy. 1996. *Sexual Subordination and State Intervention: Comparing Sweden and the United States.* Oxford: Berghahn Books.

Elson, Diane. 1995. "Male Bias in Macro Economics: The Case of Structural Adjustment." In D. Elson, ed., *Male Bias in the Development Process*, 164–190. Manchester: Manchester University Press.

Enloe, Cynthia. 1988. *Does Khaki Become You? The Militarization of Women's Lives.* London: Pandora Press/HarperCollins.

———. 1990. *Bananas, Beaches, and Bases: Making Feminist Sense of International Politics*. Berkeley: University of California Press.

———. 1993. *The Morning After: Sexual Politics at the End of the Cold War*. Berkeley: University of California Press.

———. 2000. *Maneuvers: The International Politics of Militarizing Women's Lives*. Berkeley: University of California Press.

———. 2004. *The Curious Feminist: Searching for Women in the New Age of Empire*. Berkeley: University of California Press.

Erie, Steven, Martin Rein, and Barbara Wiget. 1983. "Women and the Reagan Revolution: Thermidor for the Social Welfare Economy." In Irene Diamond, ed., *Families, Politics and Public Policy*, 94–122. New York: Longman.

Eschle, Catherine. 2005. "'Skeleton Woman': Feminism and the Antiglobalization Movement." *Signs* 30(3): 1741–1769.

Esim, Simel. 2001. "Sisters' Keepers: Economic Organizing Among Informally Employed Women in Turkey." In Vasilikie Demos and Marcia Texler Segal, eds. *An International Feminist Challenge to Theory*, 163–178. Amsterdam: Elsevier Science Ltd.

Evans, Peter. 2000. "The Eclipse of the State? Reflections on Stateness in an Era of Globalization." *World Politics* 50(1): 62–87.

Fall, Yassine. 2001. "Gender and the Social Implications of Globalization." In Rita Kelly, Jane Bayes, Mary Hawkesworth, and Birgitte Young, eds., *Gender, Globalization, and Democratization*, 49–74. Lanham, MD: Rowman & Littlefield.

Felski, Rita. 2000. *Doing Time: Feminist Theory and Postmodern Culture*. New York: New York University Press.

Ferguson, Michaele. 2005. "Home, Land, Security: Iraqi Feminists Respond to the Bush Administration." Presented at the Annual Meeting of the International Studies Association, Honolulu, Hawaii, March 5.

Fester, Gertrude. 2001. "The Way the River Flows: Feminist Activism and Politics toward Transformation in South Africa." The Wynona Lipman Lecture. Center for American Women and Politics, Rutgers University, November 5.

Foucault, Michel. 1973. *The Order of Things: An Archaeology of the Human Sciences*. New York: Vintage.

———. 1977. *Discipline and Punish*. New York: Vintage Books.

———. 1980. *The History of Sexuality*. New York: Vintage Books.

Fraser, Arvonne. 1987. *The U.N. Decade for Women: Documents and Dialogue*. Boulder, CO: Westview Press.

———. 1995. "The Convention on the Elimination of All Forms of Discrimination Against Women (The Women's Convention)." In Ann Winslow, ed., *Women Politics and the United Nations*, 77–94. Westport, CT: Greenwood Press.

Fraser, Nancy. 1992. "Rethinking the Public Sphere: A Contribution to the Critique of Actually Existing Democracy." In Craig Calhoun, ed., *Habermas and the Public Sphere*, 109–142. Cambridge, MA: MIT Press.

Freeman, Jo. 1975. *The Politics of Women's Liberation*. New York: David Mckay Company.

Friedman, Susan Stanford. 1988. *Mappings: Feminism and the Cultural Geographies of Encounter*. Princeton, NJ: Princeton University Press.

Frye, Joanne. 1987. "The Politics of Reading Feminism: The Novel and the Coercions of 'Truth.'" Paper presented at the Midwest Modern Language Association Meeting, Columbus, OH. November 6.

Fukumura, Yoko, and Martha Matsuoka. "Redefining Security: Okinawa Women's Resistance to U.S. Militarism." In Nancy Naples and Manisha Desai, eds., *Women's Activism and Globalization: Linking Local Struggles and Transnational Politics*, 239–266. New York: Routledge.

Galey, Margaret. 1995. "Forerunners in Women's Quest for Partnership." In Anne Winslow, ed., *Women, Politics and the United Nations*, 11–28. Westport, CT: Greenwood Press.

Gelb, Joyce. 1989. *Feminism and Politics: A Comparative Perspective*. Berkeley: University of California Press.

Gelb, Joyce, and Marian Lief Palley. 1982. *Women and Public Policies*. Princeton, NJ: Princeton University Press.

Geng, Veronica. 1976. "Requiem for the Women's Movement." *Harpers* (November): 49–56, 61–68.

Giddens, Anthony. 1998. *The Third Way*. Cambridge, UK: Polity Press.

Giele, Janet Zollinger. 1995. *Two Paths to Women's Equality: Temperance, Suffrage and the Origins of Modern Feminism*. New York: Twayne Publishers.

———. 2001. "In Search of the Good Life: Feminist Correctives to Modernization Theory." In Vasilikie Demos and Marcia Texler Segal, eds., *An International Feminist Challenge to Theory*, 179–195. Amsterdam: Elsevier Science Ltd.

Gilroy, Paul. 1993. *The Black Atlantic*. Cambridge, MA: Harvard University Press.

Gleadle, Kathryn. 1998. *The Early Feminists: Radical Unitarians and the Emergence of the Women's Rights Movement, 1831–1851*. New York: St. Martin's Press.

———. 2002. *Radical Writing on Women, 1800–1850*. New York: Palgrave Macmillan.

Goetz, Anne Marie. 2003. "Women's Political Effectiveness: A Conceptual Framework." In Anne Marie Goetz and Shireen Hassim, eds., *No Shortcuts to Power: African Women in Politics and Policymaking*, 29–80. London: Zed Books.

Goetz, Anne Marie, and Shireen Hassim, eds. 2003. *No Shortcuts to Power: African Women in Politics and Policymaking*. London: Zed Books.

Goldberg, David Theo. 1993. *Racist Culture*. Cambridge, UK: Blackwell.

Goldberg, Jonathan. 1992. *Sodometries: Renaissance Texts, Modern Sexualities*. Stanford, CA: Stanford University Press.

Gonzalez, Joaquin, and Ronald Holmes. 1996. "The Philippine Labour Diaspora," *Southeast Asian Affairs*, 300–317.

Goodwin Gill, Guy. 2003. "Immigration Policy." In Mary Hawkesworth and Maurice Kogan, eds., *The Routledge Encyclopedia of Government and Politics*, 738–751. London: Routledge.

Goodwin, Sarah Webster, and Elisabeth Bronfen. 1993. *Death and Representation*. Baltimore: Johns Hopkins University Press.

Gournay, Marie Le Jars de. 1622. *De l'Égalité des hommes et des femmes (On the Equality of Men and Women)*. Reprinted, Paris: Côté-femmes, 1989.

Grewal, Inderpal, and Caren Kaplan. 1994. *Scattered Hegemonies: Postmodernity and Transnational Feminist Practices*. Minneapolis: University of Minnesota Press.

Hamilton, Alexander, James Madison, and John Jay. 1961. *The Federalist Papers*. New York: New American Library.

Handler, Joel, and Yeheskel Hasenfeld. 1991. *The Moral Construction of Poverty: Welfare Reform in America*. Newbury Park, CA: Sage.

Harder, Lois. 2006. "Women and Politics in Canada." In Jane Bayes, Patricia Begné, Laura Gonzalez, Lois Harder, Mary Hawkesworth, and Laura MacDonald, *Women, Democracy and Globalization in North America*, 51–76. New York: Palgrave.

Hardt, Michael, and Antonio Negri. 2000. *Empire*. Cambridge, MA: Harvard University Press.

Hardt, Michael, and Antonio Negri. 2004. *Multitude: War and Democracy in the Age of Empire*. New York: Penguin.

Hassim, Shireen. 2003. "Representation, Participation, and Democratic Effectiveness: Feminist Challenges to Representative Democracy in South Africa." In Anne Marie Goetz and Shireen Hassim, eds., *No Shortcuts to Power: African Women in Politics and Policy Making*. London: Zed Books.

Hawkes, Jean, trans. 1982. *The London Journal of Flora Tristan*. London: Virago. (Originally published in 1840.)

Hawkesworth, Mary. 1990. *Beyond Oppression: Feminist Theory and Political Strategy*. New York: Continuum.

———. 1997. "Confounding Gender." *Signs: Journal of Women in Culture and Society* 22(3): 649–685.

———. 2003. "Congressional Enactments of Race-Gender: Toward a Theory of Raced-Gendered Institutions." *American Political Science Review* 97(4): 529–550.

———. 2004. "The Semiotics of Premature Burial: Feminism in a Postfeminist Age." *Signs* 29(4): 961–986.

Higer, Amy. 1999. "International Women's Activism and the 1994 Cairo Population Conference." In Elisabeth Prugl and Mary K. Meyer., eds., *Gender Politics in Global Governance*, 122–141. Lanham, MD: Rowman & Littlefield.

Hindess, Barry. 2003. "Class and Politics." In Mary Hawkesworth and Maurice Kogan, eds., *The Routledge Encyclopedia of Government and Politics*, 2nd rev. ed., 530–541. London: Routledge.

Hirst, Paul, and Grahame Thompson. 1999. *Globalization in Question*, 2nd ed. Cambridge, UK: Polity Press.

Hitchcock, Tim. 1997. *English Sexualities, 1700–1800*. New York: St. Martin's Press.

Hoff Sommers, Christina. 1994. *Who Stole Feminism? How Women Have Betrayed Women*. New York: Simon & Schuster, 1994.

Hogsholm, Mongaya Filomenita. 2000. "Philippine International Migration." *Forum on Philippine International Migration*. Available at http://www.philsol.nl/fora/FFON97-editorial.htm.

hooks, bell. 1981. *Ain't I a Woman? Black Women and Feminism*. Boston: South End Press.

Hoover, Kenneth, and Raymond Plant. 1989. *Conservative Capitalism in Great Britain and the United States: A Critical Appraisal*. New York and London: Routledge.

Howell, Jude. 2003. "Women's Organizations and Civil Society in China: Making a Difference." *International Feminist Journal of Politics* 5(2): 191–215.

Howell, Jude, and Diane Mulligan. 2003. "Editorial." *International Feminist Journal of Politics* 5(2): 157–162.

Hrycak, Alexandra. 2002. "From Mothers' Rights to Equal Rights: Post Soviet Grassroots Women's Organizations." In Nancy Naples and Manisha Desai, eds., *Women's Activism and Globalization: Linking Local Struggles and Transnational Politics*, 64–82. New York: Routledge.

Hsiung, Ping-Chun, Maria Jaschok, and Cecilia Milwertz with Red Chan. 2001. *Chinese Women Organizing: Cadres, Feminists, Muslims, Queers*. Oxford: Berg.

Hsiung, Ping-Chun, and Yuk-Lin Renita Wong. 1999. "Jie Gui—Connecting the Tracks: Chinese Women's Activism Surrounding the 1995 World Conference on Women in Beijing." In Mrinalini Sinha, Donna Guy, and Angela Woollacott, eds., *Feminisms and Internationalism*, 126–153. Oxford: Blackwell.

Htun, Mala. 2004. "Is Gender Like Ethnicity? The Political Representation of Identity Groups." *Perspectives on Politics* 2(3): 439–458.

Huyssen, Andreas. 1995. *Twilight Memories: Marking Time in a Culture of Amnesia*. New York: Routledge.

Hymowitz, Kay. 2002. "The End of Herstory." *City Journal* 12(3): 1–9.

Inter-Parliamentary Union. 2005. "Women in National Parliaments." Available at www.ipu.org/wmn-e/classif.htm.

Jain, Devaki. 2001. "The Problematique of South-South," *Women in Action*. No. 3. Available at http://www.isiswomen.org/pub/wia/wia301//devaki.htm .

James, Paul. 2004. "The Matrix of Global Enchantment." In Manfred Steger, ed., *Rethinking Globalism*, 27–38. Lanham, MD: Rowman & Littlefield.

Jaquette, Jane. 1995. "Losing the Battle/Winning the War: International Politics, Women's Issues, and the 1980 Mid-Decade Conference." In Ann Winslow, ed., *Women Politics and the United Nations*, 45–60. Westport, CT: Greenwood Press.

Jayawardena, Kumari. 1986. *Feminism and Nationalism in the Third World*. London: Zed Books.

———. 1995. *The White Woman's Other Burden: Western Women and South Asia During British Colonial Rule*. New York: Routledge.

Jimeno, Clara. 2001. "Implementation of Gender Demands Included in the Guatemala Peace Accords." In Sheila Rowbotham and Stephanie Linkogle, eds., *Women Resist Globalization: Mobilizing for Livelihood and Rights*, 180–198. London: Zed Press.

John, Mary. 1996. *Discrepant Dislocations: Feminism, Theory, and Postcolonial Histories*. Berkeley: University of California Press.

Joseph, Nicola. 2001. "The South Touching Base." *Women in Action*. Available at http://www.isiswomen.org/pub/wia/wia301/touching_base.htm.

Kabeer, Naila. 2003. *Reversed Realities: Gender Hierarchies in Development Thought*. London: Verso.

Kaplan, Temma. 2001. "Uncommon Women and the Common Good." In Sheila Rowbotham and Stephanie Linkogle, eds., *Women Resist Globalization: Mobilizing for Livelihood and Rights*, 28–45. London: Zed Press.

Karides, Marina. 2002. "Linking Local Efforts with Global Struggle: Trinidad's National Union of Domestic Employees." In Nancy Naples and Manisha Desai, eds., Women's Activism and Globalization, 156–171. New York: Routledge.

Katz, Michael. 1989. *The Undeserving Poor: From the War on Poverty to the War on Welfare*. New York: Pantheon Books.

Kaufman-Osborn, Timothy. 2005. "Gender Relations in an Age of Neoliberal Empire: Interrogating Gender Equality Models." Paper presented at the Annual Meeting of the Western Political Science Association, Oakland, California, March 19.

Keck, Margaret, and Kathryn Sikkink. 1998. *Activists Beyond Borders: Advocacy Networks in International Politics*. Ithaca, NY: Cornell University Press.

Kelly, Kristin. 2003. *Domestic Violence and the Politics of Privacy*. Ithaca, NY: Cornell University Press.

Kelly, Rita, Jane Bayes, Mary Hawkesworth, and Birgitte Young. 2001. *Gender, Democratization, and Globalization*. Lanham, MD: Rowman & Littlefield.

Kerber, Linda. 1980. *Women of the Republic: Intellect and Ideology in Revolutionary America*. Chapel Hill: University of North Carolina Press.

Khanna, Ranjana. 2001. "Ethical Ambiguities and Specters of Colonialism: Futures of Transnational Feminism." In Elisabeth Bronfen and Misha Kavka, eds., *Feminist Consequences: Theory for a New Century*, 101–125. New York: Columbia University Press.

Kingfisher, Catherine. 2002. *Western Welfare in Decline: Globalization and Women's Poverty* Philadelphia: University of Pennsylvania Press.

Kinsella, Helen. 2005. "Erotic Triangles in the Art of War," Workshop on the Art of Security: The Relation of Gender and Sex to Peace and Conflict. Annual Meeting of the International Studies Association, Honolulu, HI, March 1.

Koven, Seth, and Sonya Michel. 1993. *Mothers of a New World: Maternalist Politics and the Origins of Welfare States.* New York: Routledge.

Lakatos, Imre. 1970. "Falsification and the Methodology of Scientific Research Programmes." In Imre Lakatos and Alan Musgrave, eds., *Criticism and the Growth of Knowledge,* 91–195. Cambridge, UK: Cambridge University Press.

Landsberg-Lewis, Ilana. 1998. "Bringing Equality Home: Implementing the Convention on the Elimination of All Forms of Discrimination Against Women." New York: UNIFEM/United Nations Development Fund for Women. Available at www.unifem.undp.org/cedaw/cedawen0.htm.

Lang, Sabine. 1997. "The NGOization of Feminism." In Joan Scott, Cora Kaplan, and D. Keates, eds., *Transitions, Environments, Translation,* 101–120. New York: Routledge.

Laqueur, Thomas. 1990. *Making Sex: Body and Gender from the Greeks to Freud.* Cambridge, MA: Harvard University Press.

Lawless, Jennifer. 2004. "Women, War, and Winning Elections: Gender Stereotyping in the Post–September 11th Era." *Political Research Quarterly* 57(3): 479–490.

Lechner, Frank, and John Boli. 2004. *The Globalization Reader,* 2nd ed. Oxford: Blackwell.

Leijenaar, Monique. 2003. "Women's Political Empowerment in Europe: Taking Stock." Paper presented at the XIX World Congress of the International Political Science Association, Durban, South Africa, June 29–July 4.

Linkogle, Stephanie. 2001. "Nicaraguan Women in the Age of Globalization." In Sheila Rowbotham and Stephanie Linkogle, eds., *Women Resist Globalization: Mobilizing for Livelihood and Rights,* 118–133. London: Zed Press.

Lorde, Audre. 1984. *Sister Outsider: Essays and Speeches.* Trumansburg, NY: Crossing Press.

Loraux, Nicole. 1987. *Tragic Ways of Killing a Woman.* Anthony Forster, trans. Cambridge, MA: Harvard University Press.

Lyotard, Jean-François. 1990. *Heidegger and "The Jews."* Andreas Michel and Mark S. Roberts, trans. Minneapolis: University of Minnesota Press.

MacDonald, Laura. 2002. "Globalization and Social Movements: Comparing Women's Movements' Responses to NAFTA in Mexico, the USA, and Canada." *International Feminist Journal of Politics* 4(2): 151–172.

———. 2006. "Globalization and Gender in Canada." In Jane Bayes, Patricia Begné, Laura Gonzalez, Lois Harder, Mary Hawkesworth, and Laura MacDonald, *Women, Democracy and Globalization in North America,* 131–144. New York: Palgrave.

Magat, Margaret. 2001. "Rome: A Magnet for Tourists, Filipina Domestics." Women's E-News, September 10. Available at http://www.womensenews.org/article.cfm/dyn/aid/647/context/archive. (December 19, 2005).

Maguire, Patricia. 1984. *Women in Development: An Alternative Analysis.* Amherst, MA: Center for International Education.

Mandle, Jay. 2003. *Globalization and the Poor*. Cambridge, UK: Cambridge University Press.

Maracle, Lee. 1996. *I Am a Woman: A Native Perspective on Sociology and Feminism*. Vancouver, BC: Press Gang Publishers.

Martinez. Luz. 2001. "The South Touching Base." *Women in Action*. Available at http://www.isiswomen.org/pub/wia/wia301/touching_base.htm.

Marx, Karl, and Friedrich Engels. 1848 [1955]. *The Communist Manifesto*. New York: Meredith Corporation.

Mascia-Lees, Frances, and Patricia Sharpe. 2000. *Taking a Stand in a Postfeminist World: Toward an Engaged Cultural Criticism*. Albany: State University of New York Press.

Mazumdar, V. 1989. *Peasant Women Organize for Empowerment: The Bankura Experiment*. Occasional Paper 13. New Delhi: Centre for Women's Development Studies.

McClintock, Anne. 1995. *Imperial Leather: Race, Gender, and Sexuality in Colonial Context*. New York: Routledge.

Mendoza, Breny. 2000. "Unthinking State-Centric Feminisms." In Debra Castillo, Mary Jo Dudley, and Breny Mendoza, eds., *Rethinking Feminisms in the Americas*, Volume 5: 6–18. Ithaca, NY: Latin American Studies Program, Cornell University.

———. 2002. "Conceptualizing Transnational Feminism." Presented at the Transnational Feminism Conference held in conjunction with the Annual Meeting of the National Women's Studies Association, Las Vegas, Nevada, June 13.

Meyer, Mary K., and Elisabeth Prugl. 1999. *Gender Politics in Global Governance*. Lanham, MD: Rowman & Littlefield.

Miller, Francesca. 1999. "Feminisms and Transnationalism." In Mrinalini Sinha, Donna Guy, and Angela Woollacott, eds., *Feminisms and Internationalism*, 225–236. Oxford: Blackwell.

Mindry, Deborah. 2001. "Nongovernmental Organizations, 'Grassroots,' and the Politics of Virtue." *Signs* 26(4): 1187–1212.

Mink, Gwendolyn. 1998. *Welfare's End*. Ithaca, NY: Cornell University Press.

———. 1999. "Aren't Poor Single Mothers Women? Feminism, Welfare Reform and Welfare Justice." In Gwendoyn Mink, ed., *Whose Welfare*, 172–188. Ithaca, NY: Cornell University Press.

Misciagno, Patricia. 1997. *Rethinking Feminist Identification: The Case for De Facto Feminism*. Westport, CT: Praeger.

Modleski, Tania. 1991. *Feminism without Women: Culture and Criticism in a "Postfeminist" Age*. New York: Routledge.

Moghadam, Valentine. 2005. *Globalizing Women: Transnational Feminist Networks*. Baltimore: Johns Hopkins University Press.

Mohanty, Chandra Talpade. 1991. "Under Western Eyes: Feminist Scholarship and Colonial Discourses." In Chandra Talpade Mohanty, Ann Russo, and Lourdes

Torres, eds., *Third World Women and the Politics of Feminism*, 51–80. Blooming-ton: Indiana University Press.

―――. 2003. *Feminism Without Borders: Decolonizing Theory, Practicing Solidar-ity*. Durham, NC: Duke University Press.

Molyneux, Maxine. 1985. "Mobilization Without Emancipation? Women's Inter-ests and the State in Nicaragua." *Feminist Studies* 11(2): 227–254.

Muchina, Pauline. 2001. "The South Touching Base." *Women in Action*. Available at http://www.isiswomen.org/pub/wia/wia301/touching_base.htm.

Naples, Nancy. 2002. "Changing the Terms: Community Activism, Globalization, and the Dilemmas of Transnational Feminist Praxis." In Nancy Naples and Manisha Desai, eds., *Women's Activism and Globalization: Linking Local Strug-gles and Transnational Politics*, 3–14. New York: Routledge.

Naples, Nancy, and Manisha Desai. 2002. *Women's Activism and Globalization: Lin-king Local Struggles to Transnational Politics*. New York: Routledge.

Neft, Naomi, and Ann Levine. 1997. *Where Women Stand: An International Report on the Status of Women in 140 Countries, 1997–1998*. New York: Random House.

Newman, Louise. 1999. *White Women's Rights: The Racial Origins of Feminism in the United States*. New York: Oxford University Press.

Obando, Ana Elena. 2001a. "The North-South Debate: Moving Beyond Dichoto-mies." *Women in Action*. Available at http://www.isiswomen.org/pub/wia/wia301/anaelena.htm.

―――. 2001b. "The South Touching Base," *Women in Action*. Available at http://www.isiswomen.org/pub/wia/wia301/touching_base.htm.

Offen, Karen. 2000. *European Feminisms, 1700–1950*. Stanford, CA: Stanford Uni-versity Press.

Orford, Ann. 2005. Workshop on the Art of Security: The Relation of Gender and Sex to Peace and Conflict. Annual Meeting of the International Studies Associa-tion, Honolulu, HI, March 1.

Oyewumi, Oyeronke. 2003. *African Women and Feminism: Reflecting on the Politics of Sisterhood*. Trenton, NJ : Africa World Press.

Palmer, Ingrid. 1992. "Gender Equity and Economic Efficiency in Adjustment Pro-grammes." In Haleh Afshar and Carolyne Dennis, eds., *Women and Adjustment Policies in the Third World*, 69–83. Basingstoke, UK: Macmillan.

Parpart, Jane. 1995. "Deconstructing the Development 'Expert': Gender, Develop-ment and Vulnerable Groups." In Marianne Marchant and Jane Parpart, eds., *Feminism/Postmodernism/Development*, 221–243. New York: Routledge.

Parrenas, Rhacel Salazar. 2000. "Migrant Filipina Domestic Workers and the Inter-national Division of Reproductive Labor." *Gender and Society* 14(4): 560–581.

―――. 2001a. *Servants of Globalization: Women Migration and Domestic Work*. Stanford, CA: Stanford University Press.

―――. 2001b. "Transgressing the Nation-State: The Partial Citizenship and 'Imag-ined Community' of Migrant Filipina Domestic Workers." *Signs* 26(4): 1129–1154.

Patel, Pragna. 2001. "Creating Alternative Spaces: Black Women in Resistance." In

Sheila Rowbotham and Stephanie Linkogle, eds., *Women Resist Globalization: Mobilizing for Livelihood and Rights*, 153–168. London: Zed Press.

Patton, Charlotte. 1995. "Women and Power: The Nairobi Conference, 1985." In Ann Winslow, ed., *Women Politics and the United Nations*, 61–76. Westport, CT: Greenwood Press.

Pensky, Max. 2005. *Globalizing Critical Theory*. Lanham, MD: Rowman & Littlefield.

Petchesky, Rosalind. 2003. *Global Prescriptions: Gendering Health and Human Rights*. London and New York: Zed Books.

Peterson, V. Spike. 2003. *A Critical Rewriting of Global Political Economy: Integrating Reproductive, Productive, and Virtual Economies*. New York: Routledge.

Peterson, V. Spike, and Anne Sisson Runyan, 1999. *Global Gender Issues*, 2nd ed. Boulder, CO: Westview Press.

Pettman, Jan Jindy. 1998. "Women on the Move: Globalisation and Labour Migration from South and Southeast Asian States." *Global Society* 12(3): 389–404.

Pietila, Hilkka, and Jeanne Vickers. 1994. *Making Women Matter: The Role of the United Nations*. London: Zed Books.

Pizan, Christine de. 1982. *The Book of the City of the Ladies*. Earl Jeffrey Richards, trans. New York: Persea.

Poster, Winifred, and Zakia Salime. 2002. "The Limits of Microcredit: Transnational Feminism and US AID Activities in the United States and Morocco." In Nancy Naples and Manisha Desai, eds., *Women's Activism and Globalization: Linking Local Struggles and Transnational Politics*, 189–219. New York: Routledge.

Poulain de la Barre, François. 1673. *De l'Égalité des deux sexes [On the Equality of the Two Sexes]*. Reprinted, Detroit: Wayne State University Press, 1988.

Pratt, Mary Louise. 1992. *Imperial Eyes*. New York: Routledge.

Proceedings of the Woman's Rights Convention. Held at Worcester, October 15 and 16, 1851. New York: Fowler & Wells, 1852.

Prudhomme, Louis-Marie. 1791. "De l'influence de la révolution sur les femmes." *Les Révolutions de Paris* 9(83): 227.

Purewal, Navtej. 2001. "New Roots for Rights: Women's Responses to Population and Development Policies." In Sheila Rowbotham and Stephanie Linkogle, eds., *Women Resist Globalization: Mobilizing for Livelihood and Rights*, 96–117. London: Zed Press.

Quadagno, Jill. 1994. *The Color of Welfare: How Racism Undermined the War on Poverty*. New York: Oxford University Press.

Rai, Shirin. 2002. *Gender and the Political Economy of Development*. Cambridge, UK: Polity Press.

Ramusack, Barbara. 1992. "Cultural Missionaries, Maternal Imperialists, Feminist Allies: British Women Activists in India, 1865–1945." In Nupur Chaudhuri and Margaret Strobel, eds., *Western Women and Imperialism: Complicity and Resistance*, 309–321. Bloomington: Indiana University Press.

197

Razavi, Shahra. 1995. "Becoming Multilingual: The Challenges of Feminist Policy Advocacy." In Carol Miller and Shahra Razavi (eds.) *Missionaries and Mandarins: Feminist Engagement with Development Institutions*, 20–41. London: Intermediate Technology Publications/United Nations Research Institute for Social Development.

Rendall, Jane. 1985. *The Origins of Modern Feminism: Women in Britain, France, and the United States 1780–1860*. Chicago: Lyceum Books.

Riley, Denise. 1988. *Am I That Name? Feminism and the Category of "Women" in History*. Minneapolis: University of Minnesota Press.

———. 2000. *The Words of Selves: Identification, Solidarity, Irony*. Stanford, CA: Stanford University Press.

Rios Tobar, Marcela. 2003. "Paradoxes of an Unfinished Transition: Chilean Feminism in the Nineties." *International Feminist Journal of Politics* 5(2): 256–281.

Robertson, Roland. 1992. *Globalization*. London: Sage.

Rodriguez, Robyn. 2002. "Migrant Heroes: Nationalism, Citizenship, and the Politics of Filipino Migrant Labor." *Citizenship Studies* 6(3): 347.

Rodriquez, Victoria. 2003. *Women in Contemporary Mexican Politics*. Austin: University of Texas Press.

Rosca, Ninotchka. 1995. "The Philippines Shameful Export," *The Nation* 260 (15): 522–527.

Rousseau, Jean-Jacques. 1762 [1950]. *The Social Contract*. In *The Social Contract and the Discourses*, 3–141. New York: E. P. Dutton.

Rousseau, Jean-Jacques. 1762 [1955]. *Emile*. Barbara Foxley, trans. New York: E. P. Dutton.

Rowbotham, Sheila, and Stephanie Linkogle. 2001. *Women Resist Globalization: Mobilizing for Livelihood and Rights*. London: Zed Press.

Rupp, Leila. 1996. "Challenging Imperialism in International Women's Organizations, 1888–1945," *NWSA Journal* 8(1): 8–27.

———. 1997. *Worlds of Women: The Making of an International Women's Movement*. Princeton, NJ: Princeton University Press.

Said, Edward. 1978. *Orientalism*. New York: Random House.

Samanther, Meera, and Rozana Isa. 2002. "Malaysia: Foreign Domestic Workers—The Obstacles." In Rita Raj, ed., *Women at the Intersection: Indivisible Rights, Identities and Oppressions*, 39–45. New Brunswick, NJ: Center for Women's Global Leadership.

Sandoval, Chela. 2000. *Methodology of the Oppressed*. Minneapolis: University of Minnesota Press.

Sarvasy, Wendy, and Patrizia Longo. 2002. "Cosmopolitanism and Feminism: A Democratic Partnership Beyond Borders." Paper presented at the Annual Meeting of the Western Political Science Association, Long Beach, California, March 15.

Sassen, Saskia. 2002. "Global Cities and Survival Circuits." In Barbara Ehrenreich and Arlie Russell Hochschild, eds., *Global Woman: Nannies, Maids, and Sex Workers in the New Economy*, 254–274. New York: Metropolitan Books/Henry Holt.

———. 2003. "Globalization." In Mary Hawkesworth and Maurice Kogan, eds., *The Routledge Encyclopedia of Government and Politics*, 2nd rev. ed., 1089–1114. London: Routledge.

Scott, Joan. 1986. "Gender: A Useful Category for Historical Analysis." *American Historical Review* 91: 1053–1075.

———. 1988. "Deconstructing the Equality vs. Difference Debate: Or the Uses of Poststructuralist Theory for Feminism." *Feminist Studies* 14 (1): 575–599.

———. 1996. *Only Paradoxes to Offer: French Feminists and the Rights of Man*. Cambridge, MA: Harvard University Press.

———. 2002. "Feminist Reverberations." *Differences* 13(2): 1–23.

Seager, Joni. 2003. *The Penguin Atlas of Women in the World*, 3rd ed. New York: Penguin Books.

Seidman, Gay. 1999. "Gendered Citizenship: South Africa's Democratic Transition and the Construction of a Gendered State." *Gender and Society* 13(3): 287–307.

———, Gay. 2003. "Institutional Dilemmas: Representation v. Mobilization in the South African Gender Commission." *Feminist Studies* 29(3): 541–564.

Seligman, Adam. 2002. "Civil Society as Idea and Ideal." In Simone Chambers and Will Kymlicka, eds., *Alternative Conceptions of Civil Society*, 13–33. Princeton, NJ: Princeton University Press.

Sen, Gita, and Caren Grown. 1987. *Development, Crises, and Alternate Visions: Third World Women's Perspectives*. New York: Monthly Review Press.

Shaheed, Farida. 1995. "Linking Dreams: The Network of Women Living under Muslim Laws." In Margaret A. Shuler, ed., *From Basic Needs to Basic Rights: Women's Claim to Human Rights*, 305–325. Washington, DC: Women, Law, and Development International.

Shohat, Ella, and Robert Stam. 1994. *Unthinking Eurocentrism*. London: Routledge.

Sinha, Mrinalini. 1994. "Reading Mother India: Empire, Nation, and the Female Voice." *Journal of Women's History* 6(1): 6–44.

Sinha, Mrinalini, Donna Guy, and Angela Woollacott. 1999. *Feminisms and Internationalism*. Oxford: Blackwell.

Smart, Carol. 1992. "The Woman of Legal Discourse." *Social Legal Studies* 1(1): 29–44.

Snyder, Margaret. 1995. "The Politics of Women and Development." In Ann Winslow, ed., *Women Politics and the United Nations*, 95–116. Westport, CT: Greenwood Press.

Spees, Pam. 2003. "Women's Agency in the Creation of the International Criminal Court: Changing the Landscape of Justice and Power." *Signs* 28(4): 1233–1254.

Sperling, Valerie, Myra Marx Ferree, and Barbara Risman. 2001. "Constructing

Global Feminism: Transnational Advocacy Networks and Russian Women's Activism." *Signs* (26)4: 1156–1186.

Spivak, Gayatri. 1985. "Can the Subaltern Speak? Speculations on Widow Sacrifice" *Wedge* 7–8 (Winter-Spring):120–130.

Srinivasan, Viji. 2001. "Adithi: Creating Economic and Social Alternatives." In Sheila Rowbotham and Stephanie Linkogle, eds., *Women Resist Globalization: Mobilizing for Livelihood and Rights*, 86–95. London: Zed Press.

Stacey, Judith. 1992. "Sexism by a Subtler Name: Postindustrial Conditions and Postfeminist Consciousness in Silicon Valley." In Dorothy Helly and Susan Reverby, eds., *Gendered Domains: Rethinking Public and Private in Women's History*, 322–338. Ithaca, NY: Cornell University Press.

Steger, Manfred. 2002. *Globalism: The New Market Ideology*. Lanham, MD: Rowman & Littlefield.

———. 2004. *Rethinking Globalism*. Lanham, MD: Rowman & Littlefield.

Stephenson, Carolyn. 1995. "Women's International Non-Governmental Organizations at the United Nations." In Ann Winslow, ed., *Women Politics and the United Nations*, 135–154. Westport, CT: Greenwood Press.

Stetson, Dorothy McBride, and Amy Mazur. 1995. *Comparative State Feminism*. Thousand Oaks, CA: Sage.

Stichter, Sharon, and Jane Parpart. 1988. *Patriarchy and Class: African Women in the Home and in the Workforce*. Boulder, CO: Westview.

Stiehm, Judith. 2005. "Meditation on Two Photographs." Paper presented at the Annual Meeting of the Western Political Science Association, Oakland, CA, March 19.

Stienstra, Deborah. 1994. *Women's Movements and International Organizations*. New York: St. Martin's Press.

———. 1999. "Of Roots, Leaves, and Trees: Gender, Social Movements, and Global Governance." In Elisabeth Prugl and Mary K. Meyer., eds., *Gender Politics in Global Governance*, 260–272. Lanham, MD: Rowman & Littlefield.

Sylvester, Christine. 2002. *Feminist International Relations: An Unfinished Journey*. Cambridge, UK: Cambridge University Press.

Tamale, Sylvia. 2001. "Between a Rock and a Hard Place: Women's Self-Mobilization to Overcome Poverty in Uganda." In Sheila Rowbotham and Stephanie Linkogle, eds., *Women Resist Globalization: Mobilizing for Livelihood and Rights*, 70–85. London: Zed Press.

Tauli-Corpuz, Victoria. 2001. "Diversity, Universality, and Democracy: A Perspective of an Indigenous Woman." *Women in Action*. Available at www.isiswomen.org/pub/wia/wia301/vicky.htm.

Taylor, Viviene. 2000. *Marketisation of Governance: Critical Feminist Perspectives from the South*. Cape Town, South Africa: DAWN/SADEP.

Thai, Hung Cam. 2003. "Clashing Dreams: Highly Educated Overseas Brides and Low-Wage U.S. Husbands." In Barbara Ehrenreich and Arlie Russell Hochschild, eds., *Global Woman: Nannies, Maids, and Sex Workers in the New Economy*, 230–253. New York: Metropolitan Books/Henry Holt.

Thomas, Dorothy. 2000. "We Are Not the World: U.S. Activism and Human Rights in the Twenty-First Century." *Signs* 25(4): 1121–1124.

Timothy, Kristen. 1995. "Equality for Women in the UN Secretariat." In Ann Winslow, ed., *Women Politics and the United Nations*, 117–134. Westport, CT: Greenwood Press.

Tinker, Irene. 1999. "Nongovernmental Organizations: An Alternative Power Base for Women?" In Elisabeth Prugl and Mary K. Meyer., eds., *Gender Politics in Global Governance*, 88–106. Lanham, MD: Rowman & Littlefield.

Tribune des femmes [*Women's Tribune*]. 1832. "Call to Women." 1(1): 6–8. Reprinted in Claire Moses and Leslie Rabine, *Feminism, Socialism, and French Romanticism*, 286–287. Bloomington: Indiana University Press, 1993.

Tripp, Aili Mari. 2003. "Women in Movement: Transformations in African Political Landscapes." *International Feminist Journal of Politics* 5(2): 233–255.

Tristan, Flora. 1983. *The Workers' Union*. Beverly Livingston, trans. Urbana: University of Illinois Press. (Originally published 1843.)

Turpin, Jennifer. 1998. "Many Faces: Women Confronting War." In Lois Lorentzen and Jennifer Turpin, eds., *The Women and War Reader*, 3–18. New York: New York University Press.

UN, IMF, World Bank, OECD. 2000. *2000—A Better World for All*. Available at http://www.paris21.org/betterworld/home.htm.

UNDP. 1999. *Human Development Report* 1999 [on globalization]. New York: Oxford University Press.

UNDP. 2002. *Human Development Report* 2002 [on democracy]. New York: Oxford University Press.

Vas Dev, Sanjugta, and Susanne Schech. 2003. "Gender Justice: The World Bank's New Approach to the Poor." Paper presented at the XIX World Congress of the International Political Science Association, Durban, South Africa, June 29–July 4.

Waever, Ole, Barry Buzan, Morten Kelstrup, and Pierre Lemaitre. 1993. *Identity, Migration, and the New Security Agenda in Europe*. London: Pinter.

Wanyeki, Lynne Muthoni. 2001. "The South Touching Base," *Women in Action*. Available at http://www.isiswomen.org/pub/wia/wia301/touching_base.htm.

Waring, Marilyn. 1988. *If Women Counted: A New Feminist Economics*. San Francisco: Harper & Row.

Waterman, Peter. 2000. "Social Movements, Local Places and Globalized Spaces: Implications for 'Globalization from Below.'" In Barry Gills, ed., *Globalization and the Politics of Resistance*, 135–149. Basingstoke, UK: Palgrave.

Waylen, Georgina. 1996. *Gender in Third World Politics*. Boulder, CO: Lynne Rienner.

Weiss, Thomas, and Leon Gordenker. 1996. *NGOs, the UN, and Global Governance*. Boulder, CO: Lynne Rienner.

West, Lois. 1999. "The United Nations Women's Conferences and Feminist Politics." In Elisabeth Prugl and Mary K. Meyer, eds., *Gender Politics in Global Governance*, 177–196. Lanham, MD: Rowman & Littlefield.

Weldon, S. Laurel. 2002. *Protest, Policy and the Problem of Violence Against Women: A Cross National Comparison.* Pittsburgh: University of Pittsburgh Press.

———. 2004. "Democratic Policymaking on Violence Against Women in the Fifty US States." *International Feminist Journal of Politics* 6(1): 1–28.

Wells, Betty. 2002. "Context, Strategy, Ground: Rural Women Organizing to Confront Local/Global Economic Issues." In Nancy Naples and Manisha Desai, eds., *Women's Activism and Globalization: Linking Local Struggles and Transnational Politics*, 142–155. New York: Routledge.

Wichterich, Christa. 2000. *The Globalized Woman: Reports from a Future of Inequality.* London: Zed Books.

Wieringa, Saskia. 2001. "Sexual Politics in Indonesia." In Sheila Rowbotham and Stephanie Linkogle, eds., *Women Resist Globalization: Mobilizing for Livelihood and Rights*, 134–152. London: Zed Press.

Winslow, Anne. 1995. *Women, Politics, and the United Nations.* Westport, CT: Greenwood Press.

Wollstonecraft, Mary. 1792 [1975]. *A Vindication of the Rights of Woman.* New York: W. W. Norton.

Women in Black (n.d.) http://www.womeninblack.net.

Women in Black-Canberra. (n.d.). http://www.sshub.com/wibabout.htm

Women in Black-UK (n.d.) http://www.womeninblack.org.uk.

Women in Development Europe (WIDE). 1995. WIDE Bulletin: From Copenhagen to Beijing. Brussels: WIDE.

Women's Environment and Development Organization, 2000. *Women's Equality: An Unfinished Agenda: Women's Organizations Assess the U.S. Government Actions on Implementing the Beijing Platform, 1995–2000.* New York: WEDO.

Woolf, Virginia. 1938. *Three Guineas.* New York and London: Harcourt, Brace, and World.

World Bank. 2000. "Advancing Gender Equality: World Bank Action Since Beijing." Available through World Bank, Gender and Development, Other Papers, http://siteresources.worldbank.org/INTGENDER/Resources/fullreport .pdf.

World Bank. 2002a. *Attacking Poverty: World Development Report 2000/01.* New York: Oxford University Press.

World Bank. 2002b. *Integrating Gender into the World Bank's Work: A Strategy for Action.* Available at http://www.worldbank.org/gender/overview/ssp/ssppaper .htm.

World Women's Congress for a Healthy Planet Report. 1992. New York: WEDO.

Young, Iris. 2000. *Democracy and Inclusion.* New York: Oxford University Press.

Young, Iris Marion. 2003. "The Logic of Masculinist Protection: Reflections on the Current Security State." *Signs* 29(1): 1–26.

Yuval-Davis, Nira. 1997. *Gender and Nation.* Thousand Oaks, CA: Sage.

INDEX

Aachen Peace Prize, 75
AAWORD. *See* Association of African Women for Research and Development
abolitionism, 37, 38
abortion, 55, 86, 92, 166
activism, transnational, 104, 107, 111, 133, 169, 171, 178n16; agenda for, 68, 70, 80–87, 111, 126, 133, 140, 144–45, 169; change by, 30–32, 37, 39, 41–43, 44–45, 57, 63, 68; costs/consequences of, 61, 63; cross-class alliances for, 46; defining of, 26–27; economic development for, 135–36; elective/appointive office for, 92–93; elimination of colonialism by, 50, 52–53, 120; femocrat as, 150; forms of, 49; funding for, 143; future of, 169; by gender, 2, 148; gender mainstreaming for, 96–100, 135–36, 150; group characteristics of, 70–71; growth of, 130–31; historical significance of, 30–32, 65; human rights and, 80–87; as imperialist, 46–48, 50–51, 62, 124; INGOs for, 104, 105, 121; invisible labor of, 150; through journalism, 40–42; limitations of, 87, 90, 91–92, 144; marginalization of, 95, 108–9; through missionary work, 49–50;

modernization and, 127; on national level, 58, 91–92; neoliberalism and, 131, 148–52; networks for, 45, 65, 72, 130–31; NGOs for, 13, 27, 30, 53, 103–7, 121, 123, 130–31, 144, 150–51, 171, 178nn15–16; one-voice for, 132, 139–41, 144–45; pacifism by, 55–58, 67, 73; plurality of, 25; as political outsiders, 71, 87, 176n2; political quota/reservation for, 93, 95, 96, 167; politicizing of, 129–31; racism and, 62, 63, 126; representation by, 111–12; research centers for, 72; silencing of, 43–44; for social justice, 21–22, 59–60, 108, 140, 143, 148, 166; success by, 109, 140; tactics of, 62, 68, 69–70, 73–75, 92; Third Wave as, 134; tribunals by, 76–80; UN agenda by, 89; universalism and, 127–28; war's effect on, 44, 49, 55, 87, 113, 118, 157–58, 160, 161, 165–66, 171
Activists Beyond Borders (Keck, Sikkink), 68
Adithi, 71–72
adoption, international, 2
Adorno, Theodor, 147
affirmative action, 177n11
Afghan Women Lawyers Association, 167–68

ABOUT THE AUTHOR

Mary E. Hawkesworth is professor of political science and women's and gender studies at Rutgers University. Her teaching and research interests include feminist theory, women and politics, contemporary political philosophy, philosophy of science, and social policy. An award-winning teacher and scholar, Hawkesworth has published in the leading journals of feminist scholarship. Her major works include *Theoretical Issues in Policy Analysis* (1988), *Beyond Oppression: Feminist Theory and Political Strategy* (1990), and *Feminist Inquiry: From Political Conviction to Methodological Innovation* (2006). She is editor of *Signs: Journal of Women in Culture and Society.*